THE TALK IN JANE AUSTEN

The Talk
in Jane Austen

Edited by Bruce Stovel and Lynn Weinlos Gregg

THE UNIVERSITY OF ALBERTA PRESS

Published by
The University of Alberta Press
Ring House 2
Edmonton, Alberta T6G 2E1

Printed and bound in Canada by
Houghton-Boston Printers, Saskatoon,
Saskatchewan.
∞ Printed on acid-free paper.
Copyediting by Carol Berger.
Book design by Alan Brownoff.

NATIONAL LIBRARY OF CANADA
CATALOGUING IN PUBLICATION DATA

Main entry under title:
The talk in Jane Austen / edited by Bruce
Stovel and Lynn Weinlos Gregg.

Papers from the conference, Talk in Jane
Austen, hosted by the Jane Austen Society
of North America, Jasper, Alta., May 1999.
Includes bibliographical references
and index.
ISBN 0–88864–374–8

1. Austen, Jane, 1775–1817—Criticism and
interpretation—Congresses. 2. Conversation
in literature—Congresses. I. Stovel, Bruce. II.
Weinlos Gregg, Lynn, 1947– III. Jane Austen
Society of North America.
PR4037.T34 2002   823'.7   C2002–911282–6

The University of Alberta Press is committed
to protecting our natural environment. As
part of our efforts, this book is printed on
stock produced by New Leaf Paper: it contains
100% post-consumer recycled fibres and is acid-
and chlorine-free.

The University of Alberta Press acknowledges
the financial support of the Government of
Canada through the Book Publishing Industry
Development Program for its publishing activities. The Press also gratefully acknowledges
the support received for its program from the
Canada Council for the Arts.

Contents

Acknowledgements

WE WOULD LIKE TO THANK Juliet McMaster, for inspiration and guidance; our contributors, for patience and cooperation; all those who attended the "The Talk in Jane Austen" conference, for intellectual stimulation and good company; the members of the Edmonton chapter of JASNA who served on the conference planning committee; Jackie Bitz, Patricia Milligan, and Kirsten Uszkalo, for research assistance; Nora Stovel, for thoughtful advice; Kathryn Holland, for careful editing and proofreading; Carol Berger, for copyediting; and, finally, Leslie Vermeer, Linda Cameron, Alan Brownoff, Michael Luski, and Cathie Crooks of the University of Alberta Press, for help in many forms and for believing in this project.

Notes on Contributors

LINDA BREE is author of *Sarah Fielding* (1996) and editor of Fielding's *David Simple* (2002) and Jane Austen's *Persuasion* (1999). She is senior commissioning editor at Cambridge University Press.

JAN FERGUS, Professor of English at Lehigh University, has written a number of articles and two books on Jane Austen, *Jane Austen and the Didactic Novel* (1983) and *Jane Austen: A Literary Life* (1991), and is working on a study of the eighteenth-century reading public.

SARAH S.G. FRANTZ is a graduate student at the University of Michigan, Ann Arbor. Her dissertation examines how British women novelists of the Romantic era, Austen included, grappled with representing masculine emotion.

LYNN WEINLOS GREGG teaches English at a high school in Edmonton. She was, along with Juliet McMaster and Bruce Stovel, a co-convenor of the "The Talk in Jane Austen" conference held at Jasper, Alberta in May 1999.

ISOBEL GRUNDY, Henry Marshall Tory Professor at the University of Alberta, is a trustee of Chawton House Library, author of *Lady Mary Wortley Montagu: Comet of the Enlightenment* (1999), and a member of the Orlando Project team, which is producing a history of women's writing in the British Isles.

RONALD HALL read Theology and English at Oxford. He recently retired from the English Department of Rhodes University, Grahamstown, South Africa. He has published on Virgil, Shakespeare, Sir Thomas Browne, and Milton.

JOCELYN HARRIS, Professor of English at the University of Otago, New Zealand, has edited Samuel Richardson's *Sir Charles Grandison* and is the author of *Samuel Richardson* (1987) and *Jane Austen's Art of Memory* (1989).

JEFFREY HERRLE is a marketing writer in the technology industry. As a graduate student in English at the University of Alberta, he taught a course on film adaptations of Jane Austen's novels and wrote an introduction to the Juvenilia Press edition of her unfinished work *Catharine, or the Bower* (1996).

GARY KELLY is Canada Research Chair in Literature and Language in Society at the University of Alberta. His most recent work is the six-volume *Varieties of Female Gothic* (2002).

JULIET MCMASTER of the University of Alberta has published books on Thackeray, Dickens, Trollope, and Jane Austen, and she is co-editor with Bruce Stovel of *Jane Austen's Business*, and with Edward Copeland of *The Cambridge Companion to Jane Austen*.

ELIZABETH NEWARK is a Londoner by birth and a San Franciscan by choice. She writes essays on Jane Austen and Charles Dickens for the fun of it. She is the author of *Consequence* (1997), a sequel to *Pride and Prejudice*.

STEVEN D. SCOTT is an Assistant Professor in the Department of English at Brock University in St. Catharines, Ontario, specializing in twentieth-century literature, autobiography, and theory.

LESLEY WILLIS SMITH, formerly of the University of Guelph, Ontario, now lives in England. She has published articles on Jane Austen and on children's literature.

BRUCE STOVEL teaches English at the University of Alberta and is the author of many essays on Austen's novels. He edited, along with Juliet

McMaster, *Jane Austen's Business: Her World and Her Profession* (1996) and was a co-convenor of the 1999 Austen conference at Jasper, Alberta.

NORA FOSTER STOVEL is Professor of English at the University of Alberta, where she teaches twentieth-century literature. She has published books on Margaret Drabble and Margaret Laurence and essays on D.H. Lawrence.

KAY YOUNG is Associate Professor of English at the University of California, Santa Barbara. Her book *Ordinary Pleasures: Couples, Conversation, and Comedy* (2002) explores how novels (by Austen and others) and film teach us about the intimacies and happiness of everyday life.

A Note on References

QUOTATIONS FROM AUSTEN'S FICTION are from the scholarly edition by R.W. Chapman; page references are in parentheses, accompanied by abbreviations (except when there is extended discussion of a novel; in that case, the abbreviation appears with the first quotation only). Page references for quotations from books and articles about Austen's novels are given in parentheses; the full references can be found in the Works Cited section at the end of the book.

References to Jane Austen's works are to the following editions:

The Novels of Jane Austen, edited by R.W. Chapman, 5 vols., 3rd edition (London: Oxford University Press, 1953), reprinted with revisions, 1969.

Minor Works, ed. R.W. Chapman (London: Oxford University Press, 1954), reprinted with revisions by B.C. Southam, 1969.

Jane Austen's Letters, collected and edited by Deirdre Le Faye (Oxford and New York: Oxford University Press, 1995).

The following abbreviations have been used:

E	*Emma*
L	*Jane Austen's Letters*
MP	*Mansfield Park*
MW	*Minor Works*
NA	*Northanger Abbey*
P	*Persuasion*
PP	*Pride and Prejudice*
SS	*Sense and Sensibility*

Introduction

CONVERSATION IS ALL-IMPORTANT in Jane Austen's novels. The ways in which a given character speaks is our main source of knowledge about that character; changing speech habits chart her protagonists' growth, just as the unchanging speech of other characters reveals a comic inability to change. Her heroines continually judge others by the way they speak. After Emma's first, one-sided conversation with Mrs. Elton, for example, Emma has no trouble seeing that Mrs. Elton's speech displays her character in all of its gaudy glory: "A little, upstart vulgar being, with her Mr. E., and her *caro sposo*, and her resources, and all her airs of pert pretension and under-bred finery" (E 279). Even Catherine Morland, after an afternoon spent in John Thorpe's gig, listening to his "conversation, or rather talk, [which] began and ended with himself and his own concerns," begins to feel "extreme weariness of his company" and to "doubt ... of his being altogether completely agreeable" (NA 66–67). Almost all of Austen's characters, unlike those of, say, Fielding before her and Hardy after her, are ladies and gentlemen of leisure. They have no occupation that takes up their time and energy and stamps itself on their speech. Conversation is thus their major activity, and they expect it to be valuable. At the Coles' dinner party in *Emma*, "the usual rate of conversation" unfortunately prevails: "a few clever things, a few downright silly, but by much the larger proportion neither the one nor the other—nothing worse than every day remarks, dull repetitions, old news, and heavy jokes" (*E* 219). At the much grander dinner party held by John and Fanny Dashwood in *Sense and Sensibility*, things are even worse: "no poverty of any kind, except of conversation, appeared—but there, the deficiency was considerable" (*SS* 233).

It is surprising, given this primacy of speech in Austen's novels, that the topic has rarely been treated by her critics. There is a book on her use of dialogue by Howard S. Babb (1962), while Norman Page (1972), K.C. Phillips (1970), and Stuart Tave (1973) have published studies of Austen's use of language.[1] However, the latter three books give as much attention to her narrator's use of written discourse as to dialogue, Babb's analysis of dialogue largely limits itself to Austen's characters' ability to speak logically, and all four books were published more than a generation ago. More recently, Juliet McMaster, one of the contributors to this volume, has published several illuminating essays on Austen's use of speech in the novels.[2] In general, however, Jane Austen's use of speech in her novels has remained what Jim Dixon in Kingsley Amis's novel *Lucky Jim* (1953) calls "this strangely neglected topic."

To counter this strange neglect, several chapters of the Jane Austen Society of North America (JASNA) combined to hold a three-day conference on "The Talk in Jane Austen" at Jasper Park Lodge in Jasper, Alberta, in May of 1999. The editors of this volume were two of the three co-convenors of the conference; the third was Juliet McMaster.

JASNA is a unique organization: some five thousand people meet in more than fifty regional chapters across North America to discuss and celebrate the novels of Jane Austen. As at all JASNA gatherings, most of the 150 delegates at the Jasper conference were non-academic admirers of Jane Austen's novels, and the delegates came from across North America and beyond: from England, South Africa, Australia, and New Zealand. Again, as is the custom at JASNA meetings, most of the twenty-two speakers were university professors, several were graduate students, and some were non-academic devotees of the novels. The papers were scintillating and original, the setting spectacular, and the company congenial. This collection of essays consists of fifteen conference papers, some revised for publication in written form, some in their original form. Nevertheless, all the essays reveal their origin in spoken discourse: they have the bite and edge, the wit and free-spirited improvisation, of good conversation. The authors are a varied group: once again, most are university professors or graduate students, though two are "lay" members of JASNA; they come from Canada, the United States, England, South Africa, and New Zealand. (For more details, see the Notes on Contributors.)

The essays in this volume differ greatly in conception, method, and tone. We have grouped the essays under four headings: "Categories and Analysis," "Aggression and Power," "Subtexts and Ironies," and "Speculations and Possibilities." Needless to say, this grouping is tentative, after-the-fact, and hardly scientific—for one thing, it is hard to imagine an essay on Austen's novels that does not treat subtexts and ironies. Still, this ordering of the essays does suggest a primary focus for each essay and thus adds a measure of coherence and a satisfying sequence to the book. It also invites the reader to reflect on the connections within the essays in each group.

The first section, "Categories and Analysis," consists of four essays that attempt to define the nature and function of speech in Austen's novels. The collection opens with Jocelyn Harris's "Silent Women, Shrews, and Bluestockings: Women and Speaking in Jane Austen," which argues that heroines such as Elizabeth Bennet, Fanny Price, and Anne Elliot, in their poised and powerful speech, discredit "the three thousand years of misogyny that silenced women or called them shrewish, unequal, inconstant, deceiving, ignorant, or inappropriately learned" (Harris 21). Bruce Stovel, in "Asking Versus Telling: One Aspect of Jane Austen's Idea of Conversation," shows that Austen considered conversation an exchange between people, a mutual creation, and that this entails an important distinction between telling, which is one-way communication, and asking, which requires a two-way exchange. Characters such as Elizabeth Bennet and Emma thus grow when they learn to ask questions rather than merely tell their opinions. Isobel Grundy considers two contrasting excessive talkers in "Why Do They Talk So Much? How Can We Stand it? John Thorpe and Miss Bates"; the essay shows that humble, garrulous Miss Bates illuminates the function of talk within *Emma* and also the relationship of both Emma and her creator to "that common, ordinary, unadorned life which is the water in which Miss Bates swims" (Grundy 53). The final essay in this group, Kay Young's "Word-Work, Word-Play, and the Making of Intimacy in *Pride and Prejudice*," suggests that conversation as a concept contains two quite different elements: the same speakers, on the one hand, and intellectual movement, on the other. A similar duality exists in the early dialogues of Elizabeth and Darcy in *Pride and Prejudice*: they advance the plot (words at work), but they also display the couple reaching for and achieving intimacy by their creative use of conversation (words at play).

A second group of essays explores Austen's use of speech to dramatize "Aggression and Power." Juliet McMaster outlines the issues in "Mrs. Elton and Other Verbal Aggressors." She shows that characters like Mrs. Elton in *Emma* and Mrs. Norris in *Mansfield Park* not only display superlatively bad manners; they also "snarl and snatch for power" (McMaster 88). The essay demonstrates Austen's fascination with the operation of power and rank in conversations. Lesley Willis Smith, in "'Hands off my man!' or 'Don't you wish you had one?': Some Subtexts of Conversational Combat in Jane Austen," studies Austen's use of implication to give her conversations energy and substance. If the conversational surface is decorous, the hidden manoeuvring for primacy is often brutal. Jan Fergus examines the interplay of conversation, laughter, and power by considering some ordinary dinner-table conversations in "The Power of Women's Language and Laughter": she argues that both Elizabeth Bennet and Emma Woodhouse attain intimacy and equality with their mates through the use of speech laced with laughter. Gary Kelly, in "Austen's Imagined Communities: Talk, Narration, and Founding the Modern State," argues that the speech of Austen's characters and the dialect of her omniscient narrator, which frames and contains the characters' speech, allow the reader to experience another's subjectivity powerfully—and so to participate in an imagined community of novel-readers that reinforces the defining qualities of the emerging nation-state of Great Britain. The aggression and power identified in this essay are those of the novelist herself and the professional class she embodies.

The four essays in "Subtexts and Ironies" explore Austen's unparalleled skill at playing off sentences spoken by her characters against every possible variation of speech unspoken, spoken but not heard, heard but misinterpreted, echoed, repeated with variations, modulated in shapely fashion, and withheld or summarized—and all to a myriad of purposes and effects. Ronald Hall, in "Mishearing, Misreading, and the Language of Listening," focusses on the way Austen's characters underspeak and overhear or overspeak and underhear, causing a comedy of misunderstanding that ultimately resolves itself through the attainment of proper modes of listening. Linda Bree, in "Belonging to the Conversation in *Persuasion*," traces Captain Wentworth's and Anne Elliot's efforts to reconcile propriety and sincerity (or, in Elizabeth Bennet's memorable phrase, "to unite civility and truth " [*PP* 216]), a task that makes conversation exciting, complex, and dangerous. Austen's climactic proposal scenes in *Pride and Prejudice*, *Emma*, and *Persuasion*, often discussed apologetically or defensively, are explored by Sarah Frantz in "'If I loved you less, I might be able to talk about it more': Direct Dialogue and Education in the Proposal Scenes." This essay argues that these scenes are designed in each case to dramatize the hero's moral education and so prove him worthy of the heroine, whose moral growth the reader has been following thanks to Austen's decision to tell her story from the vantage point of the heroine's consciousness. Nora Foster Stovel, in "Famous Last Words: Elizabeth Bennet Protests Too Much," examines the ironies bristling from the "famous last words" uttered by Austen's most witty heroine. Considered closely, these bristles become flexible threads that form a pretty and sturdy net in *Pride and Prejudice*, reminding us that Jane Austen was herself an accomplished needlewoman.

The three essays in the final section, "Speculations and Possibilities," do indeed speculate—particularly Elizabeth Newark's entertaining foray into imagining the words not spoken by Austen's suitors and seducers, "Words Not Spoken: Courtship and Seduction in Jane Austen's Novels." Seduced herself by Austen's art, she succumbs to the temptation of writing and transposing speeches, enabling us to hear for a moment "noises off." Steven Scott, in "Making Room in the Middle: Mary in *Pride and Prejudice*," speculates about Mary, the much-mocked middle daughter of the Bennets, considering her as a disappointment to the family's expectation of a son, a post-Romantic character in a world caught up in the shift between neoclassical and Romantic paradigms, a reader who talks like a writer, a precursor of the modern woman, and even a stand-in for Austen herself. The final essay, Jeffrey Herrle's "The Idiolects of the Idiots: The Language and Conversation of Jane Austen's Less-Than-Savoury Suitors," shows just how laughable and entertaining are the distinctive speech patterns of John Thorpe of *Northanger Abbey* and Mr. Collins of *Pride and Prejudice*, while at the same time demonstrating that these speech habits contain some disturbing implications.

Taken together, the essays show the astonishing richness and subtlety that Austen has embedded in her fictional conversations. In fact, like Molière's M. Jourdain in *Le Bourgeois Gentilhomme*, who is amazed to discover he has been speaking prose all his life, the readers of this volume may find themselves startled to realize how much the everyday activity of conversation can accomplish. The essays suggest new ways of approaching Austen's art, while taking as their starting-point the nineteenth-century perception that Austen's greatest achievement is her use of dialogue to convey character. Richard Whately, in 1821, only four years after Austen's death, remarked that Jane Austen is "a thorough mistress in the knowledge of human character; how it is acted upon by education and circumstance, and how, when once formed, it shows itself through every hour of every day, and in every speech of every person. Her conversations would be tiresome but for this" (Southam 98). Or, as G.H. Lewes put it in 1859, "Instead of telling us what her characters are, and what they feel, she presents the people, and they reveal themselves. In this, she has perhaps never been surpassed, not even by Shakespeare himself" (Southam 157). Bridging the familiar and the new, the written and the spoken, the unique occasion and the printed realm of scholarly discourse, these essays celebrate the pleasures to be found in vivid, revealing, and (as Whately insisted) never tiresome speech.

NOTES

1 Howard S. Babb, *Jane Austen's Novels: The Fabric of Dialogue*; Norman Page, *The Language of Jane Austen*; K.C. Philips, *Jane Austen's English*; Stuart M. Tave, *Some Words of Jane Austen*.

2 Juliet McMaster, "The Secret Languages of *Emma*" (reprinted in her *Jane Austen the Novelist*); "Talking about Talk in *Pride and Prejudice*"; "The Talkers and Listeners of *Mansfield Park*"; "Clothing the Thought in the Word: The Speakers of *Northanger Abbey*."

Categories
and Analysis

JOCELYN HARRIS

1

Silent Women, Shrews, and Bluestockings

Women and Speaking in Jane Austen

WOMEN HAVE ALWAYS BEEN DISCOURAGED from knowing, speaking, and writing. So how did Jane Austen allow her women characters to speak, let alone risk bringing two thousand years' worth of disapproval down upon herself by raising her own voice? By looking at three common stereotypes of women in her novels—the silent woman, the shrew, and the bluestocking—I argue that Jane Austen, in the full knowledge of misogynist constructions of women as well as eighteenth-century resistance to them, deployed the dramatic conventions of the novel to undo them.

Where did these stereotypes come from? As Sidonie Smith explains in *A Poetics of Women's Autobiography*, authorities both classical and Christian declared that women were inferior. A woman, said Aristotle, was less perfect than a man. More passive and less rational because her child-bearing capacity tied her to matter, she was cold where he was hot, and therefore missed out on the virtues associated with heat, such as courage, moral strength, and honesty. Aristotle called woman a monstrous or unnatural creation, and Aquinas, though admitting that she was necessary for the preservation of the species, would name her "misbegotten man."

So too in the founding myth of Christianity, woman is less than man. In Genesis, Adam is made in the image of God, while Eve, in defiance of common logic, is made out of Adam's substance (Genesis 2.20–23).[1] Tied to procreation and therefore more irrational and vulnerable than Adam, Eve is easily persuaded to eat the fruit of disobedience—in *Paradise Lost* Milton would explain that her real crime was a transgressive desire for the knowledge that God freely gave to Adam and denied to her. For that hunger to know, Eve was punished with eternal subordination to her husband and bitter pain in childbirth. For the Church fathers, menstruation and childbirth were pollutions that women tried to cover with fancy dress, ornamentation, and cosmetics, all of which served only to expose women's vanity, seductiveness, and lechery—that is, their real involvement in the life of the senses and of matter. And because they were closely associated with the cycles of the moon, women were also thought to be fickle and inconstant. Intellectually, ethically, and morally, then, women were not only inferior, but dangerous. They must be confined to the private realm of domesticity, excluded from the public realm of action, and silenced.[2] Even at home, the good woman should say little, while a woman who said too much was labelled shrewish, vainly learned, or seductive on the assumption that a loose tongue in a woman meant loose morals. Thus where Adam was freely granted goods, words, and woman from God, Eve spoke transgressively to gain power and knowledge and to deceive. Her punishment was to become the object of representation and definition by men. And after Plato excluded women from politics, education came to be regarded as the sole preserve of men.[3]

The restrictions on women speaking and writing were therefore extraordinarily severe, as a number of Jane Austen's predecessors pointed out. Having always to be self-conscious about their gender, as men were not, they knew that critics would harp upon the fact that they were women and condemn them for it. Women's texts were seen as interchangeable with their bodies: when Katherine Philips's poems were published without her consent, she expressed her dismay in terms of bodily shame, calling herself "that unfortunate person that cannot so much as think in private, that must have my imaginations rifled and exposed to play the Mountebanks, and dance upon the Ropes to entertain all the rabble" (129). To avoid that fate, many women published anonymously, as Jane Austen herself would do. The poet Anne Finch might declare that she was impatient with "the dull manage of a servile house" and tired of painting, embroidery, and dressing to please men (24). She might boldly ask why when "Myra paints her face," she could not paint a thought (23). But caught between what she described as "the skill to write, the modesty to hide" (18), her remedy was withdrawal into solitude and depression. Others were anxious not to threaten men's customary domination of creativity and begged only for books and a space in which to speak. Even as they humbled themselves, they knew they could be labelled bluestockings. Like Eve, whose longing to know had brought sin and death into the world, learned women were thought to be as disastrous as comets, and therefore to be mocked.

By the end of the seventeenth century, however, some women writers had begun to speak out against the suppression of their voices. One reason for this may have been the ideas of John Locke in *Two Treatises of Government* (1690): his *First Treatise* contains the radical notion that slaves under tyranny have the right to rebel (1.1)—as King Charles I had discovered to his cost when he was beheaded at Whitehall. For women, Locke opened up the possibility of resisting tyrannical and arbitrary power, even the patriarchal power that descended from God to Adam to kings and then to all men.[4] His *Second Treatise* might have intrigued them all the more, for here he calls women's subordination and suffering in childbirth "curses" upon Eve and kindly suggests that women should avoid childbirth pangs if they possibly can (1.47). But although Locke pulls back from advising them to disobey their tyrannical Adams—he pleads instead the power of custom, temporal law, and nature—many women must have drawn their own conclusions. For instance, when Mary Astell, the pioneering feminist, attacked loveless marriages, she asked simply, "If all *Men are born free*, how is it that all Women are born Slaves?" (107). Samuel Richardson, who knew a great deal about

Astell, would likewise make his heroine in *Clarissa* (1747–48) question the power that her father and her brother asserted over her just because they were men. "My mind is not that of a slave," she cries (III). Some women attacked the institution of patriarchy itself, complaining, as the poet Mary Leapor put it in "Man the Monarch," that

> Sires, brothers, husbands and commanding sons,
> The sceptre claim; and ev'ry cottage brings
> A long succession of domestic kings. (203)

Others believed that before patriarchy began, women ruled the arts as well as the government. Saying that it was time to overturn men's usurpation of women's rightful place on Parnassus, they warned that with the rise of women's writing, "the Rule of Wit's now feminine."[5] Other women claimed that since all souls were equal before God, women's bodies only superinduced what Austen's favourite author Samuel Richardson called a "temporary difference" in their present transitory state. "When Sex ceases," he wrote in *Sir Charles Grandison* (1753–54), "inequality of Souls will cease; and women will certainly be on a foot with men, as to intellectuals, in Heaven" (VI.250).

Like these earlier authors, Jane Austen interrogates and rewrites the old, persistent stereotypes. It is no surprise that Fanny Price, who inhabits the most patriarchal of Austen's households, is the most wretchedly inarticulate of her heroines. Mansfield Park is founded on West Indian imperialism and ruled by a man whom Henry Crawford calls "rich, superior, long-worded, arbitrary" (*MP* 297). As a poor, young, female member of a lateral branch of the family, Fanny is indeed "the lowest and last," as Mrs. Norris reminds her (221), "exceedingly timid and shy, and shrinking from notice" (12). Fanny is the most quiet, modest, and therefore, in biblical terms, the most "truly feminine" (169) of Austen's women characters. As Mary Crawford says, she is "almost as fearful of notice and praise as other women [are] of neglect" (198). When forced to speak to prevent herself from being drawn into the play, she is "shocked to find herself at that moment the only speaker in the room, and to feel that almost every eye was upon her" (145–46). For Fanny as for Katherine Philips, body and text are one—one might almost say her body speaks for her when her tongue cannot.

As if internalizing the embargo on women's speech, Fanny finds it agonizingly difficult to speak. Her feminine sensibility often overcomes her. When Edmund helps her with her letter, "Fanny's feelings on the occasion were such as she believed herself incapable of expressing" (16); in the face of Edward's kindness over her Mrs. Norris-induced fatigue, her tears "made it easier to swallow than to speak" (74). We hear of Fanny that "though never a great talker, she was always more inclined to silence when feeling most strongly" (369). She is overpowered by a thousand feelings of pain and pleasure when Edmund gives her the plainer chain (261). When he hints at his attachment to Miss Crawford, it turns her "too sick for speech." Struggling to speak, she tells him that she herself is a listener, not an adviser, and stops him from telling her anything that hereafter he may be sorry for (268–69). Sometimes those same feelings prompt her to cry out, as when she regrets that the custom of chapel prayers has been discontinued, but the anger that makes her colour inhibits her from speech (86–87).

Then, too, Fanny constantly checks herself from commenting on other people, as if she does not want to be thought a shrew. It would be copying out half the book to show the extent of her self-censorship, but some examples must suffice. For instance, about Mary Crawford, "Fanny could have said a great deal, but it was safer to say nothing" (199). Invested with the office of judge and critic of the young people's acting, she "earnestly desired to exercise it and tell them all their faults"—and by implication their faults in real life. However,

> from doing so every feeling within her shrank, she could not, would not, dared not attempt it; had she been otherwise qualified for criticism, her conscience must have restrained her from venturing at disapprobation. She believed herself to feel too much of it in the aggregate for honesty or safety in particulars. (170)

Henry Crawford's proposal shows again how difficult it is for her to speak her mind: "She considered it all as nonsense, as mere trifling and gallantry, which meant only to deceive for the hour," but she "would not allow herself to shew half the displeasure she felt" (301). Pressed for an answer, she cries out, "No, no, no," hiding her face. "This is all nonsense. Do not distress me" (301). When Sir Thomas becomes Henry's advocate, she is "embarrassed to a degree that made either speaking or looking up quite impossible." Her very body silences her: "She could say no more; her breath was almost gone." With her face "like scarlet" and "her lips formed into a *no*, though the sound was inarticulate," she denies loving another, for "she would rather die than own the truth." When Sir Thomas asks if she has any reason to think ill of Mr. Crawford's temper, "she longed to add, 'but of his principles I have;' but her heart sunk under the appalling prospect of discussion, explanation, and probably non-conviction." Intimidated by Sir Thomas's cold sternness into apologizing through tears, she manages only to say that she could never make Mr. Crawford happy, and that she should be miserable herself (313–20). Her anger, disgust, and resentment towards Henry can never be uttered (328–29).

She is equally silenced by other people's low expectations of her, for "few young ladies of eighteen could be less called on to speak their opinion than Fanny" (48). Fanny says what others want her to say, "believing herself required to speak" (455), or being "expected to speak," and only able to say that she was "very much obliged to her aunt Bertram for sparing her, and that she was endeavouring to put her aunt's evening work in such a state as to prevent her being missed" (220). Or she speaks when she cannot escape it, as when "wearied at last into speaking" by Henry's persistent attentions (343).

Typically, Fanny is a "quiet auditor" (136), "always a very courteous listener" (164). But even if she does manage to speak at some length, nobody listens to her. She loves to hear her uncle talk of the West Indies for an hour together, but when she enquires about the important topic of the slave trade, her questions are not followed up by the others: "There was such a dead silence!" (197–98). Even more mortifying is the moment when Edmund, far from sharing her enthusiasm about the sublimity of the stars, advances by gentle degrees towards Mary's harp (113). Similarly, Mary Crawford is so "untouched and inattentive" to her friend's rhapsody on the evergreens that Fanny quickly brings her own mind back "to what she thought must interest." Mary's choice of topic, the Rushworth marriage, completes her silencing (208–10).

Only with her brother William does she know an "unchecked, equal, fearless, intercourse" (234), for although Edmund may have urged her to speak openly (15), her secret love for him and his blindness over the Crawfords combine painfully to constrain her speech. In a typical moment, Fanny "would probably have made some important communications to her usual confidant. As it was, however, she only hazarded a hint, and the hint was lost" (115). Again, when Edmund talks himself into playing Anhalt, she knows he is deceiving himself but cannot answer (154). And after Henry's proposal, she is "silent and reserved" with Edmund, for she fears they think too differently for her to find any relief in talking of what she feels (345–46). The warmth of her "never, never, never; he never will succeed with me" astonishes him with its revelation of agency in someone he thought he knew: "Never, Fanny, so very determined and positive! This is not like yourself, your rational self" (347). She tries to explain why she cannot approve of Henry's character, but Edmund scarcely hears her to the end (349).

Outwardly, then, Fanny fulfils the Western ideal of the silent woman, but although she is quiet, she is not blind, as she herself says (363). Fanny may not speak out, but Jane Austen draws on the dramatic conventions of the novel to reveal that even a silent woman can be a sentient and passionate being. Fanny's virtual soliloquy in response to Henry Crawford's fond recollections of the Mansfield Park theatricals, for instance, is powerfully forthright: "With silent indignation, Fanny repeated to herself, 'Never happier!—never happier than when doing what you must know was not justifiable!—never happier than when behaving so dishonourably and unfeelingly!—Oh! what a corrupted mind!'" (225). "Hate" is a very large word when Mr. Crawford's significant smile about Rushworth and his fair bride "made Fanny quite hate him" (224), while her opinion that "the greatest blessing to every one of kindred with Mrs. Rushworth would be instant annihilation" certainly suggests some vigour of mind (442). She can even be almost vexed into displeasure and anger against Edmund for his blindness: "Fix, commit, condemn yourself," she thinks resentfully (424), but she never says it. Gradually, though, she learns to talk (198). After her thirty-nine words to Henry Crawford about the theatricals, we are told "she had never spoken so much at once to him in her life before, and never so angrily to anyone," so that "she trembled and blushed at her own daring" (225–26)—that old fear of being thought a shrew. But Edmund's rejection of Mary Crawford finally gives her the liberty to speak openly to him (459), and ultimately to marry the cousin she loves.

"My Fanny," as Jane Austen calls her in a rare moment of narrative affection (461), exemplifies the maxim that the last shall be first and the meek inherit, if not the earth, her heart's desire. She has held vehement opinions, but because she expresses them only to herself or obliquely to Edmund, she cannot be labelled a shrew. Fanny has suffered greatly from a real shrew, Mrs. Norris, who has been to her an embodiment of Samuel Johnson's definition of the word in his *Dictionary of the English Language*: "A peevish, malignant, clamorous, spiteful, vexatious, turbulent woman." Of Fanny, Mrs. Norris says, "I shall think her a very obstinate, ungrateful girl, if she does not do what her aunt and cousins wish her—very ungrateful indeed, considering who and what she is" (147). It is a wonderful reversal when the final catastrophe to which Mrs. Norris has so largely contributed makes of her "an altered creature, quieted, stupefied" (448). In Jane Austen's revision of the stereotype, the quietness of the silent woman is recuperated as valuable. Indeed, Edmund has already spoken of sharing "the luxury of silence" with Fanny (278).

Is Mary Crawford a shrew? She calls Dr. Grant "an indolent selfish bon vivant" (111) and makes bold and bawdy jokes: "Of *Rears*, and *Vices*, I saw enough. Now, do not be suspecting me of a pun, I entreat" (60). For a woman, she knows far too much of the public realm; she certainly confirms Western suspicions that women use language for its persuasive and alluring power. When Edmund reports on her "saucy playful smile, seeming to invite, in order to subdue me" (459), he represents her as a stereotypical seductress. And yet if we admire Mary's energy and generous impulses of warmth, we may be sensing Jane Austen's support for outspokenness in a woman.

She certainly seems to admire bold speaking in *Pride and Prejudice,* which similarly spans the whole spectrum from silent woman to potential shrew. At one end lies Georgiana Darcy, silent before a rich and powerful brother who is "aweful" in his own house of a Sunday evening (PP 50). We never actually hear her speak. It is difficult to "obtain even a word ... beyond a monosyllable" from this exceedingly shy woman (261), though she sometimes does "venture a short sentence, when there was least danger of its being heard" (267). At the other extreme lies Elizabeth Bennet, whose quick verbal facility derives in no small measure from the fact that her father, having almost entirely abdicated his patriarchal authority, admires and encourages her wit, which saves her as well as getting her into trouble. From this position of strength, she can talk back to Lady Catherine, a woman made powerful by class, in spite of Mr. Collins's ludicrously oxymoronic admonition: "Your wit and vivacity I think must be acceptable to her, especially when tempered with the silence and respect which her rank will inevitably excite" (106). Lady Catherine says,

> "You will be censured, slighted, and despised, by every one connected with him. Your alliance will be a disgrace; your name will never even be mentioned by any of us."
>
> "These are heavy misfortunes," replied Elizabeth. "But the wife of Mr. Darcy must have such extraordinary sources of happiness necessarily attached to her situation, that she could, upon the whole, have no cause to repine." (355)

She can speak just as boldly to Mr. Darcy, tease him, laugh at him (57), and reject his proposal in the most vehement terms: "I have every reason in the world to think ill of you," she says, relentlessly listing "your arrogance, your conceit, and your selfish disdain of the feelings of others" as the cause for "so immoveable a dislike" (191, 193).

So is she in fact a shrew? Her close relationship to Shakespeare's Beatrice certainly lays her open to that charge (see Harris, *Memory* 109–10), and Miss Bingley thinks that Elizabeth's eyes have "a sharp, shrewish look" (271). But Miss Bingley herself is rebuked for a shrew when Mr. Darcy declares unexpectedly, in response to her attack, that for many months he has considered Elizabeth as one of the handsomest women of his acquaintance (271). Elizabeth herself comes to regret "the petulance and acrimony of her manner in rejecting him" (265), and when she knows what he has done for Lydia, she grieves over "every saucy speech she had ever directed towards him" (327), wishing earnestly that "her former opinions had been more reasonable, her expressions more moderate!" (376). Humility redeems this potential shrew, whose outspokenness, like Beatrice's, has actually been delightful: "There was a mixture of sweetness and archness in her manner which made it difficult for her to affront anybody; and Darcy had never been so bewitched by any woman as he was by her" (52). Her self-representation to Mr. Collins "as a rational creature speaking the truth from her heart" attempts to persuade him that she is not the affected coquette, the "elegant female" that he misogynistically thinks her to be (109), while her truth-telling to Lady Catherine exposes her love for Darcy: "After abusing you so abominably to your face, I could have no scruple in abusing you to all your relations" (367). She reframes her own impertinence as openness and lack of guile:

> The fact is, that you were sick of civility, of deference, of officious attention. You were disgusted with the women who were always speaking and looking, and thinking for your approbation alone. I roused, and interested you, because I was so unlike them. (380)

And in that last glimpse of Georgiana's astonished alarm at Elizabeth's "lively, sportive manner of talking with her brother" (387–88), we witness the rehabilitation of the shrew.

Given Elizabeth's independence of mind, it may seem surprising when Mr. Bennet sounds like an old-time patriarch: "I know that you could be neither happy nor respectable, unless you truly esteemed your husband; unless you looked up to him as a superior." But when he adds, "My child, let me not have the grief of seeing *you* unable to respect your partner in life" (376), he thinks rather of his own wife. He believes, in short, that partners should respect each other intellectually. He also insists that Darcy must deserve respect rather than demanding it. As a loving brother and "the best landlord, and the best master" (249), Darcy turns out to be the very model of a modern feudal patriarch. This attractive version of patriarchy depends on merit, not right, and it anticipates Captain Wentworth.

If Elizabeth effectively wins the hero by playing the shrew, Jane Austen never rescues Mary from her stereotype as a bluestocking. "'Pride,' observed

Mary, who piqued herself upon the solidity of her reflections, 'is a very common failing I believe. By all that I have ever read, I am convinced that it is very common indeed'" (20). Jane Austen tells us that "having, in consequence of being the only plain one of the family, worked hard for knowledge and accomplishments, [Mary] was always impatient for display" (25). She has "a pedantic air and conceited manner" (25); Elizabeth finds her "deep in the study of thorough bass and human nature; and had some new extracts to admire, and some new observations of thread-bare morality to listen to" (60). The narrator joins forces with Mary's father to mock her: "'What say you, Mary? for you are a young lady of deep reflection I know, and read great books, and make extracts.' Mary wished to say something very sensible, but knew not how" (7). Even Lydia's disgrace provokes from her only proverbs and clichés.

Clever women must have dreaded being caricatured like this. When Miss Bingley accuses Elizabeth of being a great reader with no pleasure in anything else, her prompt and defensive reply—"I am *not* a great reader, and I have pleasure in many things" (37)—suggests how sharply the charge could sting. Jane Austen permits her heroines a more traditional and acceptable route to learning through the experience and libraries of men— rather as Eve derived knowledge from Adam in *Paradise Lost*. Her heroes are not exactly the mentors that Mary Lascelles considers them in *Jane Austen and Her Art* but conduits to an education otherwise unavailable to women. As the narrator puts it when Elizabeth contemplates what she has lost, "From [Darcy's] judgment, information, and knowledge of the world, she must have received benefit of greater importance" (312). Darcy's definition of the truly accomplished woman includes the improvement of her mind by extensive reading, and Elizabeth, who prefers a book to a game of loo, will doubtless make quiet use of his "delightful library" at Pemberley (37–38).

In *Emma*, Jane Austen meditates feelingly on the very real "danger" of girls "coming back prodigies" from their schooling (*E* 22), for once Jane Fairfax's excellent education makes her "really accomplished" (166) and "fully competent to the office of instruction herself" (164), she is drawn inexorably to what she calls in a bitter phrase "offices for the sale—not quite of human flesh—but of human intellect" (300). Miss Fairfax argues that what she calls the "governess-trade" is equivalent to the slave-trade, "widely different certainly as to the guilt of those who carry it on; but as to the greater misery of the victims, I do not know where it lies" (300–01). Jane Fairfax is both a bluestocking and—except for this extraordinary outburst and another at Box Hill—a silent woman. Of all Jane Austen's characters she is the most private, so much so that Charlotte Brontë may have found it irresistible to enlarge her story. Why else is her own governess, Jane, greeted by Mrs. Fairfax in a book that also applies the discourse of slavery to women? Did Brontë, writing indignantly of Jane Eyre's maltreatment at the hands of the Reed children, remember Emma's sympathetic outcry, "Ah! ... if other children are at all like what I remember to have been myself, I should think five times the amount of what I have ever yet heard named as a salary on such occasions, dearly earned" (382)?[6]

Emma "has been meaning to read more since she was twelve years old," but the "great many lists of her drawing up at various times of books that she meant to read regularly through" remain largely untouched (37). Although in fact it is "rather too late in the day to be simple-minded and ignorant," like Harriet (142), Emma is as prejudiced by Jane's superior talents as by her appearance of cold caution, of being "disgustingly ... suspiciously reserved" (169). Jane is in fact silenced by the need to conceal her talents, by the intellectual disparity between herself and her aunt, and by the secret engagement, for example in the episode when Frank, in the full knowledge that she cannot speak, torments her cruelly about the real donor of the piano (241–43). Angered again by the covert meaning of "*Dixon*," the word prepared by Frank in the puzzle-game, she cannot say all she feels. Miss Bates, however, perceives it is time to be going home, "though Jane had not spoken a word" (348–49). At Box Hill, "Miss Fairfax, who had seldom spoken before, except among her own confederates, spoke now," essentially to break off the engagement (372). But in a sense she remains silenced, for in that crowd she must speak generally and obliquely. Even when Emma offers her the earnest hand of friendship, strong feelings leave her "entirely without words" (453). A prodigy among women, she is muted and marginalized, trapped by cultural stereotypes as much as by her desire for the irresponsible, the undeserving Frank Churchill.

Emma Woodhouse, like Elizabeth Bennet, speaks too freely because her father's power is weak. We may forgive her for exclaiming to herself, after her first exposure to the dreadful Mrs. Elton, "Insufferable woman! ... Worse than I had supposed. Absolutely insufferable! ... A little upstart, vulgar being, with her Mr. E., and her *caro sposo*, and her resources, and all her airs of pert pretension and under-bred finery" (279). More difficult to excuse is her mimicry of Miss Bates flying off, through half a sentence, to her mother's old petticoat. At this point, though, Emma is reeling from the idea of Jane Fairfax being mistress of Donwell Abbey, and she lashes out at the aunt to hurt the niece (225). Her attack on Miss Bates at Box Hill does real harm, however. Emma may complain that Miss Bates "never holds her tongue" (194), but she herself cannot resist the witticism about saying dull things: "Ah! ma'am, but there may be a difficulty. Pardon me—but you will be limited as to number—only three at once" (370). Mr. Knightley's rebuke renders "her tongue motionless." Unable to speak to him, she is silent on that tearful journey home (375–76).

When Mr. Knightley proposes, Emma moves comically from talking at cross purposes to astonished silence—twice. First, she who "sets [herself] up for Understanding" fails to understand that Mr. Knightley loves not Harriet, but her: "Emma could say no more. They seemed to be within half a sentence of Harriet" (427, 429). Then her offer to act as a friend prompts a proposal that silences her again. "She could really say nothing.—'You are silent,' he cried, with great animation; 'absolutely silent! at present I ask no more'" (430). Jane Austen makes one last joke about the over-talkative woman: she turns down the volume just when we want to hear. "She spoke then, on being so entreated.—What did she say?—Just what she ought, of course. A lady always does.—She said enough to show there need not be despair—and to invite him to say more himself" (431). Emma says too much too often, but her openness is better than Jane's reserve. Mr. Knightley says meaningfully of Jane that "she has not the open temper which a man would wish for in a wife. ... She is reserved, more reserved, I think, than she used to be—And I love an open temper" (288–89). But by being willing to talk, to make amends, to support her friend even against her own best interest, Emma blunders into being a wife.

Only Anne Elliot finds a truly permissible way to speak. Born to an extravagantly patriarchal environment, she walks in a favourite grove, withdrawn and reflective (*P* 25) like Anne Finch in her poem "Petition for an Absolute Retreat." Her mother is dead, and all those around her—Lady Russell, her sisters, the Musgroves—play the old male games of marriage, primogeniture, and inheritance. But her father's power wanes significantly as soon as he leaves his house, and in a climate where meritocracy is poised to supplant patriarchy, Anne speaks up for the constancy of women.

The very title *Persuasion* refers to Eve our first mother, who brought sin and death into the world because she was persuadable by the serpent. As Captain Harville observes,

> all histories are against you, all stories, prose and verse ... I could bring you fifty quotations in a moment on my side the argument, and I do not think I ever opened a book in my life which had not something to say upon woman's inconstancy. Songs and proverbs, all talk of woman's fickleness. (*P* 234)

Anne tackles this slur that women are inconstant by setting Captain Benwick's story against her own. And when she argues that the sole reason women have not been able to answer the charges against them is that they have not had access to the pen—and by implication to the telling of their own stories—she challenges the church fathers for denying women education, as the Wife of Bath had done before her. His comment, "But perhaps you will say, these were all written by men," gives Anne her chance to reply:

> Yes, yes, if you please, no reference to examples in books. Men have had every advantage of us in telling their own story. Education has been theirs in so much higher a degree; the pen has been in their hands. I will not allow books to prove any thing. (234)

Captain Harville admits, "when I think of Benwick, my tongue is tied" (236). Anne proves that in spite of all the prejudicial stories women are constant. Against all custom she defines men; against all tradition she ties the tongue of a man. But it is a measure of her difficulty that even in this scene she speaks not personally but allusively, drawing on the words of powerful "authorities"—Chaucer, Shakespeare, and Richardson—in order to speak her mind (see Harris, *Memory* 208–12).

She also challenges the assumption that men are rational and women passionate. When Captain Harville speaks "in a tone of strong feeling" about the suffering of a man taking a last look at his wife and children and of the glow of his soul when he does see them again; when he speaks of "such men as have hearts!" and presses his own with emotion, Anne confirms his warm and faithful feelings, claiming only the privilege of "loving longest, when existence or when hope is gone" (234–35). When Captain Wentworth overhears this reversal of the stereotypes, the pen actually falls down from his hand (233).[7] His reckless, incoherent letter hands all agency, rationality, and power over to her. So when Jane Austen writes that Anne Elliot and Captain Wentworth have become "more equal to act, more justified in acting" (241), she is surely hinting at their essential equality of souls, of "intellectuals," to use Richardson's word, that overrides the temporary difference in their bodies. Aristotle in his *Politics* thought that women could not possess courage, moral strength, and honesty—but Anne Elliot possesses all three of these virtues.

In this dialogue between Anne and Captain Harville, Captain Wentworth hears a declaration of love such as no woman of her time could ever have spoken directly. She both speaks and does not speak, and cannot therefore be labelled unfeminine. Through a narrative sleight of hand, Jane Austen liberates her heroine into the happiness of "belonging to that profession which is, if possible, more distinguished in its domestic virtues than in its national importance" (252), that is, the happiness of belonging to the public domain. In this extraordinary book, Jane Austen attacks patriarchy at every turn, from Sir Walter Elliot's admiration of his own lineage to the primogeniture that rewards the male heir simply for being male. For when meritocracy replaces patriarchy, a woman may speak at last.

Thus Jane Austen shields her outspoken and intelligent heroines from being labelled shrews or bluestockings. And she allows her silenced women to speak through two dramatic strategies for uncovering the mind: the soliloquy or the dialogue overheard. Her last defence is purely technical, for her famous trick of coloured narrative allows her heroines to think uncomfortable truths that they could never articulate aloud—a daughter's criticism of her parents, for instance. If Elizabeth had said that her mother was "a woman of mean understanding, little information, and uncertain temper" (*PP* 5), or pointed out her father's "continual breach of conjugal obligation and decorum which, in exposing his wife to the contempt of her own children, was so highly reprehensible" (236), we would barely tolerate such unfilial and shrewish remarks.

Elizabeth herself recognizes the difference between thinking an uncharitable thought and speaking it. When Lydia says that Wickham "never cared three straws" about Miss King and calls her "a nasty little freckled thing," Elizabeth is "shocked to think that, however incapable of such coarseness of *expression* herself, the coarseness of the *sentiment* was little other than her own breast had formerly harboured and fancied liberal!" (220). Her friend Charlotte Lucas, in order to save her female life, will likewise keep to herself her reflections that "Mr. Collins to be sure was neither sensible nor agreeable; his society was irksome, and his attachment to her must be imaginary. But still he would be her husband" (122). Although Fanny Price must and did feel that her home "was the abode of noise, disorder, and impropriety," that her father "was more negligent of his family, his habits were worse, and his manners coarser, than she had been prepared for. ... he swore and he drank, he was dirty and gross," and that "her mother was a partial, ill-judging parent, a dawdle, a slattern," she scruples to make use of the words, as the narrator says (388–90). And though Anne Elliot knows all too well that her father is "a foolish, spendthrift baronet, who had not principle or sense enough to maintain himself in the situation in which Providence had placed him" (*P* 248), she will never say so.

Such sharp comments are either coloured by the characters' views or summarize their thoughts, but an authorial persona speaks them. Unlike her characters, Jane Austen can make these judgements because her persona, like that of Fielding her mentor, is god-like, omniscient, infallible. Within the golden worlds that she herself has made, she judges her characters through their fates—what the eighteenth century would have called poetic or distributive justice: "My Fanny indeed at this very time, I have the satisfaction of knowing, must have been happy in spite of every thing" (*MP*

461). Her voice is authorial and authoritative at the same time because it comes out of nowhere and is attached to nobody in particular.

Many readers believe that they hear the "real" Jane Austen in her authorial voice, but it is only a device, another character created by the author. As Dickens would make Betsey Prig say of Mrs. Harris in *Martin Chuzzlewit*, "I don't believe there's no sich a person!" (646). That authorial voice may seem vivid and present, but it represents actual absence and is in fact pure mind. And if women's equality of souls promises equality "as to intellectuals, in Heaven," Jane Austen's authorial voice, detached from her female body, may claim an equality of knowing even on this earth. Whenever she speaks in that (literally) disembodied voice, she is invulnerable. If not woman, not shrew, however severely she judges; if not woman, not bluestocking, however much she obviously knows.

What of the real Jane Austen? In company she seems to have played the silent woman, thinking and observing. Mary Mitford said she was "perpendicular, precise, taciturn ... a poker of whom everyone is afraid. ... It must be confessed that this silent observation from such an observer is rather formidable ... a wit, a delineator of character, who does not talk, is terrific indeed!".[8] But everywhere in her letters she offers opinions that she could never have expressed publicly without sounding shrewish. In one letter alone she writes,

> I never saw so plain a family, five sisters so very plain!—They are as plain as the Foresters or the Franfraddops or the Seagraves or the Rivers' excluding Sophy. ... Mr Wigram ... is about 5 or 6 & 20, not ill-looking & not agreable.—He is certainly no addition. ... Mr R. Mascall ... talks too much & is conceited—besides having a vulgarly shaped mouth. ... Only think of Mrs Holder's being dead!—Poor woman, she has done the only thing in the World she could possibly do, to make one cease to abuse her. (*L* 236–38)

But of course she wrote only for Cassandra. As Henry Tilney knew, women kept diaries for the thoughts they could not utter, and Jane Austen wrote just as confidentially to her sister, her other self.

Sometimes she wrapped up her talents in irony. Roused beyond endurance by a self-important librarian, she claimed that she might be equal to the comic part of the character of a clergyman, but

> not the Good, the Enthusiastic, the Literary. Such a Man's Conversation must at times be on the subjects of Science & Philosophy of which I know nothing—or at least be occasionally abundant in quotations & allusions which a Woman, who like me, knows only her Mother-tongue & has read very little in that, would be totally without the power of giving.—A Classical Education, or at any rate, a very extensive acquaintance with English Literature, Ancient & Modern, appears to me quite Indispensable for the person who w^d do any justice to your Clergyman—And I think I may boast myself to be, with all possible Vanity, the most unlearned, & uninformed Female who ever dared to be an Authoress. (L 306)

But, of course, she could always read the classics in English. This, too, from a woman who based *Northanger Abbey* on Locke's theory of mind, a woman who was extraordinarily well read in the classics of English literature—Chaucer, Shakespeare, the Bible, Milton, Pope, Richardson, Fielding, Thomson, Cowper, and many more. To defend herself against the librarian's masculine superiority, she dons a mask that has been as profoundly misread as Swift's.

Her plain speaking in *Northanger Abbey* is, however, exceptional. I cannot believe this passage was written by anyone but an established author.[9] It must therefore be a late addition, written perhaps at the same time as the final chapters of *Persuasion*. Here she throws off all narrative disguise to defend—like Anne Elliot—women's right to speak and write. She especially defends the novel, which is traditionally gendered female, against history, which is traditionally gendered male, setting the imagination and feelings of women against the facts and dates of men (remember how gloriously cavalier she was with both facts and dates in her own "History of England," how partial in her preferences):

Let us not desert one another; we are an injured body. Although our productions have afforded more extensive and unaffected pleasure than those of any other literary corporation in the world, no species of composition has been so much decried. From pride, ignorance, or fashion, our foes are almost as many as our readers. ... while the abilities of the nine-hundredth abridger of the History of England ... are eulogized by a thousand pens. (NA 37)

Using the tactics of her eighteenth-century predecessors, she appeals to Frances Burney and Maria Edgeworth as the authors of works "in which the greatest powers of the mind are displayed, in which the most thorough knowledge of human nature, the happiest delineation of its varieties, the liveliest effusions of wit and humour are conveyed to the world in the best chosen language"; she calls for women to support women; and she passionately declares her preference for fiction, that upstart form written by upstart women: "There seems almost a general wish of decrying the capacity and undervaluing the labour of the novelist, and of slighting the performances which have only genius, wit, and taste to recommend them" (37–38). In fact, she goes on to "prove" in *Northanger Abbey* the superiority of the novel to history and philosophy.

In this passage, then, Jane Austen defies the three thousand years of misogyny that either silenced women or called them shrewish, unequal, inconstant, deceiving, ignorant, and inappropriately learned. She writes angrily; she knows she says forbidden things—those excessive superlatives, "greatest," "most thorough," "happiest," and "liveliest," tell us so. The constraints of custom forced her and her characters to adopt dramatic masks. But ultimately she rests her case, for her novels prove indeed that women can know and write.

NOTES

1   As St. Paul wrote to the Corinthians, "For the man is not of the woman; but the woman of the man. Neither was the man created for the woman; but the woman for the man" (I Corinthians 11.8–9).

2   St. Paul forbade them to speak during public service, and since their very presence might arouse desire, they must cover the straying tendrils of their hair (see I

Corinthians 11.13). Women might receive the gift of prophecy, but they could not use it.

3   For further discussion, see Sidonie Smith, *A Poetics of Women's Autobiography: Marginality and the Fictions of Self-Representation* 27–31.

4   Sir Robert Filmer's highly influential *Patriarcha* (1680) lays out the foundations of the patriarchal system. Locke's subtitle asserts that in the first Treatise the "false principles of Robert Filmer and his followers are detected and overthrown." He particularly attacks Filmer's basic assumption that men are *not* born free.

5   For further details, see my "Sappho, Souls, and the Salic Law of Wit" in *Anticipations of the Enlightenment in England, France, and Germany*.

6   I thank the audience at the Jane Austen Society meeting (1999) in Jasper for raising the issue of Jane Fairfax. Juliet McMaster has suggested to me that Brontë may have read and liked *Emma* without knowing it was by Jane Austen.

7   At this important moment, writes Tony Tanner, Wentworth drops "that instrument which is at once a tool and a symbol of men's dominance over women; the means by which they rule women's destinies, literally *write* (through inscription, prescription, proscription) their lives" (241).

8   This remark appears in A.G. L'Estrange's *A Life of Mary Russell Mitford, Related in a Series of Letters to her Friends* (London, 1870); it is cited here from Deirdre Le Faye, *Jane Austen: A Family Record* 198–99.

9   Since writing these words, I discovered the note in the Margaret Anne Doody, Robert L. Mack, and Peter Sabor edition of *The Wanderer; or Female Difficulties* (1814) suggesting that Frances Burney's defence of the novel "very closely resembles" Jane Austen's and that "since she revised *Northanger Abbey* as late as 1816, some parts of its fifth chapter may have been influenced by the Dedication of *The Wanderer*" (910). I shall elaborate on the relationship between Burney and Austen in my forthcoming edition of *Persuasion* for the Cambridge University Press Jane Austen Project.

2

Asking Versus Telling

One Aspect of Jane Austen's Idea of Conversation

MY TEXT FOR THIS OCCASION is drawn from *Pride and Prejudice*, Volume I, chapter one, page one:

> "My dear Mr. Bennet," said his lady to him one day, "have you heard that Netherfield Park is let at last?"
>
> Mr. Bennet replied that he had not.
>
> "But it is," returned she; "for Mrs. Long has just been here, and she told me all about it."
>
> Mr. Bennet made no answer.
>
> "Do you not want to know who has taken it?" cried his wife impatiently.
>
> "*You* want to tell me, and I have no objection to hearing it." (PP 3)

Mr. Bennet is here, for the first of many times in the novel, mocking the illogic in his wife's statements: ostensibly, she *asks* her husband two questions ("have you heard that Netherfield Park is let at last? ... Do you not want to know who has taken it?"). In reality, however, as he points out, she is bursting to *tell* him some exciting news that she has just heard. Mrs. Bennet goes on to announce, "Mrs. Long says that Netherfield is taken by a young man of large fortune from the north of England ... A single man of large fortune; four or five thousand a year. What a fine thing for our girls!" (3–4). Why doesn't she simply tell her husband the news? Because a question is more emphatic, more dramatic, than a statement, and her pseudo-questions are a transparent guise intended to induce Mr. Bennet to ask a genuine question ("Who is the new tenant of Netherfield Park?"). His question, if only he would ask it, would request information that he does not possess, and so would imply that in this matter he is dependent, needy, inferior. But Mr. Bennet, and through him Jane Austen, points out that Mrs. Bennet has tried to collapse the important distinction between asking and telling.

It is much more comfortable and comforting to tell than it is to ask, and for at least three reasons. Asking a real question of another puts one in an inferior, petitioning position: a question needs a reply from another person for its completion, and so, if you ask a question, you can never have the last word. Furthermore, to ask a question is to make an appeal to others to share a subject, a purpose, and a set of assumptions—and this appeal can always lead to a rebuff or a rejection. Mary Crawford's chances of marrying Edmund Bertram dissolve and die as soon as she asks him, "What can equal the folly of our two relations?" (*MP* 454). A third reason why questions are uncomfortable for the questioner is one that will be familiar to every classroom teacher: to ask a genuine question means waiting for an answer, and that means suspense and uncertainty until the response is forthcoming. Jane Austen often shows how hard it is to ask a real question. In *Mansfield Park*, Henry Crawford tells Edmund that while out hunting he came across Edmund's future home, the parsonage at Thornton Lacey, and adds, "for such it certainly was." When Edmund asks, "You inquired then?", Henry replies, "No, I never inquire. But I *told* a man mending a hedge that it was Thornton Lacey, and he agreed to it" (*MP* 241). A real man still hates to ask for directions. This is a passing incident, but in one of the greatest of Austen's scenes, Lady Catherine de Bourgh displays the same determination to tell, even when she has come all the way to Longbourn to ask Elizabeth a question. From the beginning of the scene, Lady Catherine tells rather than asks at every point: "That lady I suppose is your mother. ... And *that* I suppose is one of your sisters. ... You have a very small park here. ... This must be a most inconvenient sitting room for the evening, in summer; the windows are full west." (*PP* 351–52) More than a page later, Lady Catherine begins to disclose the purpose of her visit but still finds it next to impossible to ask a question, so she continues to assert: "A report of a most alarming nature, reached me two days ago. ... I instantly resolved on setting off for this place, that I might make my sentiments known to you" (353). Finally, many lines later, she is forced to ask the all-important question, "Has he, has my nephew, made you an offer of marriage?" (354).

In short, telling is easy and asking is hard, because telling is a one-way communication, a transmission of opinion and fact, while question-and-answer is a two-way exchange. Question-and-answer is thus the core element in conversation, which is, precisely, an exchange, a mutual creation by two or more people. *Conversation* is defined in *The Concise Oxford Dictionary of Current English* as "the informal exchange of ideas, information, etc. by spoken words." Samuel Johnson's definition of the word *converse* in his *Dictionary of the English Language* of 1755 is remarkably similar: "To convey the thoughts reciprocally in talk." The key notion is *exchange*: Samuel Johnson, Jane Austen's "my dear Dr. Johnson" (*L* 181), exists in Boswell's *Life of Johnson* as a hero of daily conversation, and Johnson speaks repeatedly about conversation in just these terms. At one point he says to Boswell, "That is the happiest conversation where there is no competition, but a calm quiet interchange of sentiments" (Boswell 623). Johnson frequently distinguishes between *conversation* and *talk*. When Boswell asks him if there was good conversation at a dinner Johnson went to the previous night, Johnson replies, "No, Sir, we had *talk* enough, but no *conversation*; there was nothing *discussed*" (1210).

The narrators of Austen's novels often describe the absence of conversation, of a genuine interchange of ideas. For instance, in *Northanger Abbey* Mrs. Allen and Mrs. Thorpe spend the chief part of every day together at Bath "in what they called conversation, but in which there was scarcely ever any exchange of opinion, and not often any resemblance of subject, for Mrs. Thorpe talked chiefly of her children, and Mrs. Allen of her gowns" (NA 36). Catherine Morland, in the same novel, finds herself wearied by John Thorpe, because "all the rest of his conversation, or rather talk, began and ended with himself and his own concerns. He told her of horses which he had bought for a trifle and sold for incredible sums; of racing matches, in which his judgment had infallibly foretold the winner ..." (66). The narrator of *Sense and Sensibility* tells us that at Barton Park the characters "could not be supposed to meet for the sake of conversation. Such a thought would never enter either Sir John or Lady Middleton's head, and therefore very little leisure was ever given for general chat, and none at all for particular discourse" (SS 143). In *Emma*, the heroine's "views of improving her little friend's mind, by a great deal of useful reading and conversation, had never yet led to more than a few first chapters, and the intention of going on to-morrow. It was much easier to chat ..." (E 69). As Juliet McMaster has remarked, "'Conversation,' unlike mere 'talk,' must go somewhere, must, through a process of verbal exchange and enlargement, refine on a topic and advance it" ("Secret Languages" 120).

Austen clearly thinks that conversation is different from talk or chat, and the distinction between asking and telling is a more particular instance of this difference in speech categories. One interesting point is that in Austen's novels genuine questions are relatively rare and so, correspondingly, very important. Perhaps a precise term for such real questions is that they are *consultative*: one person consults another or others to discover information, or opinion, or a preference. Think of how important it is right at the end of Volume I of *Persuasion*, when Captain Wentworth, who has, up to this point, spoken to Anne Elliot only in coldly polite terms, asks her:

> I have been considering what we had best do. [Henrietta] must not appear at first. She could not stand it. I have been thinking whether you had better not remain in the carriage with her, while I go in and break it to Mr. and Mrs. Musgrove. Do you think this a good plan? (114)

Similarly, when Darcy meets Elizabeth at Pemberley for the first time after she rejects his proposal and he has written his long letter to her, he asks her a question that is consultative in the extreme: "Will you allow me, or do I ask too much, to introduce my sister to your acquaintance during your stay at Lambton?" (*PP* 256). In much the same way, a major change happens in *Sense and Sensibility* when Marianne Dashwood, after her near-fatal illness, is transformed from a teller into an asker; she begins asking her sister Elinor what she thinks: "Shall we ever talk on that subject [of Willoughby], Elinor? ... Or will it be wrong?" (302).

Consultative questions like these are, as I have noted, surprisingly rare in Austen's novels. Most of the questions voiced by the characters resemble Mrs. Bennet's announcement to her husband: they are exclamations—statements disguised as questions, and put in question form to create more energy and intensity than a direct statement. Such a pseudo-question is traditionally known as a rhetorical question, which is, according to the *Concise Oxford Dictionary*, "a question asked not for information but to produce an effect." M.H. Abrams, in his *Glossary of Literary Terms*, adds an important point: a speaker generally uses a rhetorical question to persuade his or her audience (271). A sample rhetorical question from everyday life is, "What difference does it make?", which is simply a more emphatic way of asserting, "It makes no difference"—or, to capture the element of persuasion, "Surely we can agree that it makes no difference." Straightforward rhetorical questions are common in Austen's novels: Fanny Dashwood in *Sense and Sensibility*, for instance, convinces her husband that his widowed mother and sisters will be relatively well off through a series of rhetorical questions including, "Altogether, they will have five hundred a-year amongst them, and what on earth can four women want for more than that?" (*SS* 12). Lady Catherine believes she has dismissed once and for all Elizabeth Bennet's upstart claims with a resounding rhetorical question: "Are the shades of Pemberley to be thus polluted?" (*PP* 317).

Rhetorical questions come in many forms in the novels. There are Mrs. Bennet's *announcing* questions. There are *leading* questions, questions which lead the listener, much like a prompter in the theatre, to give a desired answer; this is the kind of question that Emma asks Harriet about Mr.

Martin's proposal: "If you prefer Mr. Martin to every other person; if you think him the most agreeable man you have ever been in company with, why should you hesitate? You blush, Harriet.—Does any body else occur to you at this moment under such a definition?" (*E* 53). A more altruistic form of the leading question is the *Socratic* question, in which the speaker tries to bring the listener to an awareness of something that the listener already knows, but is not aware of knowing: Henry Tilney, for instance, says to Catherine Morland in *Northanger Abbey*: "And did Isabella never change her mind before?" (*NA* 104). Socratic questions easily become *accusing* questions, such as those Elizabeth levels at Darcy during the proposal scene—"Can you deny that you have done it [separate Jane and Bingley]?" (*PP* 191)—or Mr. Knightley's questions to Emma at Box Hill: "How could you be so unfeeling to Miss Bates? How could you be so insolent in your wit to a woman of her character, age, and situation?" (*E* 339). We also find *browbeating* questions like those Sir Thomas asks of Fanny Price: "Am I to understand ... that you mean to *refuse* Mr. Crawford? ... Refuse him? ... Refuse Mr. Crawford! Upon what plea? For what reason?" (*MP* 315). At the other extreme are *pleading* questions; Willoughby, for instance, asks of Elinor after he has explained how he came to jilt Marianne: "And now do you pity me, Miss Dashwood?—or have I said all this to no purpose?—Am I—be it only one degree—am I less guilty in your opinion than I was before?" (*SS* 329). A more extreme form of the pleading question is the *abject* question, in which the speaker confesses mental incapacity and asks the listener to *tell* him or her what to do. Almost every question that Harriet asks Emma is an abject question, and so are most of the questions that Lady Bertram asks her husband—for instance, "What shall I do, Sir Thomas?—Whist and Speculation; which will amuse me most?" (*MP* 239).

A totally different, and insidious, kind of rhetorical question is the *strategic* question. When Lucy Steele asks Elinor Dashwood, "Pray, are you personally acquainted with your sister-in-law's mother, Mrs. Ferrars? ... Then perhaps you cannot tell me what sort of person she is?" (110), she is not *asking* for information, but beginning the process of *telling* Elinor that she has a prior claim to Edward Ferrars. One borderline kind is the *intrusive* question asked by characters such as Mrs. Jennings or Lady Catherine. These questions, often called "attacks" by the narrator, do ask for a response, but, as when Mrs. Jennings indefatigably goes on asking Colonel Brandon why he is suddenly leaving Devonshire for London (*SS* 64–66) or when Lady Catherine cross-examines Elizabeth Bennet over the way that she and her sisters have been raised (*PP* 164–66), the questioner seems interested primarily not in the content of the answer, but in asserting his or her ingenuity (Mrs. Jennings) or supremacy (Lady Catherine). It is worth noting that intrusive questions do arise out of curiosity, and curiosity is a step towards sympathy—and so a step away from self-absorption. We see in Mrs. Jennings that naked curiosity can coexist with, and grow into, kindness and sympathy.

A rhetorical question precludes a genuine answer because such a question implies that there is only one possible answer. Another common method of preventing a response is the question that does not allow for an answer because the person who asks the question immediately answers it. Mrs. Bennet says, "Well, Lizzy, ... what is your opinion *now* of this sad business of Jane's? For my part, I am determined never to speak of it to anybody" (*PP* 227). Mrs. Bennet is very fond of this way of short-circuiting conversation, as is her favourite daughter, Lydia, who brings about the plot resolution of *Pride and Prejudice* by asking Elizabeth, "Are you not curious to know how [my wedding] was managed?" and resolutely ignoring her negative response (318). This gambit I would identify by the legal term (familiar to anyone who watches *Law and Order* on TV) *asked and answered*. Miss Bingley, again from *Pride and Prejudice*, provides an example. After Elizabeth walks three miles across the muddy countryside to visit Jane, she asks the Netherfield party, "What could she mean by it? It seems to me to shew an abominable sort of conceited independence, a most country town indifference to decorum" (36).

A genuine question, like conversation itself, presupposes the speakers are equals. One of the main signs to the reader that a Jane Austen character is selfish and childishly self-absorbed is that character's use of rhetorical questions and an inability to ask consultative questions. If you can't ask and answer questions, you can't converse. Listen to Isabella Thorpe in *Northanger Abbey* as she ostensibly asks Catherine about Catherine's new friends, Henry and Eleanor Tilney, and at the same time ostensibly asks Catherine's brother James a series of lively questions. Her questions are purely rhetorical; far from waiting for an answer from her listener, she immediately provides her own reply to each question:

Was not it so, Mr. Morland? But you men are all so immoderately lazy! ... But where is her all-conquering brother? Is he in the room? Point him out to me this instant, if he is. I die to see him. ... What can it signify to you [James], what we are talking of? Perhaps we are talking about you, therefore I would advise you not to listen, or you may happen to hear something not very agreeable. ... How can you be so teasing; only conceive, my dear Catherine, what your brother wants me to do. He wants me to dance with him again. ... Nonsense, how can you say so? But when you men have a point to carry, you never stick at any thing. ... (56–57)

So far is Isabella from conversation that the narrator of *Northanger Abbey* remarks at the end of this scene, "In this common-place chatter, which lasted some time, the original subject [the Tilneys] seemed entirely forgotten" (57).

This distinction between asking and telling sharpens our understanding of two important elements in Austen's novels—the proposal scenes and the eventual achievement of self-knowledge by the heroines. In the remainder of this essay, I will consider each of these elements in turn.

First, the proposal scenes. It is all-important in Jane Austen's novels, as Henry Tilney observes to Catherine in *Northanger Abbey*, that both on the dance-floor and in marriage "man has the advantage of choice, woman only the power of refusal" (77). And because the woman's freedom is so severely limited in this arrangement, it is crucial that she exercise it wisely. Again and again in the novels we find a heroine struggling to refuse a marriage proposal *because the question has never actually been asked*. The man is so infatuated with his vision of himself as a suitor, so impressed with the wisdom of his choice, that he *tells* the woman that she is his chosen rather than *asks* her to be so.

The first, and most blissfully obtuse, of these doltish suitors is John Thorpe in *Northanger Abbey*. His idea of asking Catherine to dance is to tell her, "Well, Miss Morland, I suppose you and I are to stand up and jig it together again" (*NA* 59) or, on another occasion, "Hey-day, Miss Morland! ... what is the meaning of this?—I thought you and I were to dance together" (75). He is similarly incapable of asking her to come for a carriage ride or to go out for a walk with him and his sister. So it should be no surprise to the reader that John Thorpe actually succeeds in making what he considers to be a proposal of marriage to Catherine without even coming close to asking the crucial question. Instead, he makes a series of fatuous statements:

> You have more good nature and all that, than any body living I believe. A monstrous deal of good nature, and it is not only good nature, but you have so much, so much of every thing ... But I have a notion, Miss Morland, you and I think pretty much alike on most matters. ... My notion of things is simple enough. Let me only have the girl I like, say I, with a comfortable house over my head, and what care I for all the rest? [rhetorical question!] Fortune is nothing. I am sure of a good income of my own; and if she had not a penny, why so much the better. (123–24)

In a significant choice of words, the narrator says that Thorpe comes out of this interview with "the undivided consciousness of his own happy address, and her explicit encouragement" (124). Unfortunately, and comically, Catherine is in fact completely unaware that Thorpe's "address" is meant to be a marriage proposal.

The most egregious of Austen's suitors is Mr. Collins. The chapter in which he attempts to ask Elizabeth to marry him is introduced with, again, a significant choice of words by the novel's narrator: "The next day a new scene opened at Longbourn. Mr. Collins made his declaration in form" (*PP* 104). As Collins makes his carefully prepared "declaration," the words that he himself uses to describe what he is doing underline the fact that he is *telling* Elizabeth, not *asking* her:

> Allow me to assure you that I have your respected mother's permission for this address. ... Almost as soon as I entered the house I singled you out as the companion of my future life. ... But the fact is that, being, as I am, to inherit this estate after the death of your honoured father, ... I could not satisfy myself without resolving to chuse a wife from among his daughters. ... I am not now to learn ... that it is usual with young ladies to reject the addresses of the man whom they

secretly mean to accept. ... When I do myself the honour of speaking to you next on this subject ... You must give me leave to flatter myself, my dear cousin, that your refusal of my addresses is merely words of course. (105–08)

Author does not recognize indirect speech acts

Collins enumerates the reasons that have led him to his decision as if he were an executive reading aloud a favourite memo of his own composition. His concluding assurance, "And nothing now remains for me but to assure you in the most animated language of the violence of my affection" (106), is exorbitantly funny partly because the one thing remaining for him is to ask Elizabeth to marry him. She herself points out this omission, tactfully, when she interrupts him and says, "You are too hasty, Sir, ... You forget that I have made no answer" (106).

One of the truly brilliant aspects of *Pride and Prejudice* is the unstated but inescapable parallel between Collins's proposal and the first proposal by Mr. Darcy. A marriage proposal, broken down to its lowest common denominator, consists of seven words, "I love you. Will you marry me?"—three words of telling and four words of asking. Mr. Collins and John Thorpe fail abysmally to convey the required elements. The unreformed Darcy begins his marriage proposal auspiciously: he bursts out with a heartfelt expression of his love: "In vain have I struggled. It will not do. My feelings will not be repressed. You must allow me to tell you how ardently I admire and love you" (*PP* 189). However, as Elizabeth discovers, he is much better at telling than asking: "He concluded with representing to her the strength of that attachment which, in spite of all his endeavours, he had found impossible to conquer; and with expressing his hope that it would now be rewarded by her acceptance of his hand" (189). The grammar of this sentence sums up the situation: the subject of the sentence is "He," Elizabeth's capacity to choose is buried within the passive voice ("be rewarded") in a subordinate clause, and Darcy's asking Elizabeth to marry him has dwindled to near invisibility in the single, final word, "hand." Darcy, preoccupied with his own internal struggle, assumes Elizabeth will accept, just as Collins had. He, too, is not really asking. He tells Elizabeth at the end of the novel, "I believed you to be wishing, expecting my addresses" (369).

Collins at least makes himself understood, unlike John Thorpe, but he is unable to enter into rational conversation with his intended. Darcy, on the other hand, proves that he is capable of such an exchange, both in the proposal scene itself and in the long letter that he writes to Elizabeth (a letter that really amounts to Darcy's Proposal, Part Two). During the proposal scene, Darcy and Elizabeth ask and answer a series of blunt questions: if he asks her why with so little effort at civility she has rejected him (190), she replies, "I might as well enquire ... why with so evident a design of offending and insulting me, you chose to tell me that you liked me against your will, against your reason, and against your character? Was not this some excuse for incivility, if I *was* uncivil?" (190).

Similarly, Mr. Elton proposes to Emma by telling, not asking: "I am sure you have seen and understood me. ... Charming Miss Woodhouse! Allow me to interpret this interesting silence. It confesses that you have long understood me" (*E* 131). And in *Mansfield Park,* Sir Thomas Bertram, echoing both Mr. Collins in his deliberation and Mr. Darcy in his grammar, relates Henry Crawford's marriage proposal to Fanny in one long, pompous sentence that presents him, Sir Thomas, as the agent and Fanny as a prepositional object:

> And now, Fanny, having performed one part of my commission, and shewn you every thing placed on a basis the most assured and satisfactory, I may execute the remainder by prevailing on you to accompany me down stairs, where—though I cannot but presume on having been no unacceptable companion myself, I must submit to your finding one still better worth listening to.—Mr. Crawford, as you have perhaps foreseen, is in the house. (*MP* 314)

On the other hand, the successful proposals in Austen's novels show the man asking a genuine question—and leaving himself on tenterhooks. Mr. Knightley, ever the model, asks Emma, "Tell me, then, have I no chance of ever succeeding? My dearest Emma, ... tell me at once. Say 'No,' if it is to be said" (*E* 430). The reformed Mr. Darcy says to Elizabeth, "You are too generous to trifle with me. If your feelings are still what they were last April, tell me so at once. *My* affections and wishes are unchanged, but one word from you will silence me on this subject for ever" (*PP* 366). This time, Elizabeth is to do the telling, not Darcy. In *Persuasion*, Captain Wentworth proposes marriage in a letter to Anne that is Jane Austen's most expressive statement of love. The letter certainly contains the seven-word essence of a successful proposal: in it Wentworth tells Anne directly, "I have loved none but you," and "I offer myself to you"; he is, he says, "half agony, half hope," waiting for her reply (*P* 237).

Mr. Darcy's second proposal to Elizabeth, just cited, does not contain a question mark; Darcy's speech is in its purport a question but, literally and grammatically, it contains a series of statements. This fact leads me to an interesting point: though none of Austen's heroines overtly proposes to the man of her choice—as Amelia, the character played by Mary Crawford in *Lovers' Vows*, does so shockingly in *Mansfield Park*—several of Austen's heroines do in fact implicitly ask the crucial question. The clearest case is Elizabeth Bennet, who brings on Darcy's proposal with a carefully considered speech:

> Mr. Darcy, I am a very selfish creature; and for the sake of giving relief to my own feelings, care not how much I may be wounding yours. I can no longer help thanking you for your unexampled kindness to my poor sister. Ever since I have known it, I have been most anxious to acknowledge to you how gratefully I feel it. Were it known to the rest of my family, I should not have merely my own gratitude to express. ... Let me thank you again and again, in the name of all my family, for that generous compassion which induced you to take so much trouble, and bear so many mortifications, for the sake of discovering them. (*PP* 365–66)

Literally speaking, Elizabeth asks Darcy no questions, but implicitly she is asking him a question that she has been wondering about ever since she heard of Darcy's rescue of Lydia: has he done it for her (326)? Darcy is given the opening to make the reply she hopes for ("I thought only of *you*"), and his proposal follows immediately (366). When Elizabeth and Darcy, after the fact, talk over the sequence of events that led up to his proposal, Elizabeth admits that she took the initiative: "I wonder how long you *would* have gone on, if you had been left to yourself. I wonder when you *would* have spoken, if I had not asked you! My resolution of thanking you for your kindness to Lydia had certainly great effect" (381). Elizabeth had earlier signalled to Darcy her willingness to be asked the question when she refused Lady Catherine's request to promise that she would never become engaged to Darcy (356). By saying no, Elizabeth is letting Darcy know that she will say yes. As soon as Lady Catherine leaves, Elizabeth reflects, "From what she had said of her resolution to prevent their marriage, ... she must meditate an application to her nephew" (360). Darcy tells Elizabeth that he was greatly encouraged as soon as he was told by an outraged Lady Catherine that Elizabeth had refused to make the desired promise:

> It taught me to hope ... as I had scarcely ever dared to hope before. I knew enough of your disposition to be certain, that, had you been absolutely, irrevocably decided against me, you would have acknowledged it to Lady Catherine, frankly and openly [and, he implies, taken great delight in doing so]. (367)

Emma Woodhouse is another heroine who, in effect, asks the question that leads to her suitor asking the question. We see this acted out in the scene that leads to their dancing together at the Crown Inn. This scene foreshadows and enacts in dumb show Mr. Knightley's subsequent proposal to Emma. At the Crown Inn, Emma and Mr. Knightley have come closer together than ever before following his rescue of Harriet (and Emma) from Mr. Elton's snub on the dance floor:

> They were interrupted by the bustle of Mr. Weston calling on everybody to begin dancing again.
>
> "Come Miss Woodhouse, Miss Otway, Miss Fairfax, what are you all doing?—Come Emma, set your companions the example. Everybody is lazy! Every body is asleep!"
>
> "I am ready," said Emma, "whenever I am wanted."
>
> "Whom are you going to dance with?" asked Mr. Knightley.
>
> She hesitated a moment, and then replied, "With you, if you will ask me."

"Will you?" said he, offering his hand. (*E* 331)

Emma has clearly asked Mr. Knightley to ask, and she does as much in the proposal scene itself. When Emma tells him that she is determined to keep his friendship and to continue to enjoy his conversation, no matter what the cost to her, Mr. Knightley decides that this offer has a double meaning:

> "I stopped you ungraciously just now, Mr. Knightley, and, I am afraid, gave you pain.—But if you have any wish to speak openly to me as a friend, or to ask my opinion of any thing you may have in contemplation—as a friend, indeed, you may command me.—I will hear whatever you like. I will tell you exactly what I think."
>
> "As a friend!"—repeated Mr. Knightley.—"Emma, that I fear is a word—No, I have no wish—Stay, yes, why should I hesitate?—I have gone too far already for concealment. Emma, I accept your offer—Extraordinary as it may seem, I accept it, and refer myself to you as a friend.—Tell me, then, have I no chance of ever succeeding?" (429–30)

The proposal scene of Wentworth and Anne presents Anne as the initiator of the crucial question. Wentworth's letter is written as a running commentary on a conversation that occurs in a different part of the room between Anne and Wentworth's friend, Captain Harville, a conversation that Anne has good reason to believe that Wentworth can hear, and a conversation in which she states her belief that women's love is deeper and more constant than men's (*P* 233–35). Anne's speeches in this debate constitute her implicit answer to an equally implicit question ("Do you still love me?") that Wentworth has been asking her more and more insistently since his return to Bath—a question implied, for instance, when he asks her whether she is disgusted by the memory of their expedition to Lyme (183–84) and also when he asks if she still, after all these years, takes no enjoyment in card-parties (225). Anne's secret answer to Wentworth's secret question is clear: "Yes, I still love you, and as much as ever," and this answer, of course, implicitly asks Wentworth another question: "What are you going to do now?"

I would like to turn now from proposals to the issue of self-knowledge. If only a person who can ask genuine questions—consultative questions—

can converse, we can go one step further and say that only a person who can ask real questions can think and develop. After Mr. Bennet has read aloud Mr. Collins's letter to the Bennets, telling them that he has decided to invite himself to visit them and that he will be arriving Monday, November 18th, at four o'clock, the reactions of the Bennet family are revealing. Mrs. Bennet says, "There is some sense in what he says about the girls, ... and if he is disposed to make them any amends, I shall not be the person to discourage him." Jane remarks, "Though it is difficult ... to guess in what way he can mean to make us the atonement he thinks our due, the wish is certainly to his credit." Mary adds, "In point of composition, ... his letter does not seem defective. The idea of the olive branch perhaps is not wholly new, yet I think it is well expressed" (*PP* 63–64). Kitty and Lydia are too preoccupied with officers to take any interest in the letter or its writer. Only Elizabeth asks questions of her father: "He must be an oddity, I think, ... I cannot make him out.—There is something very pompous in his stile.—And what can he mean by apologizing for being next in the entail?—We cannot suppose he would help it, if he could.—Can he be a sensible man, Sir?" (64). Elizabeth can think, and that is evident in her ability to ask real questions.

However, for the first half of the novel Elizabeth is determined to tell, not ask, and so she abuses her intelligence and finds herself deluded about the most important events going on around her. When she and Jane are discussing whether or not to believe Wickham's account of Darcy, Jane is unable to decide, but Elizabeth tells her sister, "I beg your pardon;—one knows exactly what to think" (86). If one knows exactly what to think, questions are superfluous. Elizabeth changes once she has read Darcy's letter and admitted that she has been completely wrong in her beliefs about both Darcy and Wickham. She realizes, "As to [Wickham's] real character, had information been in her power, she had never felt a wish of enquiring" (206). Elizabeth means both that she failed to ask others about Wickham's character and that she failed to ask herself about why she was so partial to him. In other words, the question-and-answer method is not only the way that two or more people converse; it is also the way that the individual comes to understand herself or himself.

In the second half of *Pride and Prejudice*, Elizabeth asks herself a series of important questions. For instance, during her painstaking, two-hour consideration of Darcy's letter, after changing her opinion of Wickham, she turns to Darcy's explanation of his behaviour towards Jane and Bingley and asks herself, "How could she deny that credit to his assertions, in one instance, which she had been obliged to give in the other?" (208). When she is at Pemberley and hears Mrs. Reynolds, the housekeeper, praise his good nature as a child, "Elizabeth almost stared at her. 'Can this be Mr. Darcy!' thought she" (249). When a few minutes later, to the surprise of both, she meets Darcy himself, she asks herself a series of questions, ending with the most important one: "And his behaviour so strikingly altered,—what could it mean?" (252). She finds Darcy's behaviour even more puzzling when, near the novel's end, he visits the Bennets' home with Bingley, but seems strangely silent and distant. Elizabeth is no longer someone who knows exactly what to think. In fact, she asks herself a series of tough questions:

> Could I expect it to be otherwise! ... Yet why did he come? ... Why, if he came only to be silent, grave, and indifferent, ... did he come at all? ... He could be still amiable, still pleasing, to my uncle and aunt, when he was in town; and why not to me? If he fears me, why come hither? If he no longer cares for me, why silent? ... A man who has been once refused! How could I ever be foolish enough to expect a renewal of his love? Is there one among the sex, who would not protest against such a weakness as a second proposal to the same woman? (336–41)

Elizabeth, like Austen's other heroines as the plot nears its climax, is as much on tenterhooks as the man whose question she awaits.

The importance of asking oneself hard questions becomes clear if we look at two parallel chapters in *Emma*. In Volume I, chapter 16, Emma has been shocked out of her delusions about Harriet and Mr. Elton when Mr. Elton unexpectedly proposes to her. After castigating herself for her mistakes she "resolved to do such things no more" (*E* 137). As the novel nears its climax, Emma receives a much more complex series of shocks when she discovers that Frank Churchill and Jane Fairfax are secretly engaged; that Harriet, far from caring for Frank, loves Mr. Knightley and believes her love returned; and that she herself loves Mr. Knightley and has done so all along. Once again she realizes that she has been deluded and resolves to reform.

However, in the first self-discovery scene, Emma emphatically tells herself that she has been mistaken:

> The first error and the worst lay at her door. It was foolish, it was wrong, to take so active a part in bringing any two people together. It was adventuring too far, assuming too much, making light of what ought to be serious, a trick of what ought to be simple. She was quite concerned and ashamed, and resolved to do such things no more. (136–37)

The phrase "quite concerned and ashamed" signals that Emma's discoveries have barely made a dent in her complacency, and in fact half a page later she catches herself surmising that the young lawyer William Coxe might be desirable for Harriet. In the five pages devoted to Emma's thoughts in this scene, she does not ask herself a single genuine question. She does begin her attempts at self-analysis with some promising words, "How could she have been so deceived!" (134), but Jane Austen suggests that this is a pseudo-question by having the words followed by an exclamation point, not a question mark, and just ten lines later, after reviewing Elton's ingratiating manners and his charade of a courtship, Emma apparently asks herself a question, "Who could have seen through such thick-headed nonsense?" (134). However, this is a rhetorical question allowing Emma to persuade herself that questions are pointless.

Things are very different in the second self-discovery scene, in which Emma does come to understand her motives and does feel that, apart from her newly understood love for Mr. Knightley, "Every other part of her mind was disgusting" (412). During this second scene her thoughts progress by means of a barrage of questions:

> How long had Mr. Knightley been so dear to her, as every feeling declared him now to be? When had his influence, such influence begun?—When had he succeeded to that place in her affection, which Frank Churchill had once, for a short period, occupied? ... Was it a new circumstance for a man of first-rate abilities to be captivated by very inferior powers? Was it new for one, perhaps too busy to seek, to be the prize of a girl who would seek him?—Was it new for any

thing in this world to be unequal, inconsistent, incongruous—or for chance and circumstance (as second causes) to direct the human fate? ... How Harriet could ever have had the presumption to raise her thoughts to Mr. Knightley! ... Alas! was not that her own doing too? Who had been at pains to give Harriet notions of self-consequence but herself? Who but herself had taught her, that she was to elevate herself if possible, and that her claims were great to a high worldly establishment? (412–14)

These are not rhetorical questions, but consultative questions (for instance, "How long had Mr. Knightley been so dear to her?"). Emma is no longer telling, but asking herself what she thinks.

We can see the same connection between self-questioning and coming to understand oneself near the end of *Sense and Sensibility*. Marianne tells her sister Elinor, "My illness has made me think—It has given me leisure and calmness for serious recollection" (*SS* 345). Marianne's long "self-reproving" (346) speech that follows shows that, after spending the novel up to this point telling others and herself exactly what she thinks, she has begun to ask herself questions about herself: "Your example was before me: but to what avail?—Was I more considerate of you and your comfort? Did I imitate your forbearance, or lessen your restraints, by taking any part in those offices of general complaisance or particular gratitude which you had hitherto been left to discharge alone?" (304). These may sound like rhetorical questions, and they certainly have allowed Marianne to persuade herself, but it might be more satisfying to see them as an instance of a general truth, if not a truth universally acknowledged, that to ask a question is to be most of the way to arriving at the answer to it. For instance, when Emma finally reaches the point at which she can ask herself how long Mr. Knightley has been so dear to her, she quickly realizes "there never had been a time" when she did not love him (412).

In this essay, I have been in the position of telling my thoughts on asking versus telling, real questions and rhetorical questions, telling and asking in proposal scenes, and learning to ask oneself questions. My reader is in the more taxing position of asking himself or herself what to make of these ideas. And so the conversation goes on.

3

Why Do They Talk So Much? How Can We Stand It?

John Thorpe and Miss Bates

LET US FIRST TAKE A QUICK LOOK at excessive talkers in literature before Jane Austen. It seems that this tradition, like so many, began in English with Shakespeare: in, particularly, *Romeo and Juliet*. The founder of this tradition is not Mercutio or even Romeo before he meets Juliet, though the flow of language in these two young men (a fashion in their day) can well be played as excessive. There is nothing modish in the gabbiness of Juliet's nurse. We first meet her when Juliet's mother, Lady Capulet, arrives on stage to break it to Juliet that her parents have a husband picked out. She intends to talk to her daughter privately, but Nurse just refuses to leave, and Lady Capulet, knowing when she's beaten, lets her stay. Lady Capulet is then totally upstaged. Her weighty secret has to wait while Nurse delivers herself of a thirty-two-line speech of reminiscence about Juliet as a little girl. When Lady Capulet can get a word in edgeways she says, "Enough of this, I pray thee hold thy peace"—and Nurse spends another eight lines repeating her punch-line (I.iii.51–59). This is just the beginning. At later tense moments in the action, both Romeo and Juliet have to wait for her torrent of language to subside before they can get some absolutely crucial piece of information out of her.

In Shakespeare this is wonderful. It provides that famous comic relief; it keeps up suspense; it grounds the high-flown passion of the young lovers in Nurse's earthiness and total lack of moral scruples—and it obliquely questions the rigid social hierarchy that is meant to prevail in Verona. Servants—like women and children—are supposed to be seen and not heard. The infringement of propriety helps to make Nurse's gabbiness both funny and attractive.

The joke about servants' excessive talk was used by Goldsmith in *She Stoops to Conquer* and hinted at by Horace Walpole in *The Castle of Otranto* (33–36). It was picked up enthusiastically by later novelists, especially gothic novelists. Even Ann Radcliffe has a touch of it. The principle seems to be that servants *will* run on excessively and irrelevantly, holding up the action, when things are tense and haste is vital. Their loquacity is not merely insubordinate (as with Nurse), but also a clear sign of their intellectual inferiority (not like Nurse, who is nobody's fool). The talk of these later servants is characterized firstly by a mass of trivial circumstantial detail and secondly by the wildest exaggeration. These talkers have no sense of proportion, no power of prioritizing, no recognition of what's important (except that they think—wrongly—that they are themselves important). This all suggests that the authors of these novels are social conservatives: obliquely, they convey approval of the socially imposed silence of servants, since when servants are allowed to talk the results are so regrettable.

The over-talkative servant, like so many stock motifs, became grist for Jane Austen to pick up and transform. John Thorpe and Miss Bates are related to all those fictional long-winded servants, but the relationship is not one of simple family resemblance or simple contrast. Austen's juvenilia show her to have been deeply delighted both by irrelevance and by exaggeration, not when those qualities are comfortably confined to the lower classes but when they are rampant among her own class equals.

The talking-servant tradition is a reason for excluding from this essay Mr. Collins, whose talk has been so well anatomized by Juliet McMaster.[1]

Mr. Collins is certainly interminable, but his style of talk does not derive from Juliet's Nurse. Its meaning is impeded, not by circumstantial detail or exaggeration, but by an overabundance of elaborate syntax. It is clergy talk, satirizing the specialized discourse of the pulpit. Though Mr. Collins is to some extent socially disadvantaged, as his social grovelling demonstrates, it is not to his social superiors that he lets himself go in loquacity, but to unprivileged female audiences. He speaks to those below him from his authority as a clergyman. His long-windedness is in no way subversive.

Matters are obviously quite different with Miss Bates, and I believe they are different too with John Thorpe. Miss Bates is the heart of this essay, but John Thorpe provides a useful approach to it. In relation to Catherine Morland, he has the privilege of gender: his talkativeness is contrasted with that of Henry Tilney. Both claim Catherine's ear because they are male and she is female. But although Thorpe is a university student, he is as close, socially speaking, to Miss Bates as to Henry Tilney. Despite his implicit claims of having unlimited funds, his mother is "a widow, and not a very rich one" (NA 34), just like Miss Bates's mother. I believe that John Thorpe, like Miss Bates but from a different angle, may be designed as a comment on the stereotyped, novelistic, over-talkative servant.

Thorpe is introduced by his friend James Morland as "a little of a rattle" (50). Bingley in *Pride and Prejudice* is a rattle, too, but Jane Austen does not subject her readers to his rattling. Nor does she subject them to Thorpe's monologues in the way she does with those of Miss Bates. It is Catherine who gets bored to tears by John Thorpe, not the reader. And his boring talk to Catherine is insignificant, while it is other talk of his, which the reader never hears, that significantly shapes the plot.

Austen's depiction of John Thorpe is positively economical. We learn all the essential characteristics of his talk in Chapter 7, when Catherine, who has only just met him, is thoroughly supplied with information about his horse and gig. He shares with all these servants an addiction to unnecessary detail: the story of his gig purchase includes the exact spot where it took place (which means nothing to Catherine, who has not been to Oxford), the character of the vendor, exactly what was said on each side including the swear words, and the exact price. The last is presented as a punch-line, as if it is deeply significant; but then it turns out to be a boringly medium price, of no significance whatever. In this chapter, Thorpe establishes his descent from the gothic servant tradition, with irrelevant, compulsive detail and desperate exaggeration. This is the occasion on which he says of his horse, "Only see how he moves; that horse *cannot* go less than ten miles an hour: tie his legs and he will get on" (46).[2]

In conventional fiction, these characteristics—irrelevance, exaggeration, and self-centredness—distinguish the chatty servants from the sensitive, refined characters on whom the story centres. Middle- or upper-class persons do not talk like that; nor do they ever take a servant's exaggerations seriously. But in *Northanger Abbey* these qualities are not confined to the lower orders. Thorpe, who embodies them, is a person of some status and class pretension, and an individual with real status; no less a person than General Tilney takes him seriously. So does Catherine. She learns quite quickly not to take his word about social trivia, but finds it much harder to apply this lesson to more serious subjects.

After that first monologue, Austen takes to protecting her readers. In the next chapter John Thorpe is given more reported than direct speech. This is where he keeps engaging Catherine to dance and then not dancing at all, leaving her prohibited by social etiquette from dancing with anyone else, specifically with Henry Tilney. When he does return to Catherine, we hear that she is unconsoled by "the particulars which he entered into while they were standing up, of the horses and dogs of the friend whom he had just left, and of a proposed exchange of terriers between them" (55). In Chapter 9, on the drive up Claverton Down, we get some choice snippets of his conversational style: "Old Allen is as rich as a Jew—is not he?" (63) and "There is not the hundredth part of the wine consumed in this kingdom, that there ought to be" (64). But we get more summary than samples: "of horses which he had bought for a trifle and sold for incredible sums; of racing matches, in which his judgment had infallibly foretold the winner; of shooting parties, in which he had killed more birds ... than all his companions together" (66) and so on. And we get more summary than précis: "his rapidity of expression" (64), "idle assertions and impudent falsehoods" (65), "the effusions of his endless conceit" (66). We are allowed to see through John Thorpe without having to hear him out.

And so we as readers are allowed, or encouraged, to be surprised at the way General Tilney falls for Thorpe's inconsequentiality and exaggeration. Through John Thorpe, and by presenting him through authorial summary, Austen restores the potential humour in this kind of excessive talk. She also makes the point that it can have serious consequences when such talk is not safely confined to servants but becomes dangerously prevalent among middle-class idiots who expect to be listened to.

Miss Bates is equally irrelevant, equally excessive, but not in the same way exaggerated or self-centred. Talking too much is virtually her defining characteristic. The narrator sums her up at the outset as "a great talker upon little matters ... full of trivial communications [like John Thorpe] and *harmless* gossip [unlike him]" (*E* 21; emphasis added). But the narrator, who stepped forward with so many similar summaries in *Northanger Abbey* (who, as it were, talked a great deal in that novel), now steps back, or falls almost silent, leaving Miss Bates to speak for herself. Her first prodigious feat of talking is performed the first time that, as readers, we actually meet her. Six pages of print (*E* 156–62) are needed "to usher in" (156) the reading of a letter from Jane Fairfax: six pages largely devoted to Miss Bates's talk, with a bare minimum of narration and only a sentence or two from Emma.

This is a virtuoso performance, on Austen's part as well as that of her creation, in which all the inimitable characteristics of Miss Bates's talking style are not told but shown. Miss Bates has so little management of suspense or surprise that her first move in ushering in Jane's letter is to relate exactly how Mrs. Cole had thought there would not be a letter yet, and how surprised she had been to hear that there was one. She loses the letter and explains at great length how it was that she came to lose it, and how it came to be where it actually was all the time (157). Angling for a compliment to Jane's beautifully legible handwriting, she ties herself in knots over the deterioration of her mother's eyesight, coupled with a fervent Pangloss-like assertion that her eyesight is after all excellent *for her age* (157–58). And of course the brevity of Jane's letter is taken to need elaborate apology (157). Although almost nothing Miss Bates says is to the point, not a scrap of it is wasted. Every word goes towards proving some point of Jane Austen's.

Miss Bates begins as Austen meant her to go on. Later, her arrival with Mrs. Weston is the arrival of "one voice and two ladies" (235). She herself confesses only half apologetically to being "rather a talker" (346). Her constant talking becomes a running joke, like Mr. Woodhouse's valetudinarianism. She asks, "What was I talking of?", and Emma wonders "On what, of all the medley, she would fix" (237). Miss Bates leaves sentences unfinished. She twice says Mr. Knightley is, or would be, "so very" (238, 239): not very anything, just so *very*—a joke inspired by the popular rhetorical claim that a hero or heroine's charms defy the reach of language. She never fails to tell one person what she has said to another, no matter how vacuous the comment. This, too, she leaves unfinished: "I said to my mother, 'Upon my word, ma'am'" (322). Full stop. Having nothing to say is no deterrent to her: still, the other characters are pursued by "the sounds of her desultory good-will" (239), telling them to mind the step. (This is the woman who also warns of two steps when there is in fact only one [329].)

Emma finds Miss Bates even more boring than Catherine found John Thorpe. It is Emma herself, not the narrator, who both complains and jokes about this subject. She makes a joke of it not once but twice, though one occasion has been much more noticed in criticism than the other. In this novel Austen no longer protects her readers from the boring talk, as she did in *Northanger Abbey,* and it is worth considering why, if Miss Bates really is so boring, Austen makes it compulsory to listen to her for pages at a time.

A generation or two ago the stock question about this issue was: How does Jane Austen keep us interested in pages of Miss Bates, whereas in life we would be shifting in our seats like Emma, looking for a chance to escape? Because I no longer believe Miss Bates to be simply boring, I think this was the wrong question. Whole chapters might be too much, but whole pages are just right. Austen produces Miss Bates's talk through the filter of her own artistry: she achieves the paradox of apparently artless mimesis, shepherding our reactions in the direction she chooses.

Plenty of other issues arise about Miss Bates, as well as the question of her excessive talk: the matter of her moral goodness, her class position, her structural relation to the character of Emma. In each of these her loquacity is vital to her presentation.

The narrator makes much of Miss Bates's goodness, her courage in adversity, her happiness: "her own universal good-will and contented temper ... The simplicity and cheerfulness of her nature, her contented and grateful spirit ... a mine of felicity to herself" (21). This sounds like the conduct-book ideal, yet Miss Bates's constant talking is the *very reverse* of what conduct books recommend. Again, awareness of the talking-servant tradition might seem to lower Miss Bates's class position. Yet the plot of the novel insists on the parallel—neither a simple likeness nor quite a simple contrast—between her and Emma. Emma is "handsome, clever, and rich" (5); Miss Bates is "neither young, handsome, rich, nor married" (21). (Austen's silence about her lack of cleverness is a joke that becomes apparent only on a second reading.) Emma dislikes Jane Fairfax; Miss Bates dotes on her. When Emma says she could happily live unmarried, Harriet says fearfully, "But then, to be an old maid at last, like Miss Bates!" (84).

On the other side of the argument, Emma is never tedious, but says just what she ought, while Miss Bates is always tedious and says much more than she ought. These characters, however, are nothing so simple as opposites. Emma is like Miss Bates in having a "happy disposition"(57), though hers has not been tried and tested. The older woman's happiness is a paradox. On the one hand it bears out a favourite moral of contemporary fiction writers and conduct writers (indeed, of any writer addressing a female or largely female audience): that the good are always happy, indeed that nobody but the good can be happy. Austen, therefore, is calling the conventional moralists' bluff. Miss Bates's brand of goodness is not a recipe for happiness that they could afford to accept. Miss Bates as a model to follow would compromise the reliance of conventional moralists on the promised reward of happiness. Conduct books exist to guide young ladies to marriage and material comfort, not to entertain the possibility of developing into a Miss Bates.

I believe Austen is denying the morality of offering goodness as the high road to happiness, exposing the true conduct-literature lesson as a lesson in how to be a heroine. For this it is not enough to be handsome, clever, and—at least at the end of the story—rich. It is also necessary to be interesting to the reader, to have potential for change and development, which also implies potential for being unhappy. Austen requires her heroines to be teachable, but not in the manner of conduct literature. In such literature, a teachable woman is "docile." Against the simple model of education as pouring good teaching into a passive receptacle, Austen sets up an interactive model, depending on the agency of the pupil at least as much as that of the teacher. That is the point of this digression: Miss Bates's loquacity signifies that she does not and cannot learn. She never listens (being too busy putting out sound that no one is expected to listen to), while Emma learns, over the course of the action, to listen well.

Another point of relationship between Emma and Miss Bates is the unmarried status they share. Miss Bates, with her moral virtue, her happiness, and her talk, is designed as an intervention into another social debate often found in novels: the nature of the old maid. Is or is not a typical old maid sour, narrow, embittered, altogether a proof of the incompleteness of the female without the male? A key text here, though no longer new at the date of *Emma*, is William Hayley's *Essay on Old Maids* (1785). (Hayley dedicated his book, with amazing assurance, to Elizabeth Carter, whom he presents as the exception to a norm entirely lacking in goodness or happiness.) Many women writers before and after Hayley represented an opposite viewpoint, and a few of them were probably well known to Austen.[3] Some women novelists in pursuit of this ideological point allowed the courtship of their heroines to be upstaged by some other, more marginal but more unusual, unmarried female character.[4] It is not Austen's way to make ideological assertions; she offers possibilities and jokes. Nevertheless, Miss Bates's happiness is designed partly in support of the anti-William Hayley, pro-old maid side of the argument.[5]

This may sound like a paradox, since Austen is also holding up Miss Bates as a specimen for the reader's amusement. It is important in this context that Miss Bates is not presented in contrast with other, quieter characters. In *Emma* almost all the characters talk a lot, and many of them too much. Emma exchanges long speeches with almost all her friends and acquaintances. Harriet, when we first meet her, is having her "talkativeness" "encouraged" by Emma (27); she pours out desultory detail with a "youthful simplicity" (27) which sounds very like Miss Bates: "He had a very fine flock; and ... he had been bid more for his wool than any body in the country. ...

their silence than with the different loquacities of other people. Sometimes, indeed, the contrast is pointed. Take Mrs. Elton's celebrated soliloquy at the strawberry-picking, beginning with "The best fruit in England—every body's favourite—always wholesome.—These the finest beds and finest sorts" and ending with "—only objection to gathering strawberries the stooping—glaring sun—tired to death—could bear it no longer—must go and sit in the shade" (358–59). This monologue is clearly designed to contrast with two much longer soliloquies delivered earlier, just a few pages apart, by Miss Bates at a comparable social gathering: the ball (322–23, 328–30). Whereas Mrs. Elton's speech runs downhill from rhapsody into disillusion, both of Miss Bates's soliloquies sustain their enjoyment. It takes the arrival of tea the first time, and food the second time, to shut her up. Her first speech begins "So very obliging of you!—No rain at all. Nothing to signify. I do not care for myself. ... Well! This is brilliant indeed!—This is admirable!" and ends with the exclamation "Everything so good!" (322–23). Of course Miss Bates's capacity to sustain her happiness, or enjoyment, despite rain is contrasted with Mrs. Elton's reaction to sun, and it is to be counted as moral virtue. Her talk is also a constant validation of others, concern for others, and applause for others' concern for her. Miss Bates's talk weaves a web of interdependence, of reciprocity, the exchange of the trivial pleasures of gossip. When she hears the news of Mr. Elton's marriage, she rushes first to pass the story on to the Woodhouses, then back to visit with Mrs. Cole, who had told the news to her in a note (172–73, 176). She has to give thanks for the gift of news; she has to pass it on; talk is both her only wealth and her medium of exchange.

So the sheer excess is tied up with many other characteristics: those of irrelevance, of tedium, of gossip, of dailiness, of exchange and reciprocation. Although Emma's famous snub at Box Hill turns on the issue of tedium, I believe some of the other issues are more important. They are mostly issues raised in Miss Bates's very first speech, which concerns Jane Fairfax's letter, nineteen chapters into the novel. Ronald Blythe's introduction to the Penguin edition of the novel links her late entrance with the lapse of the seasons: winter comes first in *Emma*; Miss Bates's "starling chatter" heralds the spring (23). There is naturalistic observation in this: Mrs. and Miss Bates's social lives would be sharply curtailed in winter, which also restricts general social life in Highbury and gives Emma an excuse for not visiting them. But there is more to this than naturalism, for Miss Bates has another season of silence: she stops talking well before the novel's close, a silencing that I will discuss shortly.

Emma's famous Box Hill snub turns on both tedium and excess. Perhaps no scene is better known. Frank Churchill sets up his parlour game: everyone is to contribute to the conversation either one very clever thing or two things moderately clever or three things very dull indeed. Churchill here echoes the narrator describing the talk at the Coles' dinner party. Miss Bates cheerfully offers to be dull, and Emma insists on her excess as well as dullness, doubting that Miss Bates can limit herself to three dull things (370). Here the novel seems to pause: this is one of the rare moments when the silence of other people is commented on. No reader can miss the point that Emma is being unkind, and in her author's moral world that means she is being set up for rebuke and repentance. Yet I believe every first-time reader of this passage enters happily, shamelessly into Emma's joke, into her feeling of superiority (she surely feels she is saying one very clever thing), into her scoring off Miss Bates. But then Austen sharply divides herself from the Emma we have been laughing with. The moment is not allowed to pass. When Miss Bates gets the point, she registers shock and hurt: "I will try to hold my tongue. I must make myself very disagreeable, or she would not have said such a thing to an old friend" (373). And Mr. Knightley follows this up with his fierce private sentencing of Emma (374–75).

This scene is, of course, beautifully contextualized. Frank is out to make trouble; he flirts with Emma because he is beginning to quarrel seriously with Jane. Emma is drunk on flirtation and flattery, and also wound up to competitiveness by Mrs. Elton. Mr. Knightley is finding an unacknowledged outlet for suppressed jealousy. But what of Miss Bates? Is it really in character for her to be so wounded? Nowhere else in the novel do we see her behaving at all like this, but then nowhere else is she similarly provoked.

It might be possible to argue that Austen is manipulating Miss Bates's character in the interests of the plot because Emma's superiority must be punctured. Or it might be argued that in this scene Miss Bates reveals unexpected hidden depths: a capacity for unhappiness, a concern not for someone else but for her own self-esteem.

To anybody reading Miss Bates as solely a comic butt, this moment would be out of character, indeed at odds with Austen's agenda for her. In any reading of her, it is an uncharacteristic moment. Other clues to her sensitivity, such as her phrase "if any thing was to happen" (160), which must refer to the likelihood that her mother has not long to live, are clues indeed, but are half-hidden: this moment is writ large.[6] But at each of these sensitive moments, it is Miss Bates's *succinctness* that signals an abnormal situation, a shift to a different and more inward register. Again Emma and Miss Bates are obliquely linked: this crucial moment for Emma is also, if anyone has attention to spare for it, a crucial moment for Miss Bates. It offers a rare clue to motivation and character construction: a reason for Miss Bates to talk so much is that it serves to protect her from the questions, or the sneers, of others.

An unprepared reader of the Box Hill scene is likely to side with Emma and so, as it were, to share her blame. Her other witticism about Miss Bates's conversation (made out of Miss Bates's hearing) is permitted to be funny without reproof. Here Emma is talking to the wonderfully non-judgemental Mrs. Weston: in this joke she mimics Miss Bates's talk. Whereas on Box Hill Emma openly tells Miss Bates that she is both dull and prolix, she here (before the Box Hill scene happens) exhibits Miss Bates to her audience of one as clownishly trivial and irrelevant: "and, indeed, she must thankfully say that their petticoats were all very strong" (225). This comment is ribald and unlady-like if not actually improper; at the same time it is clever and wickedly perceptive, and it hurts nobody.

Given a novel so closely concerned with social pressures, it would be naive to believe that this last remark shows the real Emma, while Box Hill shows an Emma distorted by stress. But it is fair to contrast the way Emma talks before an intimate friend with the way she talks before a part-hostile audience, and perhaps also to suggest that her method on Box Hill, of telling her audience what to think, resembles Austen's method with John Thorpe, while her method with Mrs. Weston resembles Austen's method with Miss Bates. In building Miss Bates's character through a display of her talk, Austen parallels Emma's mimicry of Miss Bates. She excels in detail, verisimilitude, and insight, while Emma, rather like Austen's juvenile writing self, excels in panache, fantasy, and deliberate outrageousness.

In view of the common ground cautiously sketched between Emma and Miss Bates, we may also ask how much common ground Austen envisaged between Miss Bates and herself. The parallel between Miss Bates's discourse and that of Emma has not gone unnoticed. But the discourse of trivia (drawing detail from one's own little corner of the world, filling up emptiness, enmeshing people in tiny connections) was used by Austen herself, not in fiction but in letters.[7] In Miss Bates this tendency is artless; in Austen's letters it is a technique that deliberately ignores both scale and plot. It is a validation of that common, ordinary, unadorned life that is the water in which Miss Bates swims, and which novelists as a class, but Austen in particular, have taken as their bailiwick.

Austen brings Emma into somewhat uneasy relation with such ordinariness in the passage—another famous one—in which Emma whiles away the time, as Harriet dithers over her shopping, by looking out of the shop door. The greatest event she might hope for would be "Mr. Cole's carriage horses returning from exercise, or a stray letter-boy on an obstinate mule"; more likely would be the butcher making deliveries, an old woman shopping, "two curs quarrelling over a dirty bone, and a string of dawdling children round the baker's little bow-window eyeing the gingerbread. ... A mind lively and at ease, can do with seeing nothing, and can see nothing that does not answer" (233).

Critics have generally taken this moment as Austen's endorsement of the quotidian. But is this a moment (or, indeed, a novel) concerned with endorsement? Does the author in this passage take it upon herself to tell her readers that a lively mind at ease with itself can fill up the vacancies of life with trivia? Or is this indirect speech in which Emma tells herself these things? If these are Emma's aphorisms then they lie as open and vulnerable to criticism as do her projected reading lists elsewhere (37) and her conviction that she has plenty of resources and needs no stimulus from the outside (85). Are we really to imbibe from Emma the message that dailiness is enough?

I do not believe that Emma finds it enough. It is Miss Bates who does. This is Miss Bates's success, the key to her happiness, the thing that makes her mockable yet not pitiable, the thing, perhaps, that links her with her creator. The dogs with their bones, the children without their longed-for gingerbread, are not so trivial as Harriet's ridiculous love-tokens from Mr. Elton (338–40). They are that "every thing" which Frank Churchill believes to be readily available in female correspondence (261), and which some readers have complained of finding too much of in Austen's letters. Emma, as the heroine, can look through a door at these things and know that she moves among significant choices and important discoveries, as Miss Bates does not.

But Austen, who stands with Miss Bates, also stands with her heroine. A view from a shop door can make a letter but not a novel. In teasing Miss Bates, though not in snubbing her, Emma is doing what her creator herself has done. And indeed Austen goes further. She does what none of her characters can do and silences Miss Bates. In the bustle of closure, it is easy not to notice the full extent of her silencing. We are not allowed to hear a word from her on the match between Emma and Mr. Knightley; as if she were John Thorpe, her response is reported but not recorded. In fact all that is reported is her place in the grapevine that relays the news: the lovers tell the Westons, as a secret; Mr. Weston tells his almost-daughter-in-law, Jane, "and Miss Bates being present, it passed, of course, to Mrs. Cole, Mrs. Perry, and Mrs. Elton, immediately afterwards" (468). Miss Bates's voice is unheard.

That is not all. Miss Bates has already been stifled in her attempts to tell Emma (and through Emma the reader) about Jane's engagement to Frank. Emma "could not help being diverted by the perplexity of [Miss Bates's] first answer to herself, resulting, she supposed, from doubt of what might be said, and impatience to say every thing" (455). And Miss Bates actually keeps the secret: "Thank you, dear Miss Woodhouse, you are all kindness.—It is impossible to say—Yes, indeed, I quite understand—dearest Jane's prospects—that is, I do not mean—But she is charmingly recovered.—How is Mr. Woodhouse? ... Charming young man!—that is—so very friendly; I mean good Mr. Perry!" (455). In these broken phrases I calculate that the truth reaches the tip of Miss Bates's tongue four or five times and is bitten back every time. Miss Bates struggles heroically and successfully not to behave like John Thorpe, not to let out other people's secrets—and when it is Jane's secret, not Emma's, she actually succeeds. So within the covers of the novel she never gets to comment on either marriage.

Yet in a sense this silencing is only temporary. Miss Bates has to be quieted so that the happy ending can take place: Austen would never allow her to upstage the heroine, as certain other novelists have with their ideologically polemical single women. But Miss Bates cannot be truly silenced. Though she says nothing about these happy weddings, her earlier monologues remain in the novel, available for rereading; and she is never reproved (as Emma is) for talking too much or inappropriately. Her late silencing may even be regarded as a means of leaving the way clear for the activity critics call "writing beyond the ending," but which is actually something that happens more frequently in talk than in writing.[8] The Austen family did it by letter, but they presumably did it with equal gusto and at greater length in talk. Readers are free to read the silencing of Miss Bates as an invitation for her to talk beyond her ending: an invitation to follow in Emma's footsteps and conjure up Miss Bates's remarks, not about petticoats, but about happy endings. Austen has made us share in her put-down of Emma for mocking Miss Bates to her face. She has also allowed us to share in a different mockery, the mockery of comic imitation, not description: mockery without contempt, or reproof, or pity, but expressive of the love of the intelligent, amused, and privileged listener for the lowly, irrepressible, excessive talker.

NOTES

1 See "Talking about Talk in *Pride and Prejudice*" 87.

2 Isabella is just like her brother, waiting "these ten ages at least" for Catherine, who is not really late at all (39).

3 They included the labouring-class Mary Collier a couple of generations back, Elizabeth Hamilton in an unpublished poem, several novelists, and Elizabeth Carter herself in letters.

4 See, for example, Jane Harvey, *Memoirs of an Author* (1812); Elizabeth Benger, *The Heart and the Fancy, or Valsimore, a Tale* (1813).

5 I also wonder if Miss Bates's happiness conceals a less public joke, an in-joke. Samuel Johnson is on record as frequently maintaining that people in general are not happy. He once confessed himself much irritated by a certain lady's claim to be happy—although, as he unkindly put it, she had neither money nor youth nor brains. If she could suppose herself happy, he seemed to suggest, no sensible person would wish to

emulate her. You're wrong, says Jane Austen, look, here is a woman who *is* happy without any of those things. Despise her at your peril!

6 When I delivered this essay at the Jasper JASNA conference, a member of the audience reminded me afterwards of this vital clue. I am grateful.

7 Carol Houlihan Flynn writes well about this in her essay "The Letters."

8 See, especially, Rachel Blau DuPlessis's *Writing Beyond the Ending: Narrative Strategies of Twentieth-Century Women Writers*.

4

Word-Work, Word-Play, and the Making of Intimacy in 'Pride and Prejudice'

Though a very few hours spent in the *hard labour of incessant talking* will dispatch more subjects than can really be in common between any two rational creatures, yet with lovers it is different. Between *them* no subject is finished, no communication is ever made, till it has been made at least twenty times over. (*SS* 363–64; *emphasis added*)

CONVERSATION

Austen uses conversation perhaps more than any other rhetorical form to tell the story of *Pride and Prejudice*: it is a novel written almost wholly in scenes and the present tense. And the story she tells is "the business of getting married." Therefore, how conversations reveal what kind of business that is and what it means to be and to come to be married is of crucial importance. But what is the relation of conversation to marriage? What is it about conversation that lends itself to telling that story of intimacy?

The verb "to converse" is from the Latin root *conversare*, which means to turn around frequently or to direct. Both of these root definitions—to turn around frequently and to direct—create a picture of an active, changing verb. Turning around frequently suggests a going between, a back and forth, or a circling. The phrase also implies something that bears ongoing analysis, as in turning an idea over again and again. *Conversatio*, the Latin root of the noun "conversation," means frequent sojourn to or abode in a place or regular dealings with a person. Whereas the verb insists on movement, the noun carries with it a sense of continuity, as in the ongoing relation of one person to another or to a place. If the root meaning of "conversation" insists on the same players over time, the root of "converse" insists that those players change, move, realign. Of the definitions *The Oxford English Dictionary* cites for the meanings of "conversation," all eleven insist on some form of "engagement with" or "being in the company of." The definitions include: living in a place with others; consorting or having dealings with others; sexual intercourse; acquaintance or intimacy with a matter, company, or society; the manner of how one conducts oneself in society; the interchange of thoughts and words, familiar discourse or talk; a public debate; having an "at home" (gathering); a painting representing a group of figures; a card with the sentence for a game. Whether it is conversation as sexual intercourse or as the interchange of words and ideas or as living in the society of others, conversation carries with it some form of company and some stated or implied interaction. With regard to *Pride and Prejudice* (and really the whole Austen canon), it is conversation as "interchange of thoughts and words, familiar discourse or talk" that concerns me. In this essay, I explore how the ongoing act of *conversation* creates a groundwork of continuity between the same couple over time while, simultaneously, their particular moments of *conversing* create the ever-shifting dynamic of the couple's meaning-making. Both the conversation that goes on over time and the conversing that changes with each exchange define how Austen's couples experience what it means to talk together, which means be together.

In the way that we remember an action film by virtue of its starred, event-defining moments, we remember a marriage novel (meaning a novel that plots its way toward, through, or away from marriage) by its starred, event-defining conversations. Crux conversations function as destinations toward which a novel directs its energy; they stand out from the rest of the narrative as "keys," or as necessary points of arrival in order for the plot to come into full being. They are the moments from which we mark off how a novel charts its passing of time, path of development, or places of knowledge-gaining. In particular, they embody a partnership's turns, as in how that partnership discovers itself, understands itself, ends itself. Speech that plots, or gets things decided and hence "accomplished," makes word-acts. Literally, the words are actions and perform what I mean here by "word-work." In marriage novels, the strategies for how the narrative plots have everything to do with how the couple turns. Therefore, their conversations act as the linchpin between how the narrative works through its whole structural design and the thing it works hardest at representing, the couple. Crux conversations uncover the pleasures that accompany the experience of intimate knowledge, knowledge that unfolds in defining, often shattering (in the sense of ground-breaking) instances of speech.

Within the array of moments in a couple's history when plot turns upon the fact of a conversation, the "first meeting" requires first that words be exchanged, that each future partner hear the other speak, observe his or her manner, and in turn be observed. However, because the first-time conversation functions to define the novel, how the two individuals interact becomes a model for subsequent meetings, as well as a model for how the plot proceeds, by acting as a reference point for all that follows. It prompts from the subsequent events/exchanges questions such as: does that exchange justly define us? are we still like that? Therefore, it is a rare novel that presents what we would perceive as a generic or repeatable conversation of introduction. Instead, we find an odd exchange or strange form of meeting that shakes itself subtly or deliberately from out of the comfortable procession of plot to demand a different kind of attention. Marriage novels proceed by stopping at this meeting. Therefore, narratives cue us by marking off as distinct the first conversation between "the couple." Aware that we are hearing something unusual, we attend to this dialogue and come to know in time that it is from these opening words that the important work of the couple commences. In *Pride and Prejudice* a forestalled conversation functions to mark the first meeting of Elizabeth and Darcy. Each stands in a position to overhear the other. Elaborate plotting strategies for both bringing together and keeping apart these future lovers surround the very possibility of their first coming to speak to each other. What their first conversation plots is suspense: the ironic suspense of a meeting actually happening in that it doesn't happen, and the suspense that builds around our anticipation of what will be said when it does. First we read:

> Elizabeth Bennet had been obliged, by the scarcity of gentlemen, to sit down for two dances; and during part of that time, Mr. Darcy had been standing near enough for her to overhear a conversation between him and Mr. Bingley, who came from the dance for a few minutes, to press his friend to join it.
>
> "Come, Darcy," said he, "I must have you dance. I hate to see you standing about by yourself in this stupid manner. You had much better dance."
>
> "I certainly shall not. You know how I detest it, unless I am particularly acquainted with my partner. At such an assembly as this, it would be insupportable. Your sisters are engaged, and there is not another woman in the room, with whom it would not be a punishment to me to stand up with." (*PP* 11)

Thirteen pages later, with still no words exchanged directly between them, Darcy stages himself to overhear Elizabeth:

> He began to wish to know more of her, and as a step towards conversing with her himself, attended to her conversation with others. His doing so drew her notice. ...
>
> "What does Mr. Darcy mean," said she to Charlotte, "by listening to my conversation with Colonel Forster?"

"That is a question which Mr. Darcy only can answer."

"But if he does it any more I shall certainly let him know that I see what he is about. He has a very satirical eye, and if I do not begin by being impertinent myself, I shall soon grow afraid of him."

On his approaching them soon afterwards, though without seeming to have any intention of speaking, Miss Lucas defied her friend to mention such a subject to him, which immediately provoking Elizabeth to do it, she turned to him and said,

"Did not you think, Mr. Darcy, that I expressed myself uncommonly well just now, when I was teazing Colonel Forster to give us a ball at Meryton?"

"With great energy;—but it is a subject which always makes a lady energetic." (24)

The scene of Elizabeth's and Darcy's meeting is not set around their conversation, but rather around their acting as *eavesdroppers* to each other's conversations. Significantly, both overhear words about themselves. This picture of each character speaking of the other to his or her closest friend, while the other listens in, figures the means by which knowledge of the other is attained throughout the text. Triangles, where words are exchanged between two while a third listens, or where words are exchanged behind the scenes and the third surmises what is said, not having been a witness to them, generate the misinformation and misperception that drive the novel. The act of acquiring knowledge of and judging character is the novel's preoccupation; therefore, how that knowledge is acquired and judged is of vital importance to the workings of the plot.

For Elizabeth, her initial position of unknown surveillant will colour her perception of Darcy's character. If conversations occur directly between them, these words will not be taken at face value because Darcy can have no face value. Her first encounter with him is staged in a scene of the hidden and masked, that which she had access to because of her own position of being hidden to him. If conversations are overheard or are reported from other sources, Elizabeth takes them to be trustworthy forms of knowledge. The rules, then, for how Darcy's character is to be understood are modelled in Elizabeth's relationship to her first "conversation" with him.

Whereas Elizabeth happens accidentally to stand near enough to Darcy to overhear his rejection of the women of Longbourn and in particular his rejection of her, Darcy overhears Lizzy deliberately. Her action functions as a response to him; she confronts him for his seeming impropriety: "Did not you think, Mr. Darcy, that I expressed myself uncommonly well just now?" The progression of the plot will proceed with Darcy's deliberately generative actions: he observes Elizabeth openly, proposes, writes a letter, and proposes again. His first meeting and conversation with Lizzy is one where he places himself in the position of observable surveillant, where he acts in openness and in silence. Darcy's first known position to Elizabeth will function as a model for the ways in which his knowledge of her and his generative actions of plot will recur—through a public information-gathering about her (as if she is a kind of observable data), through the actions he takes to marry her, and through the silence in which he shrouds himself. While his is a project of collecting knowledge in a publicly observable form, hers is a collection acquired through secrets and the privately passed on. His are perceptions of her digested through observation and in silence; hers are perceptions of him collected through varied conversations in which each account provides pieces of evidence to further her privately derived understanding. Whereas his process of information-gathering leads to the events of plot to which Lizzy must respond, Lizzy's process of amassing the hidden leads her to the avoidance of generating plot between herself and Darcy. Therefore public, silent participation in conversation leads to the generating of plot, and private, verbal participation in conversation leads to reacting to plot.

The openness of his act of eavesdropping, combined with her private knowledge of his hasty evaluation of the women of Longbourn, informs Elizabeth's prejudice against him. Whatever he is to say after the two scenes of first meetings through listening will render his speech false or impertinent to Lizzy's ears until his written speech, his letter to her, forces her to see his words and therefore himself anew. Overhearing and seeing him overhear make Darcy's presence and "living words" suspect. The unseen presence of Darcy in the letter allows the words to "speak for themselves." Likewise, not knowing of Lizzy's private means of formulating her knowledge of his character enables Darcy's sense of pride. Of course she will accept his first proposal: what could she know (or have heard) of him that would make him less than wholly desirable as a suitor? Their sense of mutual surprise when Darcy first proposes and Elizabeth first refuses is the moment of conversation when their two frames for acquiring information, their rules of knowledge-collection, collide. They find, in fact, that they cannot converse, that they cannot, therefore, be a couple. They do not yet share a language because they do not yet share a means of participating in conversation, and so cannot share each other. That is, they do not yet understand what Bakhtin calls "addressivity": neither knows how to address the other ("Speech Genres" 95). Darcy's public pursuit of, as opposed to Lizzy's private involvement in, conversation keeps them worlds apart; the possibility of intimacy between them seems impossible. And yet they do share an excited focus in their misunderstanding, in that Darcy can come to love Lizzy in his open preoccupation with her and Lizzy can enjoy her dislike of Darcy in her cutting responses to him. The early pleasures they feel in response to their first conversation are the early gains that come of misreading. The work, then, that the "first meeting's words" perform is to define how the plot will proceed to the first proposal—the culminating moment of the lovers' conversations of misunderstanding.

Love stories use conversations to embody the starred moments a plot traces through the life of the relationship—the first meeting, the acknowledgment of love, the acknowledgment of the end of love, and/or the final meeting. These dialogues serve and shape linear marriage narratives by marking plot places called "the beginning," "the middle," and "the end." Only shared conversations can represent these discrete, knowable points of a love plotline, which cannot be constructed by events of a solitary "I." Dialogues are interactive, mutually made moments of a partnered story that function to mark off "our story," around which a "we" works to build the daily life that constitutes that "we." The moments of collective making that mark the turns around which a partnership moves will come to constitute that couple's history, the remembered bits that will stand for what this couple means and the pleasures that can accompany coming to that knowledge. These pleasures include experiencing an uncertainty that needs to be solved (what is happening here/between us?), the clarity of the known (this is who we are/what is), and the memory of what was made, lost, recovered (this is who we were/what was/what can be again). The narrative of an "us," whose plot is the history of a couple, relies then on rhetorical structures that tell the events of the marriage/narrative free from one controlling vision. Crux conversations "speak" the marriage narrative as a storytelling of collective consciousness.

WORD-PLAY

Plot-forming, crux conversations function as word-acts; these are the moments when a novel gets things done. Between these declarations, however, are the conversations in which a couple lives their coupleness through how they putter, tinker, and mess around together with their words. These moments of conversation that create texture or add thickness to the relationship of the couple without advancing the plot are what I call instances of word-play. How much space a novel turns over to a couple's playtime has everything to do with how "active" it takes itself to be. The "lazier" the narrative, in its avoidance of linear progression, the more complicated its structure, in that it must continuously invent some other geometry for its being in addition to the line, with its desire for action. And the difficulty of creating lazy, inactive novels has everything to do with the paucity of novels that devote themselves to the play of an established couple over time. The usual talk of couples is not a conversation that measures or marks or defines or draws lines. Instead, it is speech that functions as the "norm" in that it shows how the narrative/couple generally interacts. What makes these lines of talk less memorable has to do with their function: these conversations do not do the work of the plot; they do not get things done. Not event-connected or defining, the speech that is just about "how we talk" embeds itself inside the narrative world as part of what composes its *texture*.

Knowing the other in a novel's lengthiness is a continuous process, as is knowing the self. The world-making and world-exhibiting conversations of couples play interactively with the subtleties and ongoingness of the process of knowing. Elizabeth and Darcy spend much of their time together in conversations that do not always advance the plot, but which do always stage what it means for each to try to know and be known by the other. These are their moments of making word-play.

For instance, it is Elizabeth's sense of a joke and her critical eye that prompt her to consider, yet again, who this Darcy is, while he explores her "Elizabeth-ness" as she promenades with Miss Bingley about the room:

"Mr. Darcy is not to be laughed at!" cried Elizabeth. "That is an uncommon advantage, and uncommon I hope it will continue, for it would be a great loss to me to have many such acquaintance. I dearly love a laugh."

"Miss Bingley," said he, "has given me credit for more than can be. The wisest and the best of men, nay, the wisest and best of their actions, may be rendered ridiculous by a person whose first object in life is a joke."

"Certainly," replied Elizabeth—"there are such people, but I hope I am not one of them. I hope I never ridicule what is wise or good. Follies and nonsense, whims and inconsistencies do divert me, I own, and I laugh at them whenever I can.—But these, I suppose, are precisely what you are without."

"Perhaps that is not possible for any one. But it has been the study of my life to avoid those weaknesses which often expose a strong understanding to ridicule."

"Such as vanity and pride."

"Yes, vanity is a weakness indeed. But pride—where there is a real superiority of mind, pride will be always under good regulation."

Elizabeth turned away to hide a smile.

"Your examination of Mr. Darcy is over, I presume," said Miss Bingley;—"and pray what is the result?"

"I am perfectly convinced by it that Mr. Darcy has no defect. He owns it himself without disguise."

"No"—said Darcy, "I have made no such pretension. I have faults enough, but they are not, I hope, of understanding. My temper I dare not vouch for.—It is I believe too little yielding—certainly too little for the convenience of the world. I cannot forget the follies and vices of others so soon as I ought, nor their offences against myself. My feelings are not puffed about with every attempt to move them. My temper would perhaps be called resentful.—My good opinion once lost is lost forever."

"*That* is a failing indeed!"—cried Elizabeth. "Implacable resentment is a shade in a character. But you have chosen your fault well.—I really cannot *laugh* at it. You are safe from me."

"There is, I believe, in every disposition a tendency to some particular evil, a natural defect, which not even the best education can overcome."

"And *your* defect is a propensity to hate every body."

"And yours," he replied with a smile, "is wilfully to misunderstand them." (57–58)

Darcy's and Elizabeth's conversation takes as its goal the examination of each other's characters, or what makes each potentially ridiculous or defective. The structure of the interaction is of yet another triangle: the two women walking discuss the man who remains seated, watching them watch him. Whereas initially Darcy acts the eavesdropper to a tête-à-tête between the women, Elizabeth's assertion about Darcy, that he is "not to be laughed at," prompts Darcy to insert himself between Elizabeth and Miss Bingley. Therefore, the position of performers to audience shifts, even though Darcy remains seated and the women remain in motion. The migration of who speaks to whom and who does not creates the effect of insider and outsider, and a new delineation of who is in relation to whom and who has been dismissed from that relation.

Miss Bingley has inaugurated the topic, her inability to find anything laughable about Mr. Darcy, which she presents as her evidence to Darcy of her admiration of him. Insisting on differentiating her position from Miss Bingley's, Elizabeth reverses the evaluation of the elements juxtaposed: that laughter is the quality to be admired and that Mr. Darcy's immunity from laughter devalues him. Further, the presentation by Miss Bingley of Darcy's being above ridicule is what in fact makes him an object of ridicule. Elizabeth asserts that she wants no acquaintance who is not to be laughed at because she (apparently) dearly loves a joke. She indirectly states that because Darcy is such a case, in that his presumed arrogance leads him to imagine that he is without fault, he can be no acquaintance of hers. However, as the conversation proceeds, the subject gets the better of Lizzy: in making Darcy the object of her joke, she makes him the object of her desire.

Initially, it appears that Elizabeth controls the frame of the discussion; she seems to coerce from Darcy an admission about himself that reveals his vanity or pride, the very qualities he claims make someone worth ridiculing and that he does not possess. With the insertion of a stage direction, Elizabeth's turning away to smile, the joke is taken note of: to assert that he is not subject to the defects of vanity and pride provides further evidence that these are in fact Darcy's faults. She laughs at her partner in the conversation in such a way that neither he nor their audience, Miss Bingley, is made aware of the game. This is Elizabeth's private joke, told to herself at the expense of Darcy. She proceeds to ridicule Darcy openly by declaring that he is without defect because he has said so himself. His response, like that to her statement about his not being an object open to laughter, reveals the same note of honesty and seriousness. Admitting he has faults, namely his temper and resentment, he claims he also possesses understanding. Elizabeth cannot hear the extent of Darcy's disclosure of himself to her. Inclined to ridicule and so to find fault, she seizes on the "failing" of his resentment and extrapolates beyond that to conclude about Darcy's character that his "defect is a propensity to hate every body."

However, something has altered the tone and positions of control of the conversation—an alteration that repeats throughout the novel. When at midpoint Elizabeth turns from her partner and audience to laugh to herself—a pleasure-filled, self-congratulatory gesture about her superior wit and understanding—Darcy is the one left openly smiling. Elizabeth has so convinced herself of the shortcomings of Darcy's character that she arrives at a hyperbolic assertion of his defect. Darcy turns Elizabeth's critique of him into a gentle, thoughtful retort about her defect: "And yours ... is wilfully to misunderstand them." It is Darcy who ends their discourse with the pleasures of a smile.

Darcy's first and last comments to Elizabeth move his definition of the dangers of the "person whose first object in life is a joke" to a working-out of the specific danger to which Elizabeth falls prey. Elizabeth's discourse with Darcy is part of her ongoing acquisition of evidence to prove him to be a man of defects. While first it appears that Elizabeth's use of indirection enables her to joke at the faults of Darcy while he reveals them unawares, Darcy acts as a partner in indirection in his evaluation of how Elizabeth responds to him. Their camaraderie reveals their mutual ability to use implication as a means of evaluating each other. While theirs is not a conversation of a shared common language, it is one of "complementary schismogenesis," which Gregory Bateson describes as the simultaneous act of each member of a conversation staying within the paradigm or frame of how each views what the conversation is meaning. Neither can move into the other's gestalt because each holds vigilantly to the one he or she uses. As a result, conflicts deepen and conversation seems almost impossible because how language is used and how meaning is determined function as points of contention (Bateson 68).

Each stays within a self-determined, mutually exclusive frame of reference for understanding the other, and this results in misunderstanding. However, misunderstanding works as the means through which they relate perpetually; from the plot conversation of their first meeting to this instance of Darcy-and-Elizabeth-talk-as-usual, to misunderstand is what it means for Darcy and Elizabeth to converse. It is the life-blood of their partnership, the conversation that gets repeated. Being "present" to each other and being able to make the other "present" necessitates physical presence, time spent together, occasions in which the other is a preoccupation. To misunderstand prompts first the wrong construction of a picture of the other (but still all of the psychic energy that is required by the act of creating that misconstruction). To acknowledge that one has misunderstood is to create a new picture assembled from a negation of knowledge, an understanding based in knowing suddenly all that the other is *not*. The intimacy of knowing, then, is founded on the intimacy of having not known: this is the process that defines how Lizzy and Darcy use speech to build the sense of intimacy that redefines them as partners. They grow together from an ongoing experience of jointly shattering their misconstrued "truths." This movement from one way of knowing to another, the recognition that movement is possible because another understanding is possible, is illuminated by Ludwig Wittgenstein's description of the "'dawning' of an aspect" in his discussion of the Jastrow drawing of a duck/rabbit: "I contemplate a face, and then suddenly notice its likeness to another. I *see* that it has not changed; and yet

I see it differently. But we can also *see* the illustration now as one thing now as another.—So we interpret it, and *see* it as we *interpret* it" (193). Darcy has another face for Elizabeth when she construes him differently. He has not changed, and yet he has changed profoundly in response to the re-vision of her interpretation. Once the conversation of Darcy and Elizabeth changes to understanding, the novel must soon end: that conversation—the declaration that "we" are now an "us"—takes place silently, somewhere outside the confines of the narrative's final pages.

Language in narratives that enables partners just to talk, as opposed to making the narrative's plot, creates conversations that function as their own performances. While plot conversations may reveal how a couple repeats aspects of their linguistic engagement, these crux conversations stand out in their drive to bring the plot to new places, to do new things, to end in their full knowledge of all that there is to be known. In their memorability they function as extraordinary structures of rhetoric. It is a memorability tied to how they define certain desired moments of plot development. The conversations of repetition, or what I refer to here as the words that play, fill the text in their recurrence and work to tell the general story—to show again and again that *Pride and Prejudice* is about words misunderstood. What these repeated conversations do, therefore, is to tell the text's "usual," to function as the narrative's structural refrain. They tell of the pleasure the narrative/the couple take in these conversations, in that they are the ones repeated and hence desired, if only for a sense of being there, or being there again, though differently: these are the partnered words of the moment that creates a "now" or a lifetime together. While these conversations do not obviously advance a narrative, they do represent in their replay what a partnership is about and therefore what the narrative is about, until it shifts in direction.

When a pair shares an interest in and knowledge of how to play together through language, a boundary is drawn between those who speak in their code and those who do not, those who are in on the joke, and those who are not. This linguistic division separates a sphere of intimacy from a sphere of publicness. The moments in texts of a couple's speech comprise the scenes of their intimacy, the location of the life of their relationship discovering itself, adjusting how it knows itself, recovering itself, even ending itself. These instances of conversation in novels are the reader's means of "overhearing" or being present at that which creates, defines, and reveals the couple's intimacy. And yet linguistic speech is by no means the only conversation Austen stages to uncover that intimacy. *Pride and Prejudice's* summer chattiness grows quiet in *Persuasion's* autumn tones. Removing the annoying Walter from around Anne's neck, handing Anne into the Crofts' carriage because he sees her fatigue, blushing upon first seeing her in Bath, returning to a room so as discreetly to deliver a letter that declares the constancy of his love, Frederick Wentworth chooses to initiate a conversation of gestures to which Anne responds at first in silence, then with the return of her youth, and finally in speech. The return of the beloved and the possibility of love's open expression prompt a different conversation from the word-centred world of "firsts" of Lizzy and Darcy. Meeting again, Anne and Frederick will come to know that they love again, or rather still love, because of how his body speaks his continued care and how her body blooms for a second time in response to his touch. To first meet, to first feel attraction, to first want to know, to first love, Austen tells us in *Pride and Prejudice,* we must first risk talk—"risk" because of the capacity of words to be misunderstood. But a second chance at love affords a second chance to understand and be understood in the speech that follows words—the silent speech of bodies. If talk inaugurates the process of coming to intimacy, perhaps silence for Austen heralds the arrival at its true knowledge.

NOTE

This essay appears, in somewhat different form, as part of my book *Ordinary Pleasures: Couples, Conversation, and Company* (Columbus: Ohio State University Press, 2001).

Aggression
and Power

5

Mrs. Elton and Other Verbal Aggressors

WHEN THE NEWLY MARRIED MRS. ELTON comes to Hartfield to visit Emma Woodhouse, she lays it down as axiomatic that "Surry is the garden of England" (*E* 273). Emma, recognizing a cliché, but graciously carrying on the conversation, suggests,

> "Yes; but we must not rest our claims on that distinction. Many counties, I believe, are called the garden of England, as well as Surry."
>
> "No, I fancy not," replied Mrs. Elton, with a most satisfied smile. "I never heard any county but Surry called so."
>
> Emma was silenced. (*E* 273–74)

It is not often that confident Emma Woodhouse is stuck for something to say. The three-word sentence, "Emma was silenced," is given a whole paragraph to itself, and it speaks volumes. It is Mrs. Elton's steel-clad assumption that if she hasn't heard of it, it doesn't exist. Her answer brings civil discourse to a grinding halt. What room is there for conversation, an exchange and enlargement of ideas through speech, if one of the parties assumes a universe absolutely limited by her own perception? I would like to linger on this scene of Mrs. Elton's first visit to Hartfield. What is going on, of course, is that the great lady of the district is encountering the would-be great lady. Emma as yet doesn't feel threatened; for Mrs. Elton the exchange is all about power. And within the bounds of supposedly polite exchange, she nevertheless bristles and snarls and snatches any advantage she can.

To speak first of her *manner* of talk: Mrs. Elton espouses the exclamatory mode. Characteristic openings to her speeches are "Oh! yes" (273), "Oh! no, indeed" (276), interspersed with the occasional "Ah!" (274, 275). More frequent still is the exclamatory "so," followed by an adjective or adjectival phrase: "So extremely like Maple Grove!" strikes the keynote (273). But note also "so extremely partial," "so many happy months," "put me so exactly in mind!" (273), "so very much preferable" (274), "so cheerful a place," "so secluded a life" (275), "so many resources within myself" (276), "so truly good," "so motherly and kind-hearted," "so very lady-like," "so particular a friend," "so often mentioned" (278). Such exclamations are augmented by others beginning with "how," for example, "how very like [Maple Grove] the stair-case was," "how very delightful it is to meet" (273). As she says herself, "I really could not help exclaiming!" (273).

Whether she agrees or disagrees with a proposition, Mrs. Elton must do so with emphasis. No measly qualification for her, and nothing wishy-washy. Her speech is packed with intensifiers, adverbs co-opted from their actual meaning to provide emphasis—as, for instance, today we use "incredibly" where credibility is not really at issue. We remember how Henry Tilney takes Catherine to task for her innocent use of "amazingly" as a mere intensifier: "I really thought ... young men despised novels amazingly" (*NA* 107). Mrs. Elton could certainly have done with Henry Tilney as a commentator on her idiom, for she sprinkles such words liberally where they don't belong, like pepper in a whipped syllabub. Here is a very partial listing from the fifteen minutes' worth of dialogue: four "reallys," four "extremelys," three "entirelys," two "absolutelys," two "decidedlys," two "honestlys," plus a scattering of "particularly," "perfectly," "exactly," "astonishingly," and "strikingly." This exclamatory and emphatic mode belongs to a talker who wants to hold the stage and play the lead. "Listen to me—me—*me*," she says, by constant implication.

For this verbal practice, Mrs. Elton has some notable forebears in Austen's earlier works. The flibbertigibbet Camilla Stanley in *Catharine, or the Bower* characteristically begins speaking with an "Oh!"—as in "Oh! Yes ... and I am quite delighted with them" (MW 199). She likewise knows no moderation in her estimation of people. Each of her acquaintances, by her testimony, is "either the sweetest Creature in the world, and one of whom she was doatingly fond, or horrid, shocking and not fit to be seen" (202).

Isabella Thorpe is the next in a sequence of exclamatory and overemphatic talkers who trample on their interlocutors in the process of drawing attention to themselves. Like Camilla, who can convey "no information ... but in fashions" (MW 201), Isabella subordinates matters of real import, like love and fidelity, to the cut of a gown or the style of a bonnet. In her letter to Catherine Morland, she insists, in consecutive sentences, that Catherine's brother "is the only man I ever did or could love" and that the spring fashions are down and "the hats the most frightful you can imagine" (NA 216). She too uses "frightfully" and "amazingly" in slang senses far removed from their actual meaning and deploys an exclamatory and hyperbolic style: "Oh! I would not tell you what is behind the black veil for the world!" (39).

Both Camilla and Isabella, by their cultivated vivacity and clamorous opinions, have the effect of thrusting more sensible and discriminating speakers into the shade. Conversation as civil exchange is at an end. Those they speak to must either become their echo and follower, as Catherine Morland does, or retreat into themselves in disappointment, like Kitty when she finds there is "no variety in [Camilla's] conversation" (MW 201).

In Augusta Elton, Austen develops and refines the characteristic speech patterns of Camilla and Isabella. The three are also connected by their romantically Latinate names and their preoccupation with fashion ("Very nicely dressed, indeed," is Emma's first cautious comment on Mrs. Elton [E 271]). Like theirs, Mrs. Elton's talk is largely for show and advantage rather than for communication and exchange. But more than them, she exploits talk to generate and exert power. She comes to Highbury with the notable advantage of a husband in tow. And among single women she flourishes her *caro sposo* at every available opportunity.

To turn from the exclamatory and emphatic manner of her speech to its matter: in the speech of the verbal aggressors there is a dreary dearth of genuine subject matter. You can't, for instance, have a real discussion on which county has the best claim to be called the garden of England. Their speech is really veiled warfare. With Mrs. Elton the other speaker must either submit and be dominated, like Jane Fairfax, or resist and fume, like Emma. It is only the tactful and effective speaker, like Mr. Knightley, who can avoid being bullied without giving offence, as in the case of which guests get invited to the strawberry-picking at Donwell Abbey. As we all remember, Mrs. Elton begins her visit to Emma with a voluble comparison of Hartfield to Maple Grove. She would claim that she intends to compliment Hartfield by the comparison, but of course such a claim would be false. Transparently, she advances and supports the comparison (a) to get her main claim to social standing, "my brother Mr. Suckling's seat," into the conversation as early as possible (272) and (b) by attaching Hartfield to the skirts of Maple Grove to colonize it, to take it over. A genuine conversational *exchange* on the likeness of the two estates is of course impossible, since Emma hasn't seen one of them. Such a comparison necessarily silences the interlocutor.

A similar strain in Mrs. Elton's talk is her reference to people unknown to Emma. The oft-invoked Sucklings of Maple Grove are only the most obvious instance of this habit. She cites "Mrs. Jeffereys—Clara Partridge, that was—and ... the two Milmans, now Mrs. Bird and Mrs. James Cooper" (277). We are all familiar with this habit of talkative people, who seem to believe we are consumingly interested in people we have never heard of before. What do we, or what can Emma, know or care about Clara Partridge, even if she has succeeded in changing her status to "Mrs. Jeffereys"? Such references can only be "talk" and never "conversation." Tom Bertram of *Mansfield Park* is characterized by his penchant for anecdote, as when he speaks of Miss Sneyd, sister of "my friend Sneyd—you have heard me speak of Sneyd, Edmund" (*MP* 51). Tom has the grace to expand such references into lively anecdote, and Mary Crawford finds them entertaining. But inasmuch as most anecdote deals in matter beyond the knowledge of all but the speaker, it is a form of speech Austen ranks low. The only possible response is a counter-anecdote about someone equally unknown to the first speaker, and so it goes. There can be no enlargement of the topic through conversation. Mrs. Elton, at least, transparently parades her brother-in-law and acquaintance as a way of holding the stage herself. And since Emma is not about to compete by making reference to "my brother-in-law, Mr. John Knightley of London, with his large practice," she must again be "silenced" by the dribble of references to acquaintances not mutual.

After the conversation-stopper of the flat contradiction on Surrey as the garden of England, Mrs. Elton returns to the Sucklings, their chaise and their barouche-landau, this time with the ostensible motive of advocating the joys of "exploring." When Emma says that Highbury people are "more disposed to stay at home than engage in schemes of pleasure" (274), Mrs. Elton changes her tune from contradiction to competition. Having just extolled the joys of exploring, she eagerly claims to be a veritable couch-potato. "Ah! ... Nobody can be more devoted to home than I am. I was quite a proverb for it at Maple Grove" (274). Then again she shifts, this time to the truism: "and yet I am no advocate for entire seclusion. I think ... that it is much more advisable to mix in the world in a proper degree, without living in it either too much or too little" (275).

Next comes the intrusive advice: "Why does not [your father] try Bath?—Indeed he should"; then the intrusive patronage: "for you, who have lived so secluded a life ... I could immediately secure you some of the best society in the place" (275).

By now, of course, Emma is simply boiling with indignation: "The idea of her being indebted to Mrs. Elton for what is called an *introduction* ... !" (275). She has her own exclamatory mode but it is unspoken. As a conscientious hostess, she "restrained herself" (276), and instead of delivering the reproof that is in her mind she tactfully changes the subject to music.

Emma certainly has many faults, and many of them are committed in speech, but she has a right to claim, "I hope I am not often deficient in what is due to guests at Hartfield" (170). Her speech on this occasion is gracious and correct, and thus an appropriate contrast with Mrs. Elton's. In the face of Mrs. Elton's vociferous egotism, she holds the first person in abeyance, preferring a more generalized statement. She would never produce a flat contradiction like Mrs. Elton's, "No, I fancy not." When she must deliver a negative in response to an enquiry, "You have many parties of that kind here, I suppose, every summer?", Emma courteously qualifies it: "No; not immediately here" (274). And even though her visitor is virtually a stranger to her, she avoids the usual conversational ploy of the direct question as potentially intrusive: instead she produces a generalized statement for her guest to take up or not, as she chooses. To introduce the new subject of music, she says neither "Do you play well?" nor "I know you play well," but rather the generalized "Highbury has long known that you are a superior performer" (276). By these courtesies and restraints, she proves a point she soon has occasion to make: "Mrs. Weston's manners ... were always particularly good. Their propriety, simplicity, and elegance, would make them the safest model for any young woman" (278). Emma has learned from a good model, whereas Mrs. Elton's manners (for all her insulting patronage of Mrs. Weston as "quite the gentlewoman" [278]) "had been formed in a bad school, pert and familiar" (272). The learning of proper manners, indeed, as this bridal visit makes clear all over again, is a major part of education in Jane Austen's world.

"Propriety, simplicity, and elegance"—just the sort of things that that admirable personage, the man in the street, would expect us to find in Jane Austen! "Who cares?", one can hear the Mark Twains and D.H. Lawrences of the world shouting. What does it matter if Mrs. Elton is pert and familiar? Why *shouldn't* she call Mr. Knightley "Knightley" or refer to her husband as her *caro sposo*? *Why?*

The answer is that what Mrs. Elton speaks she *is*. Given the highly structured and formal society she belongs to, and the fullness and specificity of Austen's created world, what a character says, with the way she says it, is as salient an aspect of identity as her genetic inheritance, her body, her class, certainly her actions. Mrs. Elton is as much herself by virtue of her speech as a sonnet is a sonnet by virtue of being in fourteen lines with the right metre and rhyme scheme. Because Austen is the kind of creator she is, Mrs. Elton's conversation during a fifteen-minute visit sums her up as fully as a substantial and well-researched biography.

Although we know that Mrs. Elton, and Emma too, are mere figments, collections of inkmarks on certain sheets of paper, we, like Emma, get hot with indignation at Mrs. Elton's outrageous verbal encroachments. As she colonizes Hartfield by attaching it to Maple Grove, as she boasts of being "blessed with so many resources within myself," as she tries to take over Emma by assuming partnership in "establish[ing] a musical club" (277), she proves herself an imperialist and a self-aggrandizer on a grand scale. For a practical correlation to these verbal practices, I need only cite her campaign to take over Jane Fairfax and turn her into a mere personal appurtenance. Jane proposes to pick up her own mail. "Oh! She *shall not* do such a thing again," Mrs. Elton declares. "We will not allow her to do such a thing again" (295). She uses the emphatic form of negative, "she shall not," and she appropriates the royal "we." If Jane Fairfax only just avoids being traded by "offices for the sale ... of human intellect" (300), she as narrowly escapes becoming the virtual slave of Mrs. Elton. Emma, for all her arrogant management of Harriet and her love life, never approaches such verbal tyranny.

Of course, Emma is a self-aggrandizer, too, and conducts her own campaign to take over Harriet. In that enterprise she does much to fulfil Jane Austen's prediction that she was presenting a heroine "whom no one but myself will much like" (Austen-Leigh 157). But Emma is redeemed by her capacity for self-knowledge, and that capacity is also demonstrated by the restraint she practises in speech. Even when we see her at her worst, in steering Harriet away from accepting Robert Martin while pretending to renounce influence, her mode of speech is still courteous and still permits Harriet's responses. She never annihilates Harriet as Mrs. Elton tries to annihilate Emma by the flat denial of her "No, ... I never heard any county but Surry called so."

Mrs. Elton's godlike assumption that if she hasn't heard it, it doesn't exist is a kind of conversational hubris that is bound to have its fall. And we are not cheated of a come-uppance. There is no public trial and verdict, no hauling off to hell or the gallows, no divorce or dismissal from office: this is Jane Austen, after all. But there is an uncomfortable falling from assumed infallibility. Insisting that her husband is meeting Mr. Knightley at the Crown, because, as she characteristically puts it, "Mr. E. is Knightley's right hand," Mrs. Elton won't listen to Emma's courteous, "Have you not mistaken the day? I am almost certain that the meeting at the Crown is not till to-morrow." Notice Emma's accommodating "almost," a qualifier Mrs. Elton would disdain. "'Oh! no; the meeting is certainly to-day,' was the abrupt answer, which denoted the impossibility of any blunder on Mrs. Elton's side" (456). But *caro sposo*, when he arrives, is hot and bothered. Having walked all the way to Donwell Abbey, he has been stood up by Mr. Knightley, who has gone to visit Emma. "No, no, [the meeting at the Crown is] tomorrow," he responds irritably to his wife (457). Mrs. Elton is wrong, Emma is right, and the right people receive the demonstration. It's the appropriate punish-ment for Mrs. "I'm-right-I-always-am" Elton.

~

TALK IS ACTION, and by talk it will be rewarded or punished. To turn to another verbal tyrant: at the end of an evening spent dining at Rosings, the guests are "gathered round the fire to hear Lady Catherine determine what weather they were to have on the morrow" (*PP* 166). It is a quiet touch, but we are meant to catch the irony. Man proposes, but Lady Catherine disposes, like God; and the weather is meant to understand as much.[1] If Mrs. Elton snaps and snarls and tries to become leader of the pack, Lady Catherine considers herself superior not only in degree but in kind. She claims divine right.

In point of style and accuracy, Lady Catherine's speech is far superior to Mrs. Elton's. She is not guilty of that vulgar striving for effect that prompts Mrs. Elton's constant exclamations and slangy over-emphasis. But she is like Mrs. Elton in being determined to be first in the company, to assert her status and exert her power; and since she has much more of both than Mrs. Elton, she doesn't need to work so hard at it. She seems to have a settled belief in her own infallibility; she doesn't need to parade her knowledge.

"Oh! yes, I am quite aware of that," is Mrs. Elton's response to a cour-teous statement, a response calculated to put the last speaker in the wrong by implying she speaks the obvious (*E* 273). Lady Catherine, on the other hand, chooses to shore up a godlike omniscience by gathering information about other people, with a view to laying down the law to them. She goes in for the intrusive question. "She enquired into Charlotte's domestic concerns familiarly and minutely, and gave her a great deal of advice, as to the management of them all" (*PP* 163). Likewise she cross-questions Elizabeth about her sisters in order to reveal that the family's education has been neglected and the younger daughters have "come out" too young (165). And like Mrs. Elton, she loves to manage people and to dispose of them, again often as governesses. "It is wonderful how many families I have been the means of supplying in that way. ... 'Lady Catherine,' said [Lady Metcalfe], 'you have given me a treasure'" (165). She is proud of making gifts of human beings; she likes to trade in human autonomy.

For her aspiration to godhead Lady Catherine, of course, gets a far more developed fall than Mrs. Elton. Her fall, in fact, occupies the whole of a chapter, in which, like Milton's fallen angel, she "drop[s] from the zenith like a falling star" (*PL* 1.745). In the verbal exchange with Elizabeth at Longbourn she meets her match. And the prolonged cadence of her fall, "from noon to dewy eve" (*PL* 1.743), deserves examination.

She comes to Longbourn, she says, "with the determined resolution of carrying my purpose ... I have not been in the habit of brooking disappointment" (355–56). She thinks at first to carry her point by intimidating her adversary with thunder and lightning: "Miss Bennet, do you know who I am?" (354). But Elizabeth remains calm and firm, and even reminds this would-be deity that she is merely human, asking her reasonably, "What could your ladyship propose by [the visit]?" (353). Lady Catherine proceeds to show that she is one who *disposes*: "From his earliest hours [Mr. Darcy] *was destined* for his cousin" (355; emphasis added). Elizabeth continues to respond as to a mere human being with limited powers. "You ... did as much as you could, in planning the marriage. Its completion depended on others" (355).

From a domineering insistence on predestination, Lady Catherine tacitly admits to a limitation in her powers when she descends to persuasion, though her method is still bullying. As an appeal to Elizabeth, she invokes "honour, decorum, prudence" (355)—qualities arranged in descending order in the moral hierarchy. She adds a bribe, "interest": "Yes, Miss Bennet, interest" (355), she urges insultingly, abandoning the appeal to a higher motive for a lower one. And she can't resist turning the bribe into a threat:

For do not expect to be noticed by his family or friends, if you wilfully act against the inclinations of all. You will be censured, slighted, and despised, by every one connected with him. Your alliance will be a disgrace; your name will never even be mentioned by any of us. (355)

We all remember Elizabeth's answer: "'These are heavy misfortunes,'" replied Elizabeth. "'But the wife of Mr. Darcy must have such extraordinary sources of happiness necessarily attached to her situation, that she could, upon the whole, have no cause to repine'" (355). The human aspiration to godhead can't survive irony. To find her thunderbolts coolly surveyed and set aside as harmless is for Lady Catherine to discover her own lack of power. She continues to abuse Elizabeth as an "obstinate, headstrong girl!" (355). But now she is reduced to appealing for "gratitude" for her "attentions" to Elizabeth of last spring (355), when she has clearly cancelled all past favours by her present abuse. And it is significant that at this point she proposes sitting down. She acknowledges her own diminished stature.

If I have used imagery of the supernatural in discussing a dialogue in a realistic novel, and one so rooted in the familiar as an Austen novel, it was Lady Catherine who led the way. Since her ladyship has declared it to be "impossible" that her nephew could make an offer of marriage to one of "upstart pretensions," (353, 356), then such an impossibility can be accounted for only by a counter-magic: "*Your* arts and allurements may, in a moment of infatuation, have made him forget what he owes to himself and to all his family. You may have drawn him in" (354). Elizabeth must be a witch or a siren, figures we don't usually associate with Austen's novels. And Lady Catherine carries through in her invocation of supernatural powers: "Heaven and earth! ... Are the shades of Pemberley to be thus polluted?" (357). Heaven, shades, and unhallowed pollution: such is the mythic world in which this scion of the aristocracy locates herself.

It is part of the effectiveness of the Mrs. Eltons and Lady Catherines of Austen's world that even though they come by their fall, they aren't capable of the self-knowledge that can procure regret or a real change.[2] Their eyesight, however sharp in perceiving the shortcomings of others, is not up to seeing the error of their own ways. The fall is for the reader's satisfaction alone. At the end of her interview Lady Catherine is still asserting, "Depend upon it I will carry my point." But the narrator adds, "In this manner Lady Catherine talked on ..." (358). Blah, blah, blah, as we say irreverently today. The divine visitation to Longbourn has dwindled to a Miss-Bates-like oral leak.

~

IF A PRIZE WERE GIVEN for the most unpleasant character in Jane Austen's works, I suspect a majority of us would vote hands-down for Mrs. Norris. This wicked-stepmother figure would like to enact the role of God, like Lady Catherine, but she is short of power, and that shortage rankles. Although we are never explicitly told as much, it seems that as the oldest of the three Ward sisters she had expected to retain the superior position among her siblings. The fact that her indolent younger sister not only marries six years before her, but is also "raised to the rank of a baronet's lady, with all the comforts and consequences of an handsome house and large income" (MP 3) is a bitter pill, and though she must swallow it, the bitterness remains part of her constitution. Her hyperactive energy is chan-nelled into snatching power and status like scraps from someone else's plate, when deep down she believes that the whole meal was meant for her. Since such power as she can snatch is dependent on the goodwill of her brother-in-law Sir Thomas, she must mask her hunger for power from him and Lady Bertram, disguising it as zeal for their family. But such habitual sublimation costs her painful effort, and she needs a scapegoat. Her vindic-tive management first brings about the estrangement between the sisters; then, over many years, she vents her accumulated resentment on little Fanny Price. This is the psychological mechanism that provides the initial impulse for the action of *Mansfield Park*.

"Sticks and stones may break my bones, but words can never hurt me" runs the proverb. But Mrs. Norris's words to Fanny are so brutal as to constitute abuse. By the time "Mrs. Norris had been talking to her all the way from Northampton of her wonderful good fortune," it is no wonder that little Fanny on her arrival at Mansfield Park "knew not how to look up, and could scarcely speak to be heard, or without crying" (13). Nobody knows so well how to deliver a tongue-lashing to a subordinate. (We often hear of Mrs. Norris's triumphs over servants.) Fanny's progress in adapting to her new home is measured by the news that as she gets older and braver, "she was no longer materially afraid to appear before her uncle, nor did her aunt Norris's voice make her start very much" (17).

Mrs. Norris adapts herself endlessly to her interlocutor. She shamelessly flatters Sir Thomas and his children. Hierarchy is so important to her that for each superior she acknowledges, some inferior must suffer. She is adept at portraying herself as pathetic: "Me! a poor helpless, forlorn widow, unfit for any thing, my spirits quite broke down" (28). She has her own style in the boast: "Whatever I can do ... I am always ready enough to do for the good of those I love" (7). What she *can't* do, apparently, is shut up. She is an aggressive, indeed a compulsive, talker. On Maria's engagement, "no other attempt [was] made at secrecy, than Mrs. Norris's talking of it every where as a matter not to be talked of" (39). She is a kind of talking machine, unable to switch herself off. We hear of her "more numerous words and louder tone" (76). When Sir Thomas reproaches her about the play, we hear that "Mrs. Norris was ... as nearly being silenced as ever she had been in her life" (188). However, the speech that follows occupies two pages, and by the end she has won by pure volume of words: "Sir Thomas gave up the point, foiled by her evasions, disarmed by her flattery" (190).

But the mode of speech that Fanny experiences from her is uniformly the put-down. There is never an exchange between them. The pattern is that Mrs. Norris abuses, Fanny takes it. "That is a very foolish trick, Fanny, to be idling away the evening upon a sofa," her aunt scolds, when Fanny is caught lying down with a headache (71). And each put-down for Fanny must be a leg up for Mrs. Norris: "There is all the new calico that was bought last week, not touched yet. I am sure I almost broke my back by cutting it out. You should learn to think of other people" (71). Fanny makes no attempt at defending herself, nor answering at all: "Before half of this was said, Fanny was returned to her seat at the table, and had taken up her work again" (71). Silent obedience is her portion, as of the slaves in Antigua. Talk is Mrs. Norris's means of domination, and her calculated servility towards her superiors must be compensated by tyranny towards her inferiors.

~

Jane Austen is fascinated by the operation of power and rank on verbal exchanges between her characters. Ideally, when talk rises to the level of conversation, in which a subject is canvassed and enlarged by civil exchange, the speakers, whatever their social differences in this context, become honorary equals. In *Persuasion* William Walter Elliot, a wily social climber, urges his cousin to appreciate the vapid Lady Dalrymple and Miss Carteret as "good company." Anne memorably responds,

> "My idea of good company, Mr. Elliot, is the company of clever, well-informed people, who have a great deal of conversation; that is what I call good company."
> "You are mistaken," said he gently, "that is not good company, that is the best. Good company requires only birth, education and manners, and with regard to education is not very nice." (*P* 150)

Class consciousness and the accompanying dynamic may make for "good company" in Mr. Elliot's terms, but they virtually preclude "the best."

The talk at Mrs. Ferrars's dinner party in *Sense and Sensibility* vividly illustrates the deleterious effect of class and power structures on civil discourse. Mrs. Ferrars has plenty of money and therefore plenty of power, and moreover it is power that she enjoys wielding. However, unlike Lady Catherine, "She was not a woman of many words: for, unlike people in general, she proportioned them to the number of her ideas" (*ss* 232). Such a hostess hardly makes for a swinging party. She throws a grand dinner, with many servants: "No poverty of any kind, except of conversation, appeared—but there, the deficiency was considerable" (233).

The company assembled includes Mrs. Ferrars's daughter and son-in-law, the John Dashwoods; Sir John and Lady Middleton with Mrs. Jennings; the Steele sisters; and the Dashwood sisters. In such a gathering the criss-crossings of conflicting agendas are constant. Elinor and Lucy are highly conscious of being introduced at the same time to "this formidable mother-in-law" (231). Edward Ferrars can't face such a gathering at all and sensibly stays away. The Steele sisters are always on the alert to curry favour. Marianne will never stoop to conciliate anyone. Fanny Dashwood and Lady Middleton grow competitive on the matter of their adored little sons: "One subject only engaged the ladies till coffee came in, which was the comparative heights of Harry Dashwood, and Lady Middleton's second son

William, who were nearly of the same age" (233). Since only Harry is present, the matter can't be settled by measuring them; hence "it was all conjectural assertion on both sides, and every body had a right to be equally positive in their opinion."

> The parties stood thus [explains the narrator]:
> The two mothers, though each really convinced that her own son was the tallest, politely decided in favour of the other.
> The two grandmothers, with not less partiality, but more sincerity, were equally earnest in support of their own descendant.
> Lucy, who was hardly less anxious to please one parent than the other, thought the boys were both remarkably tall for their age, ... and Miss Steele, with yet greater address gave it, as fast as she could, in favour of each. (234)

In such an exchange, where the parties are essentially thrown into an arena to compete for favour, truth and even measurable fact go by the board, and so does real considered opinion. The "subject" of the discussion must languish, must be left far behind, as the participants verbally posture and parade their party slogans. In fact it suits them all that the fact can't be established, since that allows them to repeat their opinions "over and over again as often as they liked" (234). So in the midst of plenty, in fact *because* of the plenty and the ulterior motives it produces, conversation is poverty-stricken.

Mrs. Ferrars certainly promotes verbal aggression among her guests, as between her sons. She clearly likes the power to throw a bone among the curs and watch them snarl and fight for it. But is she a verbal aggressor herself, like Mrs. Elton, Isabella Thorpe, and Lady Catherine? Since she is short of ideas and niggardly of words, the instances of aggression aren't frequent, but they are memorably present. "Hum ... very pretty," is all she will say when Elinor's screens are shown her, and she won't even look at them (another instance in which the actual subject of discussion is set at naught). To conciliate her, Fanny Dashwood mentions "Miss Morton's style of painting," and Mrs. Ferrars, in surly distinction to her response to Elinor's artistic efforts, insists, "But *she* does every thing well" (235).

Marianne, who isn't tuned in to what is going on, loyally bursts in, "What is Miss Morton to us?—who knows, or who cares, for her?—it is Elinor of whom *we* think and speak" (235). Marianne applies a rule of relevance and of deference to present company. She doesn't know that Miss Morton is indeed highly relevant in Mrs. Ferrars's agenda, as the one she plans to be her son's bride instead of the two other candidates present. But Marianne might as well say to Mrs. Elton, "What is Mr. Suckling to us?—who knows, or who cares, for him?" Mrs. Elton, like Mrs. Ferrars, would be impervious.

In the present case Mrs. Ferrars proves her indubitable claim to the title of verbal aggressor: "Mrs. Ferrars looked exceedingly angry, and drawing herself up more stiffly than ever, pronounced in retort this bitter philippic; 'Miss Morton is Lord Morton's daughter'" (235–36).

However relevant to her own unspoken agenda, this pronouncement is so stunningly irrelevant to the surface level of the exchange as to become an effective conversation-stopper. It is like Mrs. Elton's "No, I fancy not" or Lady Catherine's "Mr. Darcy is engaged to *my daughter*" (PP 354). Each pronouncement is intended to cow the other speaker.

~~~

ARE THEY ALL WOMEN, the verbal aggressors? No indeed: John Thorpe is a perfect example of the male of the breed. Courtship and not competition is the motive of his talk with Catherine, but he too talks to bully and subdue. He too struts his stuff, and vanity is to the fore. His horse is faster and better hung than other people's, his gig is neater, his judgement on female beauty more astute. Catherine is worn down by his emphatic and self-aggrandizing talk on male subjects of which she has no experience. And when she ventures to introduce a new topic by asking timidly, "Have you ever read Udolpho, Mr. Thorpe?", his response is another conversation-stopper. "Udolpho! Oh, Lord! not I; I never read novels; I have something else to do" (NA 48). Catherine is "humbled and ashamed," as Emma is "silenced" by Mrs. Elton's aggression. I could expand further on John Thorpe's talk, but this is a subject treated "by the capital pen of a sister author" (NA 111), Isobel Grundy, elsewhere in this volume.

The sense of hierarchy is strong among Austen's verbal aggressors, whether of rank as with Lady Catherine, money as with Mrs. Ferrars, masculinity as with John Thorpe, or pretension to power not their own, as with Mrs. Elton and Mrs. Norris. They constantly strive to assert and increase their own status, to get one step higher in the pecking order, and hence to put down the person they are talking to. They address others, indeed, as though they were a superior order of being addressing an inferior, as with Lady Catherine's pretension to godhead or, to shift the metaphor, the dominant animal in the pack. Their talk is a kind of hubris, a case of "overweening pride," as the literary phrase books say, that must have its fall. And we as readers, taught to identify with the protagonists who suffer from the conversational tyrannies, also learn to rejoice in the downfall of these verbal villains.

Before I leave the overweeners, and by way of one more stroke in the definition of them, I want to say a word about their opposites: the protagonist's too-ready allies, the facile friends. I call them the underweeners. And they are sometimes as much a threat to the protagonist's identity as the overweeners.

Wickham flatters Elizabeth by too readily agreeing with her and leads her deeply into error. Emma is surrounded by yes-people; her father believes she can do no wrong and attributes prophetic powers to her: "Ah! my dear, ... whatever you say always comes to pass" (E 12). Mr. Elton is an "Exactly so!" man. And Harriet, as Mr. Knightley points out, knows "nothing herself, and looks upon Emma as knowing every thing. She is a flatterer in all her ways" (38). No wonder Emma is led into her own hubris, her tendency to believe herself infallible. It takes the exaggerated pretensions and less forgivable arrogance of Mrs. Elton to procure our forgiveness for Emma. But a developed essay on underweeners is a matter that must wait for another occasion.

In Jane Austen, talk is character, talk is action. There may be no guillotines in her novels, no French Revolution or Peninsular wars, no double-dyed villains or pictures of perfection. But among these highly socialized talkers in drawing-rooms there are those who snarl and snatch for power, those who grovel or are victimized, and those who learn to pick their way with full moral awareness through a civilized world that nevertheless occasionally affords glimpses of smothered aggressions and nature red in tooth and claw.

1   For discussion of Austen's verbal aggressors, I partly recall comments on characters I
    have published elsewhere on the subject of the talk in individual novels. On Lady
    Catherine's tendency to regard herself as divine, see "Talking about Talk in *Pride and
    Prejudice*" 87. On Mrs. Norris's compulsive talking, see "The Talkers and Listeners of
    Mansfield Park" 79. For John Thorpe's exclusionary masculine talk, see "Clothing the
    Thought in the Word: The Talk in *Northanger Abbey*" 212.

2   In two adaptations I know of, Lady Catherine and Mrs. Elton are redeemed. The Lady
    Catherine of the 1940 movie version *of Pride and Prejudice* (Edna May Oliver), after her
    stormy interview, returns to report favourably on Elizabeth to Mr. Darcy (Laurence
    Olivier), who is actually waiting in her carriage. In this version Lady Catherine
    becomes a kind of fairy godmother who has simply put on an act to test Elizabeth. In
    a recent spin-off from *Emma*, Diana Birchall's *In Defense of Mrs. Elton*, Augusta Elton
    does see the error of her ways, awakes to self-knowledge, and becomes a tolerable
    associate for Emma. Both adaptations, I suggest, essentially change Austen's charac-
    ters. I have yet to find a spin-off called *In Defence of Mrs. Norris*.

LESLEY WILLIS SMITH

6

"Hands off my man!"
or "Don't you wish
you had one?"

Some Subtexts of Conversational Combat in Jane Austen

THE GREATEST VERBAL DUEL in Jane Austen's novels is the series of skir-
mishes, culminating in a pitched battle, between Elizabeth Bennet and Mr.
Darcy in the first half of *Pride and Prejudice*; the open clashes generate electricity between them and sustain the vitality of the relationship throughout
the more reflective second half. But there are other verbal duels, notably in
Sense and Sensibility and *Emma*, that conform to a convention of indirectness in
which the antagonists do not admit what is really going on, duels that may
be as important as Lucy Steele's message to Elinor Dashwood ("Hands off
my man!") or Mrs. Elton's to Emma Woodhouse ("Don't you wish you had
one?").

Lucy's encounters with Elinor in *Sense and Sensibility* give an energy and substance to the heroine's relationship with Edward Ferrars that it would otherwise lack. Elinor and Edward are seldom together, and they are not the most obviously appealing characters in the novel. Marianne and Willoughby, who are, have a long-drawn-out conversational war of their own, but they both lose. In any case, we seldom hear them talk to each other because direct speech is powerful—and Jane Austen doesn't want their romance to dominate the novel.

Only to Elinor does either Willoughby or Colonel Brandon use "the language of real feeling" (*MP* 427) about Marianne. But Jane Austen intends Elinor to be a heroine, not a gooseberry; so what of Elinor's own romantic relationship? Its interest owes little to Edward himself. In the crucial Norland chapters, when the relationship is formed, we don't hear him say a word. During his first visit to Barton Cottage, when Elinor finds herself "extorting from him occasional questions and remarks" (*SS* 89), it is only to Marianne that he makes an arch comment: "I have been guessing. Shall I tell you my guess? ... I guess that Mr. Willoughby hunts" (100).

Everybody in this novel talks to the wrong person—everybody, that is, except Elinor Dashwood and Lucy Steele. As her last name indicates, Lucy is a born fighter, and when she hears Edward joked about as Elinor's beau she takes the first opportunity to warn her rival off. Elinor, who generally has to be her own father, is now relieved from the necessity of saying such things as "I am afraid ... that the pleasantness of an employment does not always evince its propriety" (68) or "A better acquaintance with the world is what I look forward to as [Marianne's] greatest possible advantage" (56). Surprisingly enough, she proves to be a foe worthy of Lucy's steel.

Lucy has limited powers of manoeuvre; she dare not crush Elinor out of hand by publicly announcing her engagement. That doesn't bother her too much, though; she trusts to the technique of arousing curiosity:

> "You will think my question an odd one, I dare say, ... but, pray, are you personally acquainted with your sister-in-law's mother, Mrs. Ferrars?"
> Elinor *did* think the question a very odd one.

But she is resolutely incurious, and Lucy goes on:

I am sure you think me very strange, for inquiring about her in such a way ... but perhaps there may be reasons—I wish I might venture; but however I hope you will do me the justice of believing that I do not mean to be impertinent. (128)

How Lucy longs for Elinor to question her and invite the blow! But "Elinor made her a civil reply, and they walked on for a few minutes in silence."

Changing tack, Lucy falls back on her customary form of manipulation—flattery: "I cannot bear to have you think me impertinently curious. I am sure I would rather do any thing in the world than be thought so by a person whose good opinion is so well worth having as yours" (128). But the most Lucy can extract from Elinor is "I am a little surprised, I confess, at so serious an inquiry into [Mrs. Ferrars's] character." And this has to do:

> "Mrs. Ferrars is certainly nothing to me at present,—but the time *may* come—how soon it will come must depend upon herself—when we may be very intimately connected."
>
> [Lucy] looked down as she said this, amiably bashful, with only one side glance at her companion to observe its effect on her. (129)

She can't be very pleased to find Elinor so sure of Edward's affection that she assumes Lucy must be referring to Robert. But after she has struck the definitive blow—the disclosure of her engagement to Edward—they go at it hammer and tongs, for Lucy has to convince Elinor of the truthfulness of her account, while Elinor resists such a conviction as long as possible.

Lucy also wants to give pain; after fawning and flattering all her adult life, why should she stand in awe of a woman with only one thousand pounds? "I know he ... looks upon yourself and the other Miss Dashwoods, quite as his own sisters" (130) is rather a hoary old chestnut, but her follow-up, "You must have seen enough of him to be sensible he is very capable of making a woman sincerely attached to him" (130–31), is hitting very near the bone.

Poor Elinor, "greatly shocked," can for a while be only a refrain to Lucy's chorus: "Four years! ... Your uncle! ... Four years you have been engaged!" (130–31). But she "stood firm in incredulity" (129), and though the incredulity vanishes, the firmness doesn't. She hits back: "Your secret is safe with me; but pardon me if I express some surprise at so unnecessary a communication. You must at least have felt that my being acquainted with it could not add to its safety" (132). This puts Lucy on the spot. But she's quite prepared to resort to flagrant exaggeration: "I have known you and all your family by description a great while; and as soon as I saw you, I felt almost as if you was an old acquaintance," she says (132). And before Elinor has time to do more than feel surprise, her opponent charges on with a disingenuous demand for compassion:

> "I am sure I wonder my heart is not quite broke."
>
> Here she took out her handkerchief; but Elinor did not feel very compassionate. (133)

Lucy doesn't expect compassion, of course, but taking out her handkerchief is one of the privileges of the affianced bride. And she has another blow to strike—a request for advice as to whether to terminate the engagement: "What would you advise me to do in such a case, Miss Dashwood? What would you do yourself?" (133).

The battle honours are Lucy's in this exchange; she's had to work hard for them, but the "hands off" message has come across loud and clear. The trouble with doing your worst is that, once you've done it, your enemy has nothing to lose by fighting back, and Lucy has unavoidably armed Elinor for the next encounter. While "the continuance of [Edward's] preference seemed very uncertain" when he was at Barton Cottage (96), Elinor now understands why he sent conflicting signals—and the conclusion that "he certainly loved her" is not only "a softener of the heart" (140), but a strengthener of the backbone as well.

So now it is Elinor to the charge. Making a child's basket at Barton Park, their privacy assured by Marianne's music, "the two fair rivals were thus seated side by side at the same table, and with the utmost harmony engaged in forwarding the same work" (145)—and battle commences. "I should be undeserving of the confidence you have honoured me with, if I felt no desire for its continuance," begins Elinor (146)—she who later "blushed for the insincerity of Edward's future wife" (150)! But when Lucy replies, "I was somehow or other afraid I had offended you by what I told you that Monday," one feels that one need not worry too much about *her*; especially when to Elinor's next question—"Could you have a motive for the trust, that was not honourable and flattering to me?"—she responds, "And yet I do assure you ... there seemed to me to be a coldness and displeasure in your manner, that made me quite uncomfortable. I felt sure that you was angry with me. ... But I am very glad to find it was only my own fancy" (146).

Elinor continues the dialogue on the "I feel your pain" principle, with an eloquence that could have been borrowed from John Dashwood: "Your case is a very unfortunate one ... surrounded with difficulties ... entirely dependent on his mother ... all the tediousness of the many years of suspense" (146, 147, 148). She *does* feel Lucy's pain, because it should be hers, but as soon as she gets an opening she goes straight for her adversary's weak point. "Edward's affection and constancy nothing can deprive me of I know," says Lucy, to which Elinor replies:

> "That conviction must be every thing to you; and he is undoubtedly supported by the same trust in your's. If the strength of your recip-rocal attachment had failed, as between many people and under many circumstances it naturally would during a four years' engage-ment, your situation would have been pitiable indeed."
>
> Lucy here looked up; but Elinor was careful in guarding her coun-tenance from every expression that could give her words a suspicious tendency. (147)

Unprepared for such a counteroffensive, Lucy replies with a long, angry, and unsatisfactory diatribe, the kernel of which is "I can safely say that he has never gave me one moment's alarm on that account from the first" (147). But she hasn't a hope of convincing Elinor that Edward loves her, Lucy, and they both know it: "'All this,' thought Elinor, 'is very pretty, but it can impose upon neither of us'" (148).

After one of the short silences in which *Sense and Sensibility* abounds, Elinor returns to the fray. What do Edward and Lucy plan to do? This matters much more to Lucy than Edward's affection, so she imparts her real worry—that if Mrs. Ferrars knew the truth she might give everything to Robert, "and the idea of that, for Edward's sake, frightens away all my inclination for hasty measures." Elinor ripostes, "And for your own sake too, or you are carrying your disinterestedness beyond reason" (148). (What a good thing she's had plenty of practice in trying to bring Marianne down to earth.)

Elinor wins this round on points. She's told Lucy a) that she's in a mess; b) that Edward doesn't love her any more; and c) that there's no apparent solution to her problems. But Lucy, bloody but unbowed, still has the fact of the engagement on her side. At this point the conventions of elegant skirmishing, which, thanks largely to Elinor's self-command, have so far been observed, come close to being breached. During a pause in Marianne's music, Anne Steele takes her cue from Mrs. Jennings's comments about beaux to make her one and only witty remark: "I dare say Lucy's beau is quite as modest and pretty behaved as Miss Dashwood's" (149). Both are embarrassed, but Lucy loses her composure. She makes a pointless request for Elinor's help, which allows Elinor to say, "I should be always happy ... to shew any mark of my esteem and friendship for Mr. Ferrars" (149). Lucy then falls back once more on asking for advice as to whether or not to break off the engagement, this time observing that "if you could be supposed to be biassed in any respect by your own feelings, your opinion would not be worth having" (150).

This is letting hostility get too near the surface, and "Elinor thought it wisest to make no answer to this, ... lest the fur really fly"—actually, "lest they might provoke each other to an unsuitable increase of ease and unreserve" (150). Jane Austen adds that "the confidential discourse of the two ladies was ... at an end" (151), and it is. There are some jabs from Lucy in Berkeley Street: "I should have been quite disappointed if I had not found you here *still*. ... And now to be sure you will be in no *hurry* to be gone. I am amazingly glad you did not keep to *your word*" (217). (Translation: "If you're thinking of dangling after Edward now he's coming to town, forget it.") Moments later, "returning, after a cessation of hostile hints, to the charge" (218), she is squelched by Mrs. Jennings; and soon afterwards, in a scuffle on the stairs in Harley Street, Elinor easily holds her own: Lucy says, "Pity me, dear Miss Dashwood! ... There is nobody here but you, that can feel for me. ... In a moment I shall see the person that all my happiness depends on—

that is to be my mother!" (231–32). To Lucy's amazement, Elinor assures her that she does pity her (232).

One more encounter seems promising. Lucy, thrilled by Mrs. Ferrars's affability to her, beards Elinor in her den to score a "civil triumph" (240): "You saw it all; and was not you quite struck with it? ... You shan't talk me out of my satisfaction. ... Are you ill, Miss Dashwood?—you seem low— you don't speak—sure you an't well. ... Heaven knows what I should have done without your friendship" (239–40).

Elinor is much more subdued: "Elinor wished to talk of something else, ... Elinor was obliged to go on. ... Elinor had no answer to make ... Elinor tried to make a civil answer" (239–40). She does try to burst Lucy's bubble: "'Undoubtedly, if they had known your engagement,' said she, 'nothing could be more flattering than their treatment of you;—but as that was not the case'—" (239). "'I guessed you would say so'—replied Lucy quickly" (239), and off she goes again. Elinor's best thought, that it's surprising that Lucy should feel complimented by "attention which seemed only paid her because she was *not Elinor*" (238), has to go unspoken, and Lucy then has things pretty much her own way, especially when she gets to her *coup de grâce*—a description of Mrs. Ferrars's treatment of Elinor:

> I am sure I should have seen it in a moment, if Mrs. Ferrars had took a dislike to me. If she had only made me a formal curtsey, for instance, without saying a word, and never after had took any notice of me, and never looked at me in a pleasant way—you know what I mean,—if I had been treated in that forbidding sort of way, I should have gave it all up in despair. ... For where she *does* dislike, I know it is most violent. (240)

But Elinor is rescued by the arrival of Edward, and soon afterwards Lucy is punished by the unconscious Marianne, whose praise of Edward's punctiliousness in fulfilling every engagement, "however it may make against his interest or pleasure" (243–44), is "particularly ill-suited to the feelings of two thirds of her auditors" (244), leaving Elinor, the remaining third, in possession of the field.

Lucy is not always victorious, but her conflict with Elinor allows her a refreshing change from flattering a long line of hosts and adds excitement to her relationship with Edward, a distinctly henpecked version of the romantic hero: "My mother did not make my home in every respect comfortable," he says (362); "He was always particularly afraid of his sister's suspecting any thing," says Lucy (131). But a man who is fought over can never be uninteresting. In any case Lucy has a lifetime of governesshood to avoid—and *she* wouldn't rate those "wax-candles in the school-room" to which *Emma*'s Jane Fairfax may fairly lay claim (300).

But what of Mrs. Elton? She has secured her man, so why should she try to make the heroine's life difficult? From Jane Austen's point of view Mrs. Elton is very useful: her aggression makes Emma appear less aggressive by comparison, and she forces Emma to admit the idea of change, something Emma resists almost as much as her father does. But to understand Mrs. Elton's personal motivation we must consider one of the burning questions of the novel: why does Highbury never get its promised visit from the Sucklings of Maple Grove? Because the Sucklings couldn't wait to be shot of their sister—that's why. Perhaps Mrs. Elton "conceived Miss Hawkins to have held such a place in society as Mrs. Elton's consequence only could surpass" (*E* 281), but she needed the promotion, and I'm sure her family waved her off to Bath every winter with their fingers crossed. She had seen three friends married before she met a vulnerable gentleman (277), and now that she has gained "Mrs. Elton's consequence" she is determined to dominate her new social circle.

Mrs. Elton is not a natural fighter like Lucy Steele; she's a controller and only becomes hostile when her efforts meet resistance—except in the case of Mr. Knightley, of course, but then he's a man, so she pretends it hasn't happened. For the most part Mrs. Elton concentrates on her natural sphere of influence, the women of Highbury. Only to the local heiress does she concede parity—but no more, for she makes it clear that a father can't compete with a husband in the status stakes. "Consequence I do not want," Emma tells Harriet in Volume One (84). Mrs. Elton, though, would never agree with that, and Emma can't even argue, as she can't admit to understanding Mrs. Elton's message, in her first visit to Hartfield, that "you need a husband, and I can help you get one."

Mrs. Elton strikes some of her most painful blows quite unwittingly: "'Whenever you are transplanted, like me, Miss Woodhouse,' ... Emma made as slight a reply as she could" (273). Along comes the patron saint of the passing of time—"Here is April, and June, or say even July, is very near" (300)—and blows apart Emma's illusion of the eternal present (and a very good thing too). But far more irritating is Mrs. Elton's assumption that Emma must be just as keen to find a husband as she herself was before she secured her *caro sposo*: "I perfectly understand your situation ... Your father's state of health must be a great drawback. Why does not he try Bath?" (275).

The advantage of a conversation in which neither side admits what they're really talking about is supposed to be that one can focus on the surface level if the going gets sensitive. So Emma talks about the good to be done or not done to Mr. Woodhouse in Bath, but Mrs. Elton isn't interested in Mr. Woodhouse's health and brushes this convention aside:

As to its recommendations to you, I fancy I need not take much pains to dwell on them. The advantages of Bath to the young are pretty generally understood. It would be a charming introduction for you, who have lived so secluded a life.

And Mrs. Elton goes on to assail Emma on what the heroine considers her strongest point, her social pre-eminence:

I could immediately secure you some of the best society in the place. A line from me would bring you a little host of acquaintance; and my particular friend, Mrs. Partridge, the lady I have always resided with when in Bath, would be ... the very person for you to go into public with. (275)

Emma "restrained herself ... from any of the reproofs she could have given, and only thanked Mrs. Elton coolly" (276). Changing the subject doesn't help much, for Mrs. Elton soon gets from music to marriage, as she would from any subject to marriage, and after a few impertinences about Emma's friends, she takes leave with a remark about her "caro sposo," the trophy of her triumph (278). "The dignity of Miss Woodhouse, of Hartfield, was sunk indeed!" (276), Emma reflects, stressing both "Miss" and "Hartfield."

The message that Emma needs to change and that her world will change around her is so unwelcome that Emma takes out her frustration on her father, teasing him until he grows nervous (280). And Mrs. Elton was just trying to be friendly! But when Emma rejects a proposed alliance—"You and I need not be afraid" (283)—and proves, in having designed Mr. Elton for Harriet, to have underrated his value as a catch, a "state of warfare" supervenes (282). Paradoxically, Emma is now "left in peace" (284), for Mrs. Elton only relishes hand-to-hand combat when she thinks she has already won. No wonder she says, "I am a great advocate for timidity" (283)!

Coldness and distance are Mrs. Elton's weapons of choice against a powerful foe, and the woman who is "a little shocked" at the want of savoir faire in Highbury (290) gives a dinner for seven at the Vicarage rather than return Miss Woodhouse's hospitality (343)—a dinner at which Emma's absence is underlined: "*She* was not present" (343). Mrs. Elton's animosity has been sharpened by the fear that Emma will outdo her by marrying Frank Churchill, and on no account would she bring them together. On Box Hill she is thoroughly alarmed, for Emma and Frank are indisputably together, and if "Mrs. Elton swelled at the idea of Miss Woodhouse's presiding ... 'as the *Chaperon* of the party—*I* never was in any circle—exploring parties—young ladies—married women'" (369–70), she must feel much more irritated at having afterwards to write to Maple Grove that "Mr. Frank Churchill and Miss Woodhouse flirted together excessively" (368).

Mrs. Elton's pleasure at the news of Jane Fairfax's engagement to Frank is heightened by the thought that Emma has got her come-uppance. When Emma walks into the Bates's parlour she seizes the opportunity for a direct attack—as direct as such things ever get: "Emma could have wished Mrs. Elton elsewhere; but ... as Mrs. Elton met her with unusual graciousness, she hoped the rencontre would do them no harm" (453). Emma should have been forewarned:

When they had all talked a little while in harmony of the weather and Mrs. Weston, she found herself abruptly addressed with,

"Do not you think, Miss Woodhouse, our saucy little friend here is charmingly recovered?—Do not you think her cure does Perry the highest credit? ... Oh! if you had seen her, as I did, when she was at the worst!" (454)

But there's much more to it than saying, "You're shut out of this circle":

"I have scarce had the pleasure of seeing you, Miss Woodhouse," she shortly afterwards began, "since the party to Box-Hill. Very pleasant party. But yet I think there was something wanting. Things did not seem—that is, there seemed a little cloud upon the spirits of some. ... However, I think it answered so far as to tempt one to go again. What say you both to our collecting the same party, and exploring to Box-Hill again, while the fine weather lasts?—It must be the same party, you know, quite the same party, not *one* exception." (454–55)

If she hadn't married Mr. Knightley, it would have been a case of heaven help Emma. But this speech is aimed just as much at Jane Fairfax, for Mrs. Elton hopes to gain backup; surely Jane will be spoiling for revenge after the excursion to Box Hill! After Miss Bates comes in, Mrs. Elton feels still further emboldened to refer to what has obviously been irritating her ever since the jaunt in question: Mr. Weston's feeble conundrum, "What two letters of the alphabet are there, that express perfection? ... M. and A.—Emma" (371). Mr. Weston was clumsily courting Emma on his son's behalf; Mrs. Elton has other ideas:

"I say, Jane, what a perfect character you and I should make, if we could be shaken together. My liveliness and your solidity would produce perfection.—Not that I presume to insinuate, however, that some people may not think you perfection already." (456–57)

All this is wasted because Jane Fairfax and Miss Bates aren't paying much attention and Emma is too happy to care. But Mrs. Elton's hostile behaviour gives Emma a subtle dimension of vulnerability that does her no disservice with the reader, and Jane Austen always (except in the case of Elizabeth Bennet, that worthy daughter of a doughty mother) engages our sympathy for the one who doesn't fight or who doesn't initiate the combat. Yet in the end it is not "poor Emma," but "poor Mrs. Elton," for Emma Woodhouse carries off the most eligible bachelor of all—and she's not going to move to Yorkshire. The woman who exults in her status of bride now has three newer ones to contend with, and she has nothing to do but withdraw into the Vicarage and vent her feelings on her husband, the only audience she now dares address:

> Poor Knightley! poor fellow!—sad business for him.—She was extremely concerned ... How could he be so taken in?—Did not think him at all in love—not in the least.—Poor Knightley! ... How happy he had been to come and dine with them whenever they asked him! But that would be all over now. ... Oh! no; there would be a Mrs. Knightley to throw cold water on every thing. (469)

Mrs. Elton is much less fortunate than Lucy Steele, for not only does Lucy, in her own estimation, out-husband Elinor, but her relish of the fray finds expression in an endless cycle of containable conflict:

> Setting aside the jealousies and ill-will continually subsisting between Fanny and Lucy, in which their husbands of course took a part, as well as the frequent domestic disagreements between Robert and Lucy themselves, nothing could exceed the harmony in which they all lived together. (*SS* 377)

But poor Mrs. Elton has lost both substance and shadow, dominance of her social world and conquest of her enemy. "A little quickness of voice there is which rather hurts the ear," Mr. Woodhouse once says of her (*E* 279). However, by the end of *Emma* she's been metaphorically silenced. When we take leave of her in the final paragraph of the novel she's writing to Maple Grove: when *will* the Sucklings visit Highbury?

JAN FERGUS

7

The Power of Women's Language and Laughter

ALTHOUGH JANE AUSTEN'S MASTERY OF LANGUAGE is universally acknowledged, and although many books have been written about her use of language in dialogue and narration, only recently have critics described her novels as actually *about* language, particularly *Emma*.[1] My interest lies in adjacent territory: the extent to which her novels are about talk and power. I wish to investigate Austen's representations of talk at dinner tables, dinner parties, and so forth, that is, at social occasions where a number of different voices appear, where various sorts of hierarchies are taken for granted, and where the rules of polite behaviour are more or less observed, in order to address the question of what sorts of power her female characters are able to exercise through language and sometimes through laughter. I also wish to address the question of how we are supposed to regard the power of language and laughter when so exercised: for instance, when a character like Elizabeth Bennet in *Pride and Prejudice* can ironically call into question the judgement of someone like Darcy. In such cases, are we to see Elizabeth as a successful subverter of the social order or is she simply working within it, becoming one of the boys? In other words, is Austen more or less approving when her characters, in a Foucauldian manner, gain access to power by using the established systems of power (here, the power of and in language); or does she, rather like a Marxist or in particular a Marxist feminist, demonstrate that in occupying a class position that grants power, women simply become more patriarchal than the patriarchs (like Lady Catherine de Bourgh, for example)? This last approach assumes that without a complete revolution or a newly invented language, women who gain access to the power of language or class are not changing or subverting anything. What then is going on in such exchanges, and how does Austen view it?

Before I move to women's talk and laughter in the later novels, I propose to look in some detail at an early scene in *Pride and Prejudice*: Elizabeth's most complex encounter with Darcy at Netherfield. This scene occurs once Elizabeth advises Caroline Bingley to laugh at Darcy; Miss Bingley's reply, as Elizabeth summarizes it, is that "Mr. Darcy is not to be laughed at!" (*PP* 57). "Laughter at" is certainly a form of discipline that individuals can deploy against one another, and Michel Foucault has taught us to pay attention to these operations:

> In reality, power in its exercise goes much further [than the State apparatus], passes through much finer channels, and is much more ambiguous, since each individual has at his disposal a certain power, and for that very reason can also act as the vehicle for transmitting a wider power. (72)

"Laughter at" participates in the complexities of power that Foucault outlines here; notably, it is a recourse for the disempowered, a tactic whereby the laugher can gain what Thomas Hobbes in *Leviathan* called "*Sudden Glory*" (284), identifying "laughing at" as a strategy of domination.[2] But "laughing at" is not simply a matter of a superior laugher and an inferior butt. Hobbes and some other analysts of laughter seem to ignore the more complicated strategies of "laughter with" or indeed laughter at *oneself*—strategies that create communal feeling instead of establishing dominance.[3] Although in the exchange I will analyze Elizabeth Bennet deploys only the "laughter at" that aims at dominance, at other times she uses laughter to produce community—as do some female characters in the other novels, for Austen reserves these two modes of laughter primarily for women, with some exceptions among her male charmers, Henry Tilney, Henry Crawford, and Frank Churchill. Certainly, laughter of various kinds is so crucial to Elizabeth that she responds to the notion that Darcy cannot be laughed at by remarking, "That is an uncommon advantage, and uncommon I hope it will continue, for it would be a great loss to *me* to have many such acquaintance. I dearly love a laugh" (*PP* 57). If Darcy is not to be laughed at, he is exempt from the disciplinary power of Elizabeth Bennet's ridicule. Elizabeth then takes up this challenge, and she succeeds, in the exchange on laughter and ridicule that follows, not simply in laughing at Darcy in complex ways but also in challenging his language and, I would argue, in modifying it.

Although we may be inclined to consider that both Elizabeth and Darcy are witty in this passage, they actually exercise judgement as opposed to wit according to John Locke's influential deployment of these terms: judgement separates by making fine distinctions between similar elements, while wit yokes together elements that seem distinct.[4] Thus, both Elizabeth and Darcy use language to make distinctions between what can properly excite laughter and what cannot. Darcy acknowledges the disciplinary power of laughter, particularly against those who represent patriarchal systems: "The wisest and the best of men, nay, the wisest and best of their actions, may be rendered ridiculous by a person whose first object in life is a joke" (57). This somewhat abrasive response aligns Darcy with wise, good men and implies that Elizabeth belongs in the class of ridiculous people interested only in jokes. She responds by denying the implication and by distinguishing among objects of laughter: "I hope I am not one of *them*. I hope I never ridicule what is wise or good. Follies and nonsense, whims and inconsistencies *do* divert me, I own, and I laugh at them whenever I can.—But these, I suppose, are precisely what you are without" (57). Darcy does not reply as Elizabeth did, in the first person, saying, "I hope I am not capable of supposing any such thing." Instead, he rejects her ironic supposition that he is without follies and nonsense by elevating himself into generalization: "Perhaps that is not possible for any one." Generalization is the dominant discourse of eighteenth-century moralists, almost exclusively a male discourse. Darcy has brought out his biggest linguistic guns here, then, and he attempts to stand to them in his next sentence, which only admits the personal pronoun "my" into a balanced generalization about his own life: "But it has been the study of my life to avoid those weaknesses which often expose a strong understanding to ridicule" (57). Weakness is banished, strength embraced in this antithetical formulation.

Elizabeth shows in her response that she too can adopt the language of eighteenth-century moralists, if not their style, by ironically suggesting what those banished—actually "cherished"—weaknesses might be: "Such as vanity and pride." Darcy replies by distinguishing between the two, calling vanity "a weakness indeed. But pride—where there is a real superiority of mind, pride will be always under good regulation" (57). Again, the generalization elevates Darcy into the class of those with real superiority of mind, free of vanity and rejoicing in only well-regulated pride; as we know, at the end of the novel Darcy admits that he was "properly humbled" by Elizabeth (369). Here Elizabeth does not explicitly humble him: instead, she "turned away to hide a smile" (57). She dissembles her amusement, as the rules of politeness demand. But this moment of dissembling or disguise is present in her next and most ironic remark: "I am perfectly convinced ... that Mr. Darcy has no defect. He owns it himself without disguise" (57). The doubleness of irony has seldom been more perfectly exercised. While staying completely within the bounds of polite discourse, Elizabeth has managed to say—without saying it—that Darcy is full of defects and that he has been doing his unsuccessful best to hide them.

After this utterance, I will argue, Darcy's discourse must undergo a radical shift. But what Elizabeth's words are doing here requires more attention. Her irony has performed just the trick that a feminist theorist like Luce Irigaray, in Judith Butler's analysis, performs on Plato's philosophy: "repetition and displacement of the phallic economy" (Butler 45). Elizabeth's irony, in other words, like all female irony to some extent, repeats the terms of the dominant male discourse, but displaces them: it can be read "straight" as repetition (Mr. Darcy has no faults) and ironically as displacement (Mr. Darcy has many faults). Just as in Butler's account of Irigaray, Elizabeth's irony "refuses the notion of resemblance as copy" (Butler 45).

This refusal to "copy" the dominant discourse, this insistence on ironically displacing while duplicating it, means that Elizabeth disrupts what can be called Darcy's "regime of truth" in Foucault's terms:

Each society has its regime of truth, its "general politics" of truth: that is, the types of discourse which it accepts and makes function as true; the mechanisms and instances which enable one to distinguish true and false statements, the means by which each is sanctioned; the techniques and procedures accorded value in the acquisition of truth; the status of those who are charged with saying what counts as true. (131).

I would argue that Elizabeth's irony destabilizes Darcy's regime of truth, the "mechanisms ... which enable one to distinguish true and false statements, ... the techniques and procedures accorded value in the acquisition of truth." Darcy must alter his discourse to engage with Elizabeth's. He therefore abandons the generalizing, moralizing discourse that has failed him hitherto. In response to her supremely ironic announcement of his faultlessness, Darcy has to admit his faults; he must retreat from a language that pretends to be above the fray, that has pretensions to objectivity. He thus responds, "No ... I have made no such pretension [an admission that indirectly acknowledges that he has been guilty of other pretensions]. I have faults enough, but they are not, I hope, of understanding" (58). For the first time in the scene, Darcy utters the pronoun "I" (he has employed "me" and "my" once each until now). That is, he has descended to the particular and the personal. More, he has begun to echo Elizabeth's language, her direct use of "I hope I am not one of them."

"Begun" is accurate, however: the rest of his speech, unlike hers, is full of an inflated self: "I cannot forget the follies and vices of others so soon as I ought, nor their offences against myself" (58). Nonetheless, although Darcy reinstates in their final exchanges the generalizing language that he briefly abandons here, he does so with a difference. His language continues to approach Elizabeth's. She first redefines his admittedly "resentful" temper as "implacable resentment," noting that it "*is* a shade in a character. But you have chosen your fault well.—I really cannot *laugh* at it. You are safe from me" (58). She ironically concludes that Darcy is indeed exempt from disciplinary laughter: his faults are too grave for ridicule, though of course she is applying ridicule as she speaks. This pretended exemption leads Darcy to reply, "There is, I believe, in every disposition a tendency to some particular evil, a natural defect, which not even the best education can overcome" (58). The insertion of "I believe" into this general statement about "every disposition" is a noteworthy qualification, perhaps indicating Darcy's sense that the discourse he usually resorts to is ineffective against irony and laughter. In any case, he positions himself differently in the rest of the scene. His descent, too, from the general to a "particular" evil or defect allows Elizabeth to make a personal and dismissive remark: "And *your* defect is a propensity to hate every body" (58).

Darcy achieves his most complete echo of Elizabeth's language in the response that closes their exchange: "'And yours,' he replied with a smile, 'is wilfully to misunderstand them'" (58). Smiling signals the good humour of this riposte; Darcy's smile here is open, almost a communal gesture— unlike Elizabeth's hidden, superior smile earlier. Darcy's achievement of this moment of equality or community is underscored by his better judgement of Elizabeth's character than she has pronounced of his. She does wilfully misunderstand. That is, I would argue that in this scene Austen allows Elizabeth's power to laugh at Darcy—and at his pretensions to superiority—to influence not only his choice of words, but also how he positions himself in language as well as body language: Darcy finally attempts to establish community rather than distance and dominance, but he does not succeed. Elizabeth remains distant and dominant.

Elizabeth's irony is so successful at disrupting and deflecting the power built into Darcy's male, moralizing discourse, its regime of truth, that the only way he can engage her is by abandoning his own system and trying to enter hers. In this sense, in answer to my original question, Elizabeth's laughter and irony does successfully subvert the social order, though only temporarily. And although in this scene she maintains distance and dominance, these are supported by laughter and irony, not by a more privileged class position or by socially privileged language (even if her irony can press that language into service at need). But her stance is limited: she is blind to Darcy's attempts to adopt her discourse and blind to her wilful misunderstanding. She maintains this epistemological blindness until she receives

Darcy's letter—as if only in his absence can she pay attention to his words. (This fact has something to do, I believe, with the sexual tension between Elizabeth and Darcy, extant even when she dislikes him; his bodily presence tends to preoccupy her, as when she ignores her needlework at Netherfield and watches him write a letter while Miss Bingley observes and flatters him [47–49].)

Darcy is treated with parallel irony at the end of this exchange: the alteration in his discourse does not bring him closer to Elizabeth, but Darcy is altogether too powerful, too privileged, too sure of himself, and too vain to recognize her distance. He thinks she likes him. As he later admits, "What will you think of my vanity? I believed you to be wishing, expecting my addresses" (369). In short, the challenge from below has temporarily deflected and reformed the powerful man but has not dethroned him. Although the end of the novel effects a more stable reformation in Darcy's language and conduct, so that Darcy has learned "how insufficient were all my *pretensions* to please a woman worthy of being pleased" (369; emphasis added), he has not yet learned to laugh at himself. Learning to accept the discipline of laughter is a process; it occurs within marriage, when Darcy is "the object of open pleasantry" (388). Here, I believe, we can see Austen's attitude to the power of laughter to disrupt discourse and the regimes of truth that discourse registers: the subversive effects of laughter on a dominant discourse are powerful but temporary. Laughter must be reiterated, reinforced, repeated in order to reform, to make a difference, and it works best in intimacy. Furthermore, as we know, even its temporary effects are only rarely subversive. Lydia Bennet's "violence" in laughing is inane, silly, mindless—indicating only her high spirits and self-satisfaction.[5] Mr. Bennet's laughter and irony are corrosive rather than subversive, allowing him to deny intimacy and to embrace patriarchal irresponsibility. That is, Austen always critiques the devices she deploys so well in her novels. I believe, however, and have argued elsewhere (*Didactic Novel* 133–42), that her later novels find techniques to move toward rendering greater intimacy among characters (and creating greater intimacy with readers) in part to intensify the subversive, indeed reforming effects laughter and irony can produce.

I have spent so much time on this brief but extremely rich exchange between two characters in *Pride and Prejudice* (studiously ignoring, too, Miss

Bingley's necessary contributions to it) that I obviously cannot explore the way Austen renders the group exchanges of table talk in any of the novels except superficially. But I want to suggest that during her novel-writing career Austen becomes increasingly adept at rendering such scenes, in part because she is interested in the ways in which language permits power to be exerted, shared, undermined, and redistributed within the intimacies of small social groups. And I would argue that these operations of language and power are more obvious in exchanges that I will call "table talk" than in more dramatic exchanges, like the brilliant visits to Sotherton in *Mansfield Park* or to Box Hill in *Emma*. The visit to Sotherton in *Mansfield Park*, for example, has been much discussed, partly because it neatly adumbrates so much of the succeeding action: Maria's liaison with Henry Crawford, the angry exclusion of Rushworth and Julia, Edmund's captivation by Mary Crawford, Mrs. Norris's obliviousness, and Fanny's painful position as observer of all. Although language remains polite, the characters' speeches reveal their desires, jealousies, and irritations quite openly under the generally decorous surface—as when Maria expresses her "feeling of restraint and hardship" while waiting at the locked gate with Henry for Rushworth to fetch the key (*MP* 99). Speech expresses character, exposes clashing motives, and sometimes forwards or foreshadows the action.

These functions for dialogue—expression, exposure, forwarding, or foreshadowing—are usual in comic fiction like Austen's and evident in all Austen's dialogues, including the conversations between Elizabeth and Darcy and those I am calling table talk. But table talk as Austen renders it generally has something more, ironically enough because it is ostensibly something less. The "something more" is attention to talk *as* talk among a greater number of characters at once; that is, attention is diffused among many. Action is almost absent; after all, the characters are usually fixed to chairs and tables. They do not range. Their only recourse is talk or silence. And the talk is generally ordinary: therein lies its interest. When the table talk of a wit like Samuel Johnson or Samuel Taylor Coleridge is collected, readers expect brilliant conversation—what Elizabeth Bennet calls, in another exchange with Darcy, "something that will amaze the whole room, and be handed down to posterity with all the eclat of a proverb" (*PP* 91). This is not what Austen records in her social talk. The irony that can destabilize established discourses is generally absent as well. Austen is concerned instead with the usual table talk that occurs in her social world: highly conventional, polite, agreeable, light conversation adapted to people who do not know each other well—or who do not wish to know each other better.

This sort of talk occurs around the dinner table when the visit to Sotherton is agreed upon. To trace how that important decision comes about in language is striking, for it arises amid the table talk that deliberately avoids what Edmund Bertram calls "serious subjects" (*MP* 87). It is not even small talk, a term that appears only once in Austen's novels, here in *Mansfield Park*: Tom Bertram is full of "the gaieties of small talk," according to Mary Crawford, and Edmund is not (65). A late-nineteenth-century anonymous etiquette book called *Society Small Talk: Or What to Say and When to Say It* defines small talk by negatives: it is not "intimate," not "private," not "an important communication," and above all it has no "purpose" beyond the agreeability of the moment (2–3).[6] Small talk is meaningless, superficial, but—ideally—entertaining conversation. Table talk as Austen presents it is seldom entertaining to the participants, though observers (including distanced characters and readers) will find it amusing; in this sense, Austen's table talk is less than small talk. It includes what the narrator in *Emma,* adopting Emma's viewpoint, calls "the usual rate of conversation; a few clever things said, a few downright silly, but by much the larger proportion neither the one nor the other—nothing worse than every day remarks, dull repetitions, old news, and heavy jokes" (219).

Accordingly, in Tom Bertram's absence, Mary Crawford expects no entertainment except as an observer of others' foolishness in the scene at the dinner table where, eventually, the visit to Sotherton will be planned. Tom Bertram's "gaieties of small talk" will be missing:

In comparison with his brother, Edmund would have nothing to say. The soup would be sent round in a most spiritless manner, wine drank without any smiles, or agreeable trifling, and the venison cut up without supplying one pleasant anecdote of any former haunch, or a single entertaining story about "my friend such a one." (52)

The narrator here has slipped into Mary's point of view in order to register her self-conscious assessment of talk, ultimately sliding into Mary's parody of Tom's recent story about "my friend Sneyd" (51). This self-reflexive attention to talk, to narrative, to stories reappears throughout the scene that follows. When Mikhail Bakhtin discusses the way experience is mediated by language in so-called "real life, " he describes something very close to what Austen renders in the table talk at Mansfield:

> In real life people talk most of all about what others talk about—they transmit, recall, weigh and pass judgement on other people's words, opinions, assertions, information; people are upset by others' words, or agree with them, contest them, refer to them and so forth. ... At every step one meets a "quotation" or a "reference" to something that a particular person said, a reference to "people say" or "everyone says," to the words of the person one is talking with, or to one's own previous words, to a newspaper, an official decree, a document, a book and so forth. (*Dialogic Imagination* 338)

In the remarkable scene around the Mansfield dining table, we hear most of what Bakhtin outlines here. Talk mediates talk; as Bakhtin says, one's words sometimes even require the echo of one's "previous words"— and others' previous words too, as when Mrs. Norris cites the absent: "If dear Sir Thomas were here, he could tell you what improvements we made" at the parsonage, improvements limited only by "Mr. Norris's sad state of health ... and *that* disheartened me from doing several things that Sir Thomas and I used to talk of" (54).[7] Nine people are present: three young Bertrams, Lady Bertram, Mrs. Norris, Fanny, the two Crawfords, and Mr. and Mrs. Grant.[8] Ultimately everyone speaks, even Lady Bertram (to recommend a shrubbery); several topics of conversation succeed one another; many of them constitute talk about words (spoken and written); and ultimately the decision to visit Sotherton is reached, a decision achieved by the efforts of four women—Julia Bertram, Mrs. Grant, Maria Bertram, and Mrs. Norris.

The decision takes place in the space opened up in dialogue when Edmund ends the conversation between himself, Mary, and Fanny, changing the subject from Mary's dislike and criticism of her uncle—a subject that she has addressed twice but that is inappropriate to the occasion and audience, not proper table talk—to the appropriate topic of her harp-playing, also addressed earlier. Repetition of words and of topics has been important in the scene, starting with Mr. Rushworth's endlessly repeated wish for improvement at Sotherton. Alastair Duckworth has taught us to be sensitive to the complex political and social implications of estate improvement,[9] but my concern with it here is as a topic of conversation that allows Mr. Rushworth simply to repeat himself over and over—a notable feature of table talk. As Edmund and Mary's conversation closes, the other end of the table commands attention, and women direct the discourse. Two voices have not yet been heard, Henry Crawford's and Julia's, though we may confidently assume that they have been flirting all the while. Mrs. Grant calls for Henry's words by asking, "Have *you* nothing to say?" and by noting the words she has heard of his own improvements: "From what I hear of Everingham, it may vie with any place in England" (60–61). Henry, in turn, replies, "Nothing could be so gratifying to me to as to *hear your opinion of it*" (61; emphasis added), but regrets that no further improvement is possible at Everingham. Julia flatters Henry for his ability to "resolve quickly and act quickly" and proposes that "instead of envying Mr. Rushworth, you should assist him with your opinion" (61). Mrs. Grant enforces that suggestion, as does Maria, and when Rushworth invites Crawford to pay him a visit, Mrs. Norris, "as if reading in her two nieces' minds their little approbation of a plan which was to take Mr. Crawford away," amends the proposal, suggesting that she, Maria, and Julia drive with Henry to Sotherton, Edmund accompanying them on horseback (62). "As if" is a wonderful ploy of the narrator here: Mrs. Norris is generally oblivious to her nieces' thoughts and is stimulated instead, as always, by the prospect of a carriage to appropriate—here for a free ride to Sotherton.

Perhaps the most powerful of the four women who produce this important decision is Maria, who is engaged to Mr. Rushworth. He has been full of the wish to improve his estate and "could talk of nothing else" in both the drawing-room and the dining-parlour (52), and the narrator tells us that "Miss Bertram's attention and opinion was evidently his chief aim" (52). When he says, "I hope I shall have some good friend to help me" with

improvements (52), his hope is evidently aimed at obtaining Maria's "attention and opinion," but she "calmly" snubs him, saying, "Your best friend
upon such an occasion" would be the improver Humphrey Repton (53).[10]
Her slight play on the word "friend" distances herself from Rushworth—a
decorous move that allows her to direct him at the same time that she
disclaims interest. Maria enjoys, at this point in courtship, the only socially
approved power accorded young women: her fiancé is supposed to court
her, defer to her, in short, demonstrate to her that, when he obtains all the
legal and social power that marriage affords him, he will be generous rather
than tyrannical. But Maria prefers to exercise her temporary power indirectly, under the guise of polite indifference. Rushworth seizes upon her
recommendation of Repton, however, and appropriates it: "That is what I
was thinking of. As he has done so well by Smith, I think I had better have
him at once. His terms are five guineas a day" (53). Maria is much more
direct in her subsequent recommendation that Rushworth seek Henry
Crawford's advice on improvements; she thoroughly contradicts her earlier
advice and abandons her indifferent stance. We hear her speech indirectly:

> Miss Bertram caught at the idea likewise, and gave it her full support,
> declaring that in her opinion it was infinitely better to consult with
> friends and disinterested advisers, than immediately to throw the
> business into the hands of a professional man. (61)

To give contradictory pieces of advice that are both accepted in the course
of a dinner is perhaps unremarkable when the listener is as stupid and
pliable as Rushworth, but it still represents power—not unlike Darcy's
power successfully to advise Bingley first to abandon Jane Bennet and then
to court her. And Maria is adept at using language that will move Rushworth:
she finally offers her "opinion"; she adapts his expressed desire for a friend
to help him and offers a "friend" in Crawford; and she snobbishly alludes to
the "disinterestedness" of such an adviser as opposed to a professional,
responding to Rushworth's earlier allusion to Repton's high price. She also,
for herself, speaks in the plural: she clearly intends to join Crawford as a
friend and adviser. That is, she aligns herself in language with Crawford
rather than Rushworth, yet her skill in offering repetition of Rushworth's

terms with a difference renders this result invisible to him and to others. Elizabeth Bennet is only one of several female characters in the novels, then, who can use this device to her advantage, though of course Elizabeth's motives do not resemble Maria's.

Mrs. Norris's proposal forms the last spoken words in the scene. Edmund answers her proposal, which excludes not only Fanny but Mary, with silence. He "heard it all and said nothing" (62). Certainly one reason that women obtain power in this exchange—primarily through flattery or Maria's power in courtship and in language—is because men are at least temporarily silenced. Edmund, after all, later modifies the visiting plan so that Fanny may come. The most powerful silenced man at the Mansfield dinner table is, of course, not Edmund nor his absent brother, Tom, but the equally absent Sir Thomas. His absence allows women like Maria Bertram, Mrs. Norris, and especially Mary Crawford more power through language than they otherwise have. Sir Thomas remains insulated from laughter, particularly female laughter.

Austen sets up a later dinner party at the Grants that closely parallels this early one at Mansfield. Like the Mansfield dinner that produces the visit to Sotherton, the Grants' party results in a previously unplanned social occasion (the ball at Mansfield Park). But unlike it, Sir Thomas dominates the scene and ultimately the discourse at the Grants', and as a result, Mary Crawford cannot bring herself to throw ridicule on his cause when he insists that his son Edmund must be a resident clergyman at Thornton Lacey (248). Sir Thomas's control extends beyond vetoing Henry Crawford's renting Thornton Lacey from Edmund: he monitors Henry's courtship of Fanny and then her conversation on promotion with her brother William Price (249–50); and, after William's query to Sir Thomas about Fanny's dancing, Sir Thomas hints that all will have an "opportunity" to observe her dancing (250)—in short, as we later learn, he plans the ball because of his "suspicions" of Crawford's attachment to Fanny (280). His power and his powerful discourse help to make him blind to women here and throughout the novel: he misreads the language and the conduct of Mrs. Norris, Maria, Julia, Mary Crawford, and Fanny, in part because he is, like Darcy, so sure of himself, and in part because he is, unlike Darcy, so susceptible to the flattery of a woman like Mrs. Norris. He has never learned to laugh at himself or others; his discourse has evidently never been challenged by laughter or irony; *he* is therefore diminished, though his power in language is not.

Laughter of all kinds is much more evident in *Emma* than in *Mansfield Park,* and so are social occasions that give rise to talk. *Emma* is full of morning calls; of dinners or lunches at Hartfield, Randalls, the Coles', the vicarage, Donwell Abbey, Box Hill, the ball at the Crown; of chance meetings of groups in Highbury that produce events like the game of charades around the "large modern circular table" at Hartfield (*E* 347). This incomplete list suggests how many scenes of table talk and laughter *Emma* has, and how impossible it would be to analyze any of them fully here, in part because all talk so quickly becomes dramatic talk in this novel, forwarding and foreshadowing plot, but also because these scenes also incorporate talk *as* talk in complex ways. Consider, for example, the Hartfield dinner for Mrs. Elton that Emma reluctantly gives, the dinner that briefly courts disaster when John Knightley's presence threatens to expand the table to nine, whereas "Mr. Woodhouse considered eight persons at dinner together as the utmost that his nerves could bear" (292). This gathering occupies three chapters at the end of Volume Two, all those present talk (some quite extensively), and a close analysis of the table talk, parlor talk, and tea talk could easily exhaust three chapters of a book on the subject.

The most comical exchanges are those between Mr. Weston and Mrs. Elton, in which each seizes the conversational stage from the other at the slightest pretext, he to talk of his son Frank Churchill, she to parade Maple Grove and her marriage. Here the power of language to effect desire is most blatantly demonstrated: the desire, that is, to gratify vanity—one's supreme self—by talking of one's dearest concerns as if they interest others equally, despite ample proof that they do not. Strikingly, even this very broad comedy allows Austen to investigate some of the ways in which women's language may achieve dominance, may alter men's language through repetition with a difference. For what is surprising here is how far Mr. Weston's language and style echo Mrs. Elton's. Her self-assertion, her repetition, her self-congratulation call forth the same from him. Just as she brags of Maple Grove and the Sucklings, he brags about Enscombe and the Churchills, particularly his son, of course, but even Mrs. Churchill, for complaining about her caprices and faults becomes a form of boasting, an assertion of his superiority to the "great Mrs. Churchill" (387). Mrs. Elton instigates their competition in boasts when Mr. Weston's reference to Mrs. Churchill's delicacy prompts Augusta to cite her sister Selina Suckling's delicacy (306). But Mr. Weston is quite ready to take up the implied comparison and to speak of Mrs. Churchill as unable to "be second to any lady in the land" (306). By the end of their exchange, they sound remarkably similar:

> "I hope [says Mr. Weston] ... I have not been severe upon poor Mrs. Churchill. ... She was nobody when he married her, barely the daughter of a gentleman; but ever since her being turned into a Churchill she has out-Churchill'd them all in high and mighty claims: but in herself, I assure you, she is an upstart."
>
> "Only think! [replies Mrs. Elton] well, that must be infinitely provoking! I have quite a horror of upstarts. Maple Grove has given me a thorough disgust to people of that sort; for there is a family in that neighbourhood who are such an annoyance to my brother and sister from the airs they give themselves! ... and yet by their manners they evidently think themselves equal even to my brother, Mr. Suckling, who happens to be one of their nearest neighbours. It is infinitely too bad. Mr. Suckling, who has been eleven years a resident at Maple Grove, and whose father had it before him—I believe, at least—I am almost sure that old Mr. Suckling had completed the purchase before his death." (309–10)

Since most readers don't see Mr. Weston as resembling Mrs. Elton in general, I believe that Austen is showing us here a more crude and obvious and common instance of the power that women's language can exercise than we have observed in Elizabeth Bennet's or Maria Bertram's exchanges with their admirers. We have here the repetition with a difference that Elizabeth Bennet and Maria Bertram employ against male discourses, but we also have something we did not see in those earlier examples: a female discourse that succeeds in setting or altering the terms of the debate in the absence of sexual attraction. Admittedly, Mr. Weston is not wholly altered in his dialogue with Mrs. Elton, nor is his language, which never gushes as hers does. He does not fish for compliments nor laugh "affectedly" (305), favourite ploys of Mrs. Elton. Her laughter, of course, is neither disciplinary nor communal, but, like Lydia Bennet's, a form of self-assertion and display. Furthermore, Mr. Weston remains himself in that he has always bragged about Frank, after all, and he retains with Mrs. Elton his favourite speech habits, particularly his self-contradictions and his completely false claims that he would not say what he is saying to "every body" (307). But I would argue nonetheless that his language in this scene makes him seem nearly as pretentious, snobbish, and vulgarly self-absorbed as Mrs. Elton.

Not surprisingly, Emma and Mr. Knightley offer the most interesting examples in *Emma* of the manner in which male and female languages can exercise power upon each other. I will limit myself to examining the opening of one of another long, complex dinner-party scenes, the dinner at the Coles'. Our attention is directed to this opening by Emma herself, who refers back to her own words when she talks to Mrs. Weston after dinner about how Jane Fairfax arrived at the ball: Mrs. Weston has learned that Mr. Knightley's carriage brought Jane and suspects that "it was for their accommodation the carriage was used at all" (223). Emma agrees, saying, "I know he had horses to-day—for we arrived together; and I laughed at him about it" (223–24). In the opening exchange, then, we have an intelligent, witty woman laughing at an intelligent, patriarchal man, something, in short, rather like what Elizabeth and Darcy enact for us at Netherfield, and what Mary Crawford does not produce in relation to Sir Thomas at the Grants'. But the result of this reprise is quite different.

The exchange begins with Emma "speaking her approbation while warm from her heart": "This is coming as you should do, ... like a gentleman.—I am quite glad to see you" (213). Emma deploys a term of great significance in this novel, for redefining the English gentleman, English manhood, according to Mr. Knightley's model is central to it, as Claudia L. Johnson has recently established (201–02). But for the first and only time, Emma implies here that Mr. Knightley is *not* the model gentleman that he appears to be elsewhere: he evidently arrives at other social occasions *unlike* a gentleman, in Emma's terms, that is, without his equipage, without the accoutrements of his station. She does not generalize about gentlemanliness, however; she simply applies her definition to this occasion with complete confidence.

Furthermore, her frequent use of the second-person pronoun "you" announces their intimacy at the same time that it commands what he "should do." His response echoes hers in several ways. He does not resort to generalization; he resorts to irony at the expense of Emma's perceptions and her definition. "How lucky that we should arrive at the same moment! for, if we had met first in the drawing-room, I doubt whether you would have discerned me to be more of a gentleman than usual.—You might not have distinguished how I came, by my look or manner" (213). Furthermore, like Emma, he proclaims intimacy through the pronoun "you," but less assertively: "I doubt whether you" and "You might not have." By suggesting, however, that Emma might not perceive him to be "more of a gentleman than usual," Mr. Knightley repeats her charge while deflecting it. He comfortably places himself in the class of those who are gentlemanly; he reformulates Emma's destabilization of his position. Furthermore, he calls attention to the superficiality of her criteria by citing look and manner—outward and visible signs of gentlemanliness, like a carriage.

Emma ought to be squelched by Mr. Knightley's irony, but instead she carries his accusation of superficiality much further. She re-echoes his terms, modifying them also, as soon as she reiterates her confidence that she is right: "Yes I should, I am sure I should" (213)—meaning that she would be able to distinguish Mr. Knightley's mode of arrival, even if she had not seen it. Emma the imaginist indeed; she is busy in the activity that Mr. Knightley later fears for himself—"myself creating what I saw"—when he recalls the line from William Cowper's *The Task* (E 344). Taking up Mr. Knightley's word "look," Emma produces first a snobbish generalization, not about gentlemen but about manner and hierarchy: "There is always a look of consciousness or bustle when people come in a way which they know to be beneath them" (213). She takes up the criteria for gentlemanliness that he has attributed to her and justifies them by verbal images. Going further, she elaborates on Mr. Knightley's look and manner, generalizing about Knightley himself: "You think you carry it off very well, I dare say, but with you it is a sort of bravado, an air of affected unconcern; I always observe it whenever I meet you under those circumstances" (213–14). Emma laughs at look and manner even more directly in her final sentences, which poke fun at, literally, a "height" in his manner, while insisting on a difference that arraigns his former style and while defining him even more decidedly through the pronoun "you":

> *Now* you have nothing to try for. You are not afraid of being supposed ashamed. You are not striving to look taller than any body else. *Now* I shall really be very happy to walk into the same room with you. (214)

Mr. Knightley's reply abandons argument and resorts to epithet: "Nonsensical girl!" In a sense, of course, this answer simply proclaims their deep intimacy. Nonetheless, Emma's play with the terms that he himself has proposed, look and manner, appears to leave him with no recourse but to accuse her of talking nonsense—a favourite accusation of his—and to attack her power in language further by calling her a girl. He responds, we are told, "not at all in anger" (214), unlike his response to Emma's earlier assertion that Harriet Smith is too good for Robert Martin: "Nonsense, errant nonsense, as ever was talked!" (65). Here at the Coles', even though he takes refuge in the dismissive phrase, Mr. Knightley is willing to let Emma have the last laugh; at the end, when they are engaged, he refers casually to Emma's laughing at him: "You laugh at me about William Larkins" (473). Unlike Darcy, Mr. Knightley does not have to learn to be laughed at; Emma has long laughed at him, and in their casual encounters like this one, I believe it is possible to detect the intimacy that allows them a reciprocal exchange of the kind of irony, and the attendant modification of language, that we see operating only one way between Elizabeth and Darcy. In this sense, too, Mr. Knightley may be a new model of an English gentleman whose manliness is defined and modified by woman's language—Emma's and of course Jane Austen's.

NOTES

I want to thank my colleagues Patricia Ingham and Alexander Doty for inspiration and aid in thinking through the issues addressed in this essay, Ruth Perry for incisive critique and indispensable encouragement, and Ruth Portner for phone help at every stage. I am also grateful for helpful readings from Alastair Duckworth and Claudia L. Johnson.

1   See André Brink 5–6, 19, 104–35. I disagree with Brink's reading that language in *Emma* shows that "men decide and act; women submit" (124), as my subsequent discussion of the novel indicates.

2   Hobbes, *Leviathan* (1651), 1.6; cited here from *The Idea of Comedy*, ed. Wimsatt.

3   See, for example, Sigmund Freud on comedy: "Our laughter expresses a pleasurable sense of the superiority which we feel in relation to" the other (Lauter 406–07). Similarly, Susanne K. Langer summarizes Marcel Pagnol's theory as "Laughter always—without exception—betokens a sudden sense of superiority" (Lauter 511).

4   One of the more well-known statements of this idea, not original with Locke, occurs in his *Essay Concerning Human Understanding* II.11.2.

5   I am thinking of the narrator's description of Lydia after receiving Mrs. Forster's invitation to Brighton: "Lydia flew about the house in restless ecstasy, calling for every one's congratulations, and laughing and talking with more violence than ever" (230).

6   This book, in its eighth edition, has no date, but the British Library dates a seventh edition in 188-?. The anonymous author also wrote *The Manners and Tone of Good Society* and *Party Giving* and is there alleged to be a member of the aristocracy; the author's extended examples of small talk are stunning in their blandness and in the way a supreme blandness seems best attained by reverting to general and particular remarks about men and women. These imagined, supposedly exemplary and proper conversations suggest that without this topic, mixed groups of comparative strangers would have absolutely nothing to say once they had exhausted the weather. The book thus sheds fascinating light on Victorian notions of gender.

7   Unlike Rushworth, who in this scene alludes only to his words to his friend Smith, Mrs. Norris refers to Sir Thomas's testimony to her improvements as well as to alleged talks with him.

8   As we shall see, nine is one too many for Mr. Woodhouse (*E* 292).

9   See Alastair Duckworth, *The Improvement of the Estate: A Study of Jane Austen's Novels.*

10 She has heard him mention Repton many times in the drawing-room, no doubt.

8

GARY KELLY

Jane Austen's Imagined Communities

Talk, Narration, and Founding the Modern State

IN THIS ESSAY I argue that Jane Austen uses narration to master talk and in so doing helps found the modern state in the (idealized) image and interests of people like herself—broadly, the novel-reading (and -writing) public, and more particularly, gentrified professional middle-class Anglicans. For it was people like herself in the broad sense who, beginning in the decades after her death and continuing to our present, founded modern states in Britain, Europe, and beyond. In order to support this argument, I historicize Austen's novels in particular ways: in the context of the social, cultural, and political crises and changes they were designed to address, and in relation to the way other novels were addressing the same context. By historicizing Austen's novels in this way, we can more fully understand several things about them: why they became and remained classics throughout the period of the founding of modern states; why they remain popular and seem to have continued relevance now, when the modern (liberal) state seems triumphant everywhere; and yet why these novels can still disclose contradictions in a form of the state that remains persistently inadequate to the central human, social, and even ecological needs of our time.

In his ground-breaking book *Imagined Communities*, Benedict Anderson argues that the modern nation-state was and is made possible by what he calls "print capitalism"—forms of mass-market, commercialized print, of which the two most important and widely read kinds are newspapers and novels. Anderson argues that the modern nation-state, unlike earlier forms of community and national identity based predominantly on face-to-face interaction (talk), is made possible through reading. Individuals believe that others reading the same form of mass print as themselves have similar responses and thus a common nature and identity—an imagined community. Anderson fixes on the form of novel with the widest circulation during the founding of nation-states and Romantic nationalism in the early nineteenth century, the social novel, which not only affords the experience of imagined community through reading but also represents the nation through use of characters, settings, descriptions, and plots. What Anderson does not point out is that this representation is in a form of "national" speech that had been standardized as a written form only recently in England and that would accompany modern state-formation elsewhere in Europe and beyond.

Austen practised one version of the social novel of her time and pioneered a textual structure in which narration masters talk or representation of speech. In this structure, the narrator uses the form of written English we still know but which was only established as the standard about the time Austen was a child. The narrator's "voice" contains and frames a variety of individual and group dialects or written representations of speech, thereby mastering them by implying that the only "national" dialect is this standardized written form. The same linguistic structure calls the reader into a community of understanding, identity, and values with the narrator. Austen masters talk, and community based on talk, in the interests of a community that, in her time, owned the standard form of the language and that was constituted as a community by exchanging the very kind of thing Austen wrote. She did so by specialized use of "free indirect discourse" or reported inward speech and thought. This device was then fairly new, only recently fully developed by Austen's near- contemporary, Frances Burney; it was perfected for her time by Austen, employed by the majority of Victorian social novelists from Dickens to James, and significantly extended only by early-twentieth-century Modernist writers such as Katherine Mansfield, Virginia Woolf, and James Joyce. The device enables the reader to have the otherwise (i.e., in real life) unobtainable experience of another's talk to herself, within herself (in Austen, this is rarely himself). The resulting illusion of experiencing another's subjectivity powerfully reinforces the sense of imagined community obtained by reading in itself, as described by Anderson.

The imagined community evoked by the narrative structure of Austen's novels is that of the novel-reading (and -writing) public of her time. This community—or rather its adult male property owners—also became the "political nation" by the Reform Act of 1832. By no coincidence it was at this time that Austen began to achieve the status of "classic" writer, with the republication of her novels in 1833 in Bentley's Standard Novels (where "Standard" has the force of "classic"). Certain linked historical developments made it possible for Austen to use the novel to participate in this process of state-formation by cultural revolution. The modern state is based on the ideology and culture of the professional middle class to which Austen herself belonged and which increased rapidly in numbers, prosperity, and power in the eighteenth century. Historically, this class had a complex dependence on the culture of writing and print. Not only did most professionals, and especially the most prestigious "learned" professions, practise some form of remunerated reading, interpretation, and writing, they also depended on reading and writing for their sense of social distinctness.

Reading and writing in themselves helped construct this class's identity, for, as historians of literacy argue, reading transforms individual identity from being primarily social or communal to being primarily subjective.[1] Reading temporarily isolates the individual from the face-to-face community and enables a sense of communication with the physically absent but imaginatively and powerfully present selves to be found in texts, though never met personally or known socially. When reading is laid aside and sociability resumed, the individual remembers the encounters in reading and feels possessed of a self apart from that known in the immediate social world. There is a new or increased sense of identity that is inward and distinct from or even opposed to the social self. We can speculate, then, that the eighteenth-century increase in the number of readers and rise in the social and cultural status of reading were driven by and helped to drive another major cultural change—the emergence of new discourses and practices of subjectivity, or what Michel Foucault calls "technologies of the self" (*Technologies* 145–62). Professional middle-class ideology and culture emphasized not only these technologies but also disciplines of the self, including what were then termed "reason" and "virtue" and the acquisition of knowledges, over a prolonged formal education, that constituted both the utilitarian and the cultural capital needed in professional life.

Unlike the upper and lower classes, then, the ideology, culture, and collective identity of the professional middle class depended less for affirmation and reaffirmation on face-to-face socializing and sociability, with shared forms of speech and talk, than on a shared culture of reading, writing, and print. By the late eighteenth century this class had succeeded in forming and imposing a new dialect to serve this culture. Accompanying the rise of the professionals was the rise of standard written English, followed by a standard spoken English partly based on the written standard. By Austen's childhood, approved usage in written English had become more restricted and standardized in spelling, punctuation, and lexicon; spelling was reformed to reflect the historical etymology of the written form of words; there was greater emphasis on correctness; and a form of spoken English was developed based on spelling pronunciations and "freed" from local characteristics.[2] Standardized written English served the vocational practices of the professionals; emergence of a standardized spoken English, deferring to the written standard, created an ostensibly classless, supposedly national form of the language, but one that reduced all other spoken forms of the language to dialects or "second speech." In fact, this new form of written and spoken English was only another dialect—that of a self-appointed, self-consciously "national" class comprised of a relatively small number of professional middle-class people scattered across Britain.

These developments in the social politics of language were both enabled and reinforced by another cultural and social transformation. Many commentators of the time remarked on the "rise of the reading public," and the professional middle class were pre-eminently people of the book. Their vocations and status depended on possession of practical knowledge, intellectual skills, and cultural capital acquired largely from books. Their increase in numbers and prosperity enabled the rapid expansion of publishing, bookselling, authorship, and related professions as print culture's "gate-keepers"—editors, reviewers, journalists, scholars, popularizers, and educational writers. The proliferation of metropolitan publishers, linked to increasingly numerous provincial booksellers, the rapid increase in commercial lending libraries, and the greater circulation of books and magazines enabled the users of standardized written English to communicate with each other more often and, more importantly, to receive frequent confirmation that they were the "national" class—the only class with more of a trans-local than a local identity. Affirmation of social identity through a standardized form of language could not depend on the circulation of merely professional kinds of writing and print, however, and the rise of the reading public stimulated interest in certain kinds of print.

These were the so-called books of the day or books of current interest—predominantly genres referred to at the time as "belles-lettres," including poetry, drama, fiction, essays, and certain learned discourses, and later termed literature in the sense of written and printed verbal art or writing ostensibly as an end in itself rather than for professional or practical use. Thus the belles-lettres subsumed professional writing and raised the status of the entire domain of written discourses. The belles-lettres were also widely recommended as necessary recreation from the intellectual rigours of professional education and practice. The belles-lettres gave literary form to the knowledges that were the cultural and social capital of the professional class. Such cultural capital was shared with the well-to-do and the gentry for whom the professionals worked and helped distinguish them from the mercantile and industrial middle class and the lower classes. Consequently, the belles-lettres became an indispensable avocation or cultural complement to professional middle-class vocational practices of reading and writing. Not surprisingly, many of these readers also aspired to be writers—like Austen herself. They filled the pages of the new miscellany magazines, provided booksellers with work to be published by subscription (a favourite medium of the genteel amateur), and occasionally they went on to become professional writers of belles-lettres. The belles-lettres, reconstructed in the early nineteenth century as the national and educational institution of "British" literature, became a major cultural discourse of the professional middle class as they engaged in the complex process of modern state-formation.

Austen intervened in this process through one of the most widely read forms of the new print culture and the belles-lettres. Literary historians have shown how Austen's novels play off those of her predecessors and contemporaries.[3] They do so because she wants to reform the ideology and culture of the reading public in the interests of her own vision of state-formation. In this project she reconstructed a particular form of novel—the novel of manners or (as I have argued elsewhere[4]) of manners, sentiment, and emulation. As the novel of manners it represented for professional middle-class readers the manners of most interest to them—the social codes and conduct, from conversation to courtship, where upper and middle classes met. As the novel of sentiment it constructed characters' identity as authentic subjectivity different from or opposed to "merely" social identity based on ascribed status of rank, birth, or wealth. This model of subjectivity sustained Sensibility's ideology of economic individualism, individual rights, meritocracy, and the sovereign subject and informed the constitutional representative democracy of the modern state. Finally, as the novel of emulation it depicted the relationship between the professionalized middle class and the upper class as emulative or combining imitation and rivalry—plotting the social recognition and accommodation of the meritorious subject in a gentry-dominated social system that is renewed by the accommodation.

Such renewal is Austen's concern in the face of the national and imperial crisis that she lived through and wrote under, and she emphasizes and alters particular elements of this form of the novel accordingly. Central to the novelistic realization of her political vision is a particular development of omniscient narration through free indirect discourse or reported inward thought and speech. This technique was devised in the late eighteenth century partly in response to the "war of ideas" over the significance for Britain of the French Revolution.[5] Many earlier eighteenth-century novelists of manners chose first-person epistolary form; later, novelists of Sensibility often favoured first-person autobiographical form. During the

French Revolution debate, reformist novelists such as William Godwin, Thomas Holcroft, Mary Wollstonecraft, and Mary Hays used first-person narration to give greater immediacy and emotiveness, and thus rhetorical force, to the protagonist's personal story of injustice and oppression. Novelists supporting moderate reform or the established system avoided and often burlesqued these forms, as Austen did in her juvenilia. They also preferred a form of omniscient third-person narration in which an authoritative narrator represents fallible characters with sympathetic superiority—stylistically appropriate for proponents of a hierarchical yet benign social structure supposedly dominated by enlightened people like the novel's narrator and—implicitly—the author and the reader.

In the Revolutionary aftermath, many in Britain sought means of social reconciliation. Austen's form of omniscient third-person narration with free indirect discourse may be seen as a compromise between the more democratic implications of first-person narrative and the more implicitly hierarchical omniscient third-person narration. There were other such formal compromises, including first-person narrative set in a third-person narrative frame. In the following decades, however, while Britain was reconstructed as a modern liberal state, the form chosen by Austen became predominant. She adapts this form for her own purposes. She applies the technique to her protagonist—always a young female—rather than to a range of characters as most other novelists of manners, such as Frances Burney, did. Austen places this protagonist in the conventional social terrain of the novel of manners—the border between professional and middle classes in contemporary civil society; representatives of other classes appear only on the periphery of her novels' social world. Characters are accordingly those found in civil society and are presented through the narrator's description, other characters' remarks, dialogue, action, and—in a few cases—letters. Settings are the places of domestic and public resort of civil society, including social gatherings, public assemblies, dinners, and outings; professional, business, or political encounters are excluded. The incidents of Austen's novels are those largely commonplace ones of such civil society, and also excluded are sensational events of the kind found in some novels of manners and routinely in Gothic and historical romances of Austen's day. Most importantly, however, Austen ensures that direct character self-expression through the usual means of talk and letters is dominated by narration.

Talk as a major element in the practice of civil society among the upper and middle classes was also a major element in the novel of manners, supposedly showing how to converse in the social terrain of most interest to novel readers of the time. In the prolonged crisis of the Revolutionary and Napoleonic period, however, the practices of civil society, indeed civil society itself, seemed more threatened, more fragile, and therefore more valued. In the Revolutionary and Napoleonic aftermath, novelistic representations of the maintenance of civil society, largely through talk and despite differences in individual character, social class, regional, or national background, and religious and political ideology, promoted the belief or hope in the possibility of social harmony, if not unity. Such social differences were increasingly represented in literature, and especially fiction, through certain kinds of idiosyncratic speech, especially idiolect, sociolect, and dialect. Idiolect is the distinctive style and lexicon of the individual—in drama, characteristic speech—and sociolect is the distinctive speech of a social group or class; dialect was associated especially with regional Englishes, including Welsh, Irish, and Scots. Representations of socially differentiated speech had long been used in English literature for ideological purposes, going back to Chaucer. In Austen's day, however, there was rapid development of novelistic representation of such differences, as writers addressed the prolonged crisis of social stability and national unity.

From 1814 on, Scott's Waverley Novels established a highly influential model for this technique, not only in Britain, but throughout Europe and beyond. Central to this novel form is the relation between narration and forms of English speech that are distributed by character and class. Usually, the comic, lower-class, and "merely" local or provincial "folk" use dialect, and the "serious" and upper-class characters use speech in written standard. Just as Austen began publishing novels, Maria Edgeworth published a tour de force in novelistic representation of social and regional speech. "The Absentee" (1812), one of her *Tales of Fashionable Life*, is set in London and Ireland and combines the novel of manners with the emergent "national tale" or fiction of regional life. The novel contains numerous varieties of spoken

English, representing groups from London high society through urban middle classes to Irish peasants, all framed by omniscient third-person narration in standard written English. Edgeworth was the most respected novelist in Britain from publication of her *Castle Rackrent* (1800), an experiment in first-person dialect narration, until Walter Scott began publishing his Waverley Novels in 1814. Both Edgeworth and Scott set important characters (especially protagonists) apart by having them "speak" in standard written English, thereby indicating their transcendence of "merely" social kinds of identity, such as class or region, and their participation in a "national" identity. Narration is in standard written English, so that protagonists, socially important characters, and narrator share the same English, implying shared ideology, values, and identity in which the reader is invited to participate.

Austen reworks this structure to give formal embodiment to her own politics of state-formation. She reduces the range of represented speech to idiolect, the peculiar style of individuals; speech styles of region and class are not represented. She shows a dramatist's skill in creating characteristic speech, or idiom appropriate for each character, and does so for moral significance. From Lucy Steele through Mr. Collins and Mrs. Elton to Sir Walter Elliot, characters with a noticeable idiolect are usually comic, intellectually limited, ethically flawed, and socially insensitive. Moreover, the idiolect of the important and "serious" characters is closer to standard written English, and Austen rarely uses free indirect discourse to represent the subjectivity of anyone other than the protagonist; consequently, most other characters seem limited to their talk, to their social self-representation. In Austen's novels, then, there is significant linguistic convergence if not overlap between the talk of protagonists and important characters and the discourse of the narrator. There are also significant similarities in their styles in a specifically literary sense. Central characters' talk and epistolary style resemble the flexible, elegant prose recommended in conduct manuals for conversation and writing in the civil society shared by gentry and professional middle classes. The narrator, too, uses that style, but usually with more noticeably belletristic traits, such as syntactic balance, "literary" diction, hypotactic construction, frequency of periodic sentences, and epigrammatic turn.

Cultivated middle-class readers would recognized these traits as those of "good" prose from *The Spectator* through Samuel Johnson, a tradition seen as characteristically English and a model for gentrified professionals practising non-vocational writing, especially the belles-lettres. By the time Austen began writing novels in the 1790s this model was being publicly challenged by a religious and political counter-culture within the professional and commercial middle class, led by liberal Dissenters still excluded from the establishment of church and state to which Austen belonged. For example, Joseph Priestley, scientist, rhetorician, Dissenter, leader of the Midlands Enlightenment, and political reformer, advocated a plain style as more demotic and "democratic"; this style was practised during the political debates of the 1780s and 1790s by reform polemicists such as Richard Price, Tom Paine, and Mary Wollstonecraft. The Austen family seem to have sympathized with Tory and Anglican loyalism during that period, but in the Revolutionary and Napoleonic aftermath many writers sought ways of accommodating ideological, political, and cultural differences, including stylistic ones. It is highly suggestive, then, that while Jane Austen generally eschews the oppositional plain style in her narrator's discourse, she does have the narrator use plain style to good effect at times, and that these times seem more frequent as she, her novels, and Britain move farther from the confrontations, political and literary, of the 1790s.

In Austen's novels, as in social-historical novels of the time, differentiated Englishes comprise a linguistic universe that is disciplined, or framed and ordered, by third-person omniscient narration in standard written English. The variety of Englishes is more restricted than in other novels of a similar kind, however, and it is dominated by a belletristic style that was in turn restricted to gentrified professional culture, though it was also becoming more flexible during her writing and publishing career. This linguistic and stylistic restrictedness in Austen's novels reinforces that of the story material, with three important implications. First, the imagined community of the nation is or should be comprised of those who can master the language of Austen's novels, practise it, and feel at home with and in it. Secondly, and consequently, moral, social, cultural, and political models for the present and future of a Britain in crisis, external and internal, are to be found in the kind of civil society that was inhabited by and served the interests of people like the narrator/author and most of her readers and that was maintained by the kind of talk and by writing in the kind of style represented in Austen's novels. Finally, therefore, such models are presumably not to be found in the eccentric characters, extreme situations, exotic settings, and sensational incidents, expressed in exaggerated language and represented in idiosyncratic and individualistic style, that were practised by many of Austen's contemporaries, from Gothic romancers to English Jacobin political novelists.

These implications are reinforced by the particular way in which Austen uses third-person omniscient narration with free indirect discourse.[6] "Free indirect discourse" translates unhelpfully the French technical term *style indirect libre*. The German expression for the same device is more accurate: *erlebte rede*—"lived or experienced thought." By this technique the omniscient narrator represents a character's thoughts and feelings indirectly rather than as a quotation of inward speech. This use of free indirect discourse by Austen and other novelists of the period has two important and related effects. It implies that a certain form of language—standard written English—is the language of thought and feeling and thus the language of the sovereign subjectivity on which the modern liberal state was to be based. As I have argued, this form of the language was in fact class property; consequently, use of free indirect discourse implies that sovereign subjectivity is restricted to those who have access to that form of the language. It is not surprising, then, that omniscient narration with free indirect discourse remained the dominant though not the only form of fictional narration through the era of founding modern states. Austen uses the technique differently from most of her contemporaries, however, in two important and interdependent ways, and she does so to promote a specific kind of sovereign subjectivity as the basis for a particular version of the modern state. First, by restricting the use of free indirect discourse to represent the thoughts and feelings of the protagonist—rarely of another character—Austen places greater emphasis on the protagonist's subjectivity and gives it greater interest for the reader. Second, by intermittently introducing irony into the narrator's representation of the protagonist's thoughts and feeling, Austen complicates the reader's task, making it parallel the protagonist's task of reading her world and herself.

A characteristic passage occurs late in *Emma*; the heroine is both listening to Mr. Knightley's surprising marriage proposal and reflecting on its implications for Harriet Smith:

> While he spoke, Emma's mind was most busy, and, with all the wonderful velocity of thought, had been able—and yet without losing a word—to catch and comprehend the exact truth of the whole; to see that Harriet's hopes had been entirely groundless, a mistake, a delusion, as complete a delusion as any of her own—that Harriet was nothing; that she was every thing herself; that what she had been saying relative to Harriet had been all taken as the language of her own feelings; and that her agitation, her doubts, her reluctance, her discouragement, had been all received as discouragement from herself.—And not only was there time for these convictions, with all their glow of attendant happiness; there was time also to rejoice that Harriet's secret had not escaped her, and to resolve that it need not and should not.—It was all the service she could now render her poor friend; for as to any of that heroism of sentiment which might have prompted her to entreat him to transfer his affection from herself to Harriet, as infinitely the most worthy of the two—or even the more simple sublimity of resolving to refuse him at once and for ever, without vouchsafing any motive, because he could not marry them both, Emma had it not. She felt for Harriet, with pain and contrition; but no flight of generosity run mad, opposing all that could be probable or reasonable, entered her brain. She had led her friend astray, and it would be a reproach to her for ever; but her judgment was as strong as her feelings, and as strong as it had ever been before, in reprobating any such alliance for him, as most unequal and degrading. Her way was clear, though not quite smooth.—She spoke then, on being so entreated.—What did she say?—Just what she ought, of course. A lady always does.—She said enough to show there need not be despair—and to invite him to say more himself. (430–31)

As in most passages of free indirect discourse, much of this can be attributed safely to the character as her inward speech filtered through, rather than directly reported by, the narrator. In the filtering process, third-person pronouns replace first-person ones and the past tense replaces the present. For example, "She had led her friend astray, and it would be a reproach to her for ever …" supposedly replaces "I have led my friend astray, and it will be a reproach to me for ever …". Other statements seem more likely attributable to the narrator, as with the opening phrases and the closing sentences of the passage. Narrator's discourse often blends into protagonist's, however, and certain passages seem attributable to either narrator or character, or both, as in, "Her way was clear, though not quite smooth." These passages suggest three things to the reader: that the narrator strongly identifies with the protagonist, that the narrator approves the protagonist's thoughts and feelings, and that the reader should share in this identification and approval. Such passages may also, however, create ambiguity and thereby test the reader's judgement, as in the phrases on "heroism of sentiment" or the statement "Her way was clear, though not quite smooth." To understand these passages as representations of Emma's thought would assume her to be capable of self-reflexive irony, and the whole passage emphasizes Emma's self-exculpation for misleading a friend and protégée— something the reader should disapprove. If attributable to the narrator, the sentences on "heroism of sentiment" and on the "clear" but unsmooth way strike a note of irony.

As elsewhere in Austen, the irony may be easy to miss but warns the reader not to identify as closely with the protagonist's thoughts and feelings—and consequently to approve them—as free indirect discourse tends to encourage. Such encouragement is unrelenting in most of those women's novels of the period that use this kind of narrative technique. These novels range from the "trash of the circulating libraries" or commonplace formula fiction through novels whose heroines Austen found improbable, such as Mary Brunton's *Self-Control* (1811), to novels by widely read or controversial contemporaries whose work Austen knew, such as Ann Radcliffe and Madame de Staël. Austen's attitude is indicated in this passage in the clichéd exaggeration "a reproach to her for ever" and the passage on "heroism of sentiment," which warn the reader obliquely not to read *this* novel as if it were one of those. As she pointed out to her niece Fanny Knight on hearing that a Kentish squire objected to the heroines of her novels, Austen meant to represent something other than the "pictures of perfection" found in the novels of others (*L* 335). Yet she uses free indirect discourse in such a way as to make it easy for readers to miss the narrator's irony and consequently to misread the heroine or rather to misread the novel's world and the heroine as the heroine herself does.

In doing so, Austen embodies in novelistic form the central tenets of her own Anglican faith. In England this faith had long been the state religion, and Austen would believe that it must continue to be so. It was the faith of her favourite, Samuel Johnson, and of most writers in the tradition of prose belles-lettres that her own style emulates, from Addison to Johnson. This faith views humanity as radically flawed and needing not only true faith and a rational, educated mind in order to choose good over evil, but also divine grace—a decisive God-given moment of opportunity for the believer to exercise her faith and reason and choose the good, cost herself what it might, and so perhaps to achieve happiness here and salvation hereafter. Such a moment of grace is afforded Emma just before the passage cited above, when, tempted to protect her own feelings and perhaps mislead Knightley, she believes he is about to disclose that he loves Harriet Smith. Emma's self-abnegation in then encouraging Knightley to speak, whatever the pain to her, enables him to propose to her and so earns her the earthly happiness she was close to missing. Such happiness is not only a desirable end in itself but also, as Anglican religion teaches and as the novel has already amply illustrated in the wise and benevolent landlordism of Knightley, a chance for Emma to make the best of herself and those around her and not the worst and thereby, again, to save her soul.

Moreover, by using free indirect discourse to entice the reader to err with the heroine—at least in first reading—Austen reminds the reader of her or his human fallibility and implicates him or her in the novel's theological vision of humanity's destiny in history. That destiny may include founding a modern state, as a form of good works also enjoined by Anglican religion, though not itself sufficient to win salvation. According to an Anglican vision, however, such a state could not be the utopia of perfectibility envisaged by some of Austen's contemporaries. Austen's modern state would be one that, peopled by flawed mortals, still needs the established church. That may be one reason why reformist Anglican contemporaries, men implicated in the formation of the modern state, were among the first to recognize Austen's novels as classics.[7] Austen did aim to represent the language of people like herself as the language of both civil society and sovereign subjectivity; but she also aimed to make apprehension of that language a challenge for the reader—a challenge in discriminating reading, just as the characters in the novel, and especially the protagonist, are challenged in reading the language—speech, talk, letters—and actions of others. Austen constructs her narration and free indirect discourse so that protagonist and reader sometimes fail that challenge, usually in the same instance, and then learn that they have done so—as Emma, in the passage above, has just learned that she misread Knightley only a few moments before, thinking he was about to speak of his love for Harriet.

This kind of ironic narrative makes Austen's novels eminently re-readable because it makes them a different read the second (or more) time through—and one definition of the classic or "standard" text is that it is re-readable.[8] Recognition of that quality made Colburn and Bentley republish Austen's novels in their "Standard Novels" in the early 1830s, at the time of the Great Reform Bill that began the process of reforming Britain as a modern state. Thus Austen's narrative form is her way of claiming literary status for her novels, against the common opinion of her day and long after that most novels were sub-literary at best, if not actually harmful, vitiating the reader's intellectual discrimination and literary taste. In Austen's day it was widely assumed that reading played a large role in forming the individual subject, for better or worse. Austen's novels are meant to be an education in reading, and re-reading, better. In that way, they are designed to participate in founding the modern state in and on the consciousness or collective subjectivity of the reading public. Austen has a specific kind of reading public in view, however. This is an Anglican reading public, actual and prospective, and her novels are designed to help constitute that reading public, before any other or others, as the imagined community of the modern state.

1 See Walter J. Ong, *Orality and Literacy*, and François Furet and Jacques Ozouf, *Reading and Writing*.

2 See James Milroy, *Linguistic Variation and Change*.

3 See Kenneth Moler, *Jane Austen's Art of Allusion*, and Jocelyn Harris, *Jane Austen's Art of Memory*.

4 Gary Kelly, *English Fiction of the Romantic Period 1789–1830*.

5 See Marilyn Butler, *Jane Austen and the War of Ideas*.

6 For a full account, see Monika Fludernik, *The Fictions of Language and the Languages of Fiction*.

7 For example, two early champions of her novels were Walter Scott, who sympathized with Episcopalianism, the Scottish version of Anglicanism, and Richard Whateley, Anglican clergyman and later archbishop of Dublin.

8 See Gary Kelly, "Jane Austen's Real Business: The Novel, Literature, and Cultural Capital."

Subtexts
and Ironies

9

Mishearing, Misreading, and the Language of Listening

HALFWAY THROUGH *PERSUASION* Captain Harville is discussing Captain Benwick with Anne Elliot and says, in a voice confidentially lowered, "Miss Elliot, ... you have done a good deed in making that poor fellow talk so much" (107). We know that Anne and Benwick have had two conversations about books and reading, but if we search for any quotable direct-speech dialogue from Captain Benwick, we will find nothing at all. Jane Austen chooses to give us only a wryly humorous summary of his talks with Anne, allowing him to remain a "mute" character as far as direct speech is concerned. And this in spite of the fact that he is an important figure for the resolution of the plot (by becoming engaged to Louisa Musgrove) and an important focus of thematic contrasts (in his relationships with the dead Fanny Harville and the live Louisa Musgrove, so eagerly discussed by Captain Harville and Anne Elliot near the end of the novel). So it comes about that the poor fellow who talks so much, and is the subject of so much talk, is never directly heard by us, the readers, to utter a single syllable. In fact, he never reappears in person after the two chapters set at Lyme.

Austen's strategic offering or withholding of direct-speech dialogue deserves a whole book. (If one already exists, I must plead ignorance of it.) The point of interest is not how much her characters can be imagined talking, but how much she allows us to *hear* them talk and to what effect; and why we sometimes hear them so seldom, or almost entirely in summary or in that peculiar *oratio obliqua* that, despite its quotation marks, is not direct dialogue. Confining ourselves to direct speech, we may find on a rough count that one-third of all Anne Elliot's dialogue occurs in one chapter of conversation with Mrs. Smith (vol. 2, ch. 9) and that in this chapter the voluble and informative Mrs. Smith says more than Captain Wentworth does in the entire novel.

In considering "The Talk in Jane Austen," I want to offer a slight variation by commenting on the significant *lack* of "talk"—of quoted direct-speech dialogue—in a few areas of her work. I will focus mainly on the hero and heroine of *Persuasion*, and then more briefly on Fanny Price and Emma Woodhouse. This essay might well be subtitled "Underspeaking and Overhearing," for reasons that will soon appear. In Austen's work, as we know, characters often misunderstand their own feelings or those of others, and such misunderstanding is often resolved by the proper modes of listening rather than by speaking. The author's distribution of talk and relative silence strongly affects our impressions of the relationships and discoveries she presents.

~~

IN VOLUME I, chapter 8 of *Persuasion* we hear from the narrator that Anne and Wentworth "had no conversation together, no intercourse but what the commonest civility required." This is immediately followed by one of those fine touches of irony: "Once so much to each other! Now nothing!" (*P* 63). (I will not follow up the interesting question of how much we assign this mental exclamation to the consciousness of Anne or Wentworth or the narrator.) What is clear is that for most of the novel we hardly ever hear Anne and Wentworth speak to each other and that we are made acutely aware of the tension caused by their broken engagement years earlier.

Before their final understanding we hear only one conversation between them of any substance—their two-and-a-half-page encounter in the octagon room before the concert (181–84). Before that, their entire direct-speech dialogue with each other would, if brought together, occupy about one page of print; since they share in a variety of social occasions at Uppercross and Lyme, this limitation is tonally very significant.

What do their audible exchanges amount to? Anne says the Musgrove sisters are upstairs with Mary (79); in the crisis at the Cobb, she recommends a surgeon and makes a few other practical suggestions (110, 111, 113–14); months later, in Bath, she expresses her preference for walking in the rain, says she is waiting for Mr. Elliot and, not needing Wentworth's assistance, wishes him good morning (176–77). This is literally all from Anne. And besides his few lines in the same exchanges, Wentworth's total direct-speech offerings are the following words: "I beg your pardon, madam, this is your seat" (72). This is virtually the sum total of what we hear them say to each other in the first nineteen of the novel's twenty-four chapters. To emphasize the extreme impression of reticence the author creates, I may mention in comparison that the quiet little Fanny Price of *Mansfield Park* is barely out of her girlhood when she has said more to Edmund Bertram than Anne does to Wentworth in the whole of *Persuasion*, and this although Fanny is the other of Jane Austen's quiet observers and great listeners.

I call the lack of explicit exchange between Anne and Wentworth "underspeaking," but it is certainly not understatement: a high emotional electricity invests their few exchanges, which stand out in strong relief. So too do the instances of Wentworth's concern and attention expressed in physical terms without any verbal exchange: his relieving Anne of the troublesome child (80) and his handing her into the Crofts' gig (91). Silent agitation is her response to these gestures: a quiet preparation, of course, for her later growing conviction that he still cares for her after all.

~

FANNY PRICE of *Mansfield Park* is another largely silent observer-heroine— relatively silent, that is, in comparison to the volubility around her. In the sequence of rehearsals for the home theatricals, the production of *Lovers' Vows*, Fanny refuses to "speak" in that she refuses to play a role (up to the very last minute, that is). Her refusal does not prevent her from helping the others learn their parts: she helps them rehearse despite her doubts about the rightness of what they are doing. And in helping them, she shows herself very willing to "hear" as they try to memorize their lines—until, ironically, she knows many of their parts better than they do themselves. This situation (quite apart from other issues raised by the theatricals) offers itself as a metaphor suggesting the strong need for good listeners and sparing speakers among those who speak much and hardly listen at all. Most of the cast of *Lovers' Vows* are eager speakers and poor listeners, even Edmund in his preoccupation with Mary Crawford and his comparative deafness to Fanny's feelings.

Earlier in *Mansfield Park*, during the visit to Sotherton, character and circumstance have combined to cast Fanny in a slightly different role: not so much a willing hearer as a reluctant and distressed *over*hearer of other people's conversations that do not really include her—notably those of Mary Crawford with Edmund and Henry Crawford with Maria. In *Persuasion* Anne Elliot, too, is on some occasions a patient hearer (especially of her sister Mary's complaints) and on one notable occasion a distressed *over*hearer in the specific sense of hearing when not known to be doing so, yet accidentally overhearing rather than deliberately eavesdropping. She over-hears, through the hedgerow, Wentworth's conversation with Louisa Musgrove, a highly significant conversation about those who are too "easily persuaded," who "have not resolution enough to resist idle interference," who are of "too yielding and indecisive a character"; Wentworth pays tribute to Louisa's "character of decision and firmness" (*P* 87–88). He also hears from Louisa that Anne had refused Charles Musgrove before he married her sister, a refusal attributed by the Musgrove family to Lady Russell's powers of persuasion (88–89). The experience of overhearing is very painful for Anne, because in hearing Wentworth's strictures on lack of firmness she applies them negatively to herself, thinking how he must despise her for having yielded to her godmother's persuasion, whether in the (true) first instance or the (untrue) second one. Meanwhile, she is unaware of other feelings Wentworth may be having (about her refusal of Charles, for instance). As so often in Austen, the moment we are invited to share the heroine's consciousness of "seeing" or "understanding" something is the very moment of our ironic grasp that her awareness, though partly correct, is incomplete. This irony occurs here when we read "She saw how her own character was considered by Captain Wentworth" (89) and also shortly afterwards, when he has handed her into the Crofts' gig and she thinks, "She understood him. He could not forgive her,—but he could not be unfeeling" (91). Only at the end does she hear from Wentworth that it was an encouragement to him to know "that you had refused one man at least, of better pretensions than myself: and I could not help often saying, Was this for me?" (244).

This episode is beautifully—and I believe designedly—balanced with the other overhearing scene in *Persuasion*, which takes place at the White Hart in Bath. This time it is Wentworth who is overhearing, while Anne has an animated discussion with Captain Harville. It begins mildly enough with Harville's account of Benwick's portrait drawn by an artist in South Africa, but soon develops into an exchange of opinions about Benwick's feelings for the dead Fanny and the living Louisa, expanding into general comment on the respective constancy of women and of men. It rises to Anne's moving and justly famous climax, "All the privilege I claim for my own sex (it is not a very enviable one, you need not covet it) is that of loving longest, when existence or when hope is gone" (235). This time the overhearer, Wentworth, applies *positively* what he overhears, interprets it correctly, and under cover of writing other letters, writes his new proposal to Anne, including the confession, "Unjust I may have been, weak and resentful I have been, but never inconstant" (237). We have in fact already heard Wentworth's own sentiments on Benwick's affections: "A man does not recover from such a devotion of the heart to such a woman!—He ought not—he does not" (183), and so his response to the Anne-Harville conversation carries its own emotional logic. The postscript to his proposal ends with "A word, a look will be enough" (238). We know from Austen's fiction, with its many comic or poignant misunderstandings, that they are *not* always enough. But in the right circumstances they will be: the design of the novel is to create and present those right circumstances.

Fanny in *Mansfield Park* is in general an attentive listener and a sparing talker; in *Persuasion* Anne and Wentworth are, in rather more specialized ways, "underspeakers" and "overhearers," as we have seen.

IN CONTRAST to this "underspeaking and overhearing" is what we may call "*over*speaking and *under*hearing" in many minor characters, but also notably in the heroine herself for a substantial part of *Emma*. An eager talker, planner, interpreter, and organizer, Emma repeatedly fails to listen properly and therefore misapplies and "misreads" the very words she hears. She blinds (or should we say deafens) herself to the truth of Harriet's feelings about Robert Martin, Mr. Elton's feelings about Harriet and herself, Frank Churchill's feelings about herself, other people's feelings about Jane Fairfax, Harriet's feelings about Frank Churchill—and, finally and most significantly, her own feelings about Mr. Knightley and his feelings about her. Eagerness to organize and deafness to the responses of others are not, of course, limited to Emma. By now I think it is commonly agreed that the unspeakable Mrs. Elton, patronizing and planning for her dear Jane, is a ghastly yet valuable parody of Emma, absorbing much of the reader's potential dislike of Emma and her patronizing and planning for her dear Harriet. Mrs. Elton may be unspeakable but she is seldom unspeaking—and her speech, though less voluble than Miss Bates's, shows far less warmth and observation of the world about her. Miss Bates is herself an important foil to Emma, whose famous rudeness to her at Box Hill is implicitly and ironically self-reflexive: it is Emma, not Miss Bates, who talks too impulsively and unthinkingly without true attentive listening to others.

What Emma especially needs to learn is to listen, and she does. This is aptly and movingly shown in her climactic encounter with Mr. Knightley. She has by now discovered her own love for him but is afraid that he loves Harriet, so she stops him speaking when he is about to unburden himself. In doing so, she nearly misses his proposal altogether. But her generosity of heart (which has always been a feature of Emma, in spite of her faults) impels her to decide that no matter how painful it may be, she *must* in friendship hear him out about his love for Harriet: "Emma could not bear to give him pain. He was wishing to confide in her—perhaps to consult her;—cost her what it would, she would listen" (*E* 429). So she reopens the conversation—to find him declaring his love for herself. Perhaps nowhere else in Jane Austen's work does she make so beautifully clear (and so clearly beautiful) the importance of readiness to listen rather than readiness to talk or even to hasten to interpretation. The novel's comedy of misunderstanding is resolved in a moment of profound recognition. It is as if, through this image of the finally listening Emma, the author is telling us something about how to read her work.

This remarkable chapter warrants a few more comments, specifically on Jane Austen's methods of conveying dialogue. Its first paragraph includes Emma's going to walk in the shrubbery, Mr. Knightley's unexpectedly joining her there, just arrived from London, *and* a quietly staccato series of sentences conveying the initial exchanges in indirect speech: "The 'How d'ye do's' were quiet and constrained on each side. She asked after their mutual friends; they were all well.—When had he left them?—Only that morning. He must have had a wet ride.—Yes.—He meant to walk with her, she found" (424). And so on. The sense of constraint is palpable, thanks to the *oratio obliqua*. The next paragraph takes us inside Emma's thoughts and fears—fears of a conversation about his love for Harriet. She feels unequal to giving him the opening, yet after a silence she begins the next phase, which the author gives us in direct-speech dialogue. It runs through the engagement of Frank Churchill and Jane Fairfax, which leads to Mr. Knightley's anger at Frank's misleading behaviour. Then comes another, more painful, pause. He offers to tell her why he envies Frank, but she (for the reasons we already know) moves closure on the subject. After an awkward silence, Emma bravely reopens the conversation, expecting to hear the worst, and her readiness to listen is rewarded beyond all expectation.

The direct-speech dialogue culminates in Mr. Knightley's fine speech beginning "I cannot make speeches, Emma" (430)—and then stops. The chapter has about three more pages to run, but notice that once. the climactic revelation has been made, direct dialogue gives way to the narrator's privileged account of the feelings of each, while we maintain a courteous and tactful distance, as it were, from the final privacies of the conversation. Instead, we are treated to delightful indirection: "What did she say?—Just what she ought, of course. A lady always does. ... Seldom, very seldom, does complete truth belong to any human disclosure" (431). The chapter which began with Emma's melancholy ends with the deftly ironic resolution of Mr. Knightley's long-standing jealousy of Frank into the generous tolerance born of complete happiness:

He had found her agitated and low.—Frank Churchill was a villain.—He heard her declare that she had never loved him. Frank Churchill's character was not desperate.—She was his own Emma, by hand and by word, when they returned into the house; and if he could have thought of Frank Churchill then, he might have deemed him a very good sort of fellow. (433)

~

A FICTIONAL CHARACTER'S "misreading" of others can be seen as analogous to our own potential misreadings. "Reading" is itself a species of "listening," and the two easily become metaphors of each other. We hear or mishear according to our capacity for listening, and we may easily misread because we are overeager to interpret and don't listen patiently enough before speaking. In the literal sense we may notice that Fanny Price and Anne Elliot are both avid readers who can discuss their reading with intelligence and spirit. Emma, on the other hand, with all her honourable intentions and book-lists, is not much of a reader. These details are suggestive, yet Austen's touch is light and unmoralistic. We think with pleasurable amusement of Anne Elliot counselling the forlorn Captain Benwick on the proper diet of reading (more prose, less verse) in the wake of his bereavement (P 101) or of Anne discoursing to Captain Harville on the paucity of books by women compared with those by men (234)—perhaps an indirect hint, after all, that women have long been far more accustomed to listening to men than men have been to listening to women.

My main concern has been to draw attention to the notion, implied in Jane Austen's work in a number of ways, that dialogue—if we are to take the prefix *dia* seriously—is not merely talk, but communication involving the silence of listening. Without this, so-called dialogue becomes merely a series of alternating monologues (as Austen herself so often entertainingly shows). It is characteristically only after a proper process of listening that her plots find their resolutions, her characters their destinies, and her readers their satisfaction.

10

Belonging to the Conversation in 'Persuasion'

TOWARDS THE END of Jane Austen's *Persuasion*, Anne Elliot is visiting Mrs. Musgrove and other friends from Uppercross and Lyme at the White Hart Inn in Bath. She is hoping that somehow she and Captain Wentworth will find a way to declare their renewed love for each other. And yet, as Wentworth is absorbed in writing at the other end of the room, and as Captain Harville, the only other person present, "seemed thoughtful and not disposed to talk" (P 230), she has no alternative but to listen to Mrs. Musgrove telling Mrs. Croft about Louisa's recently announced engagement to Captain Benwick.

The engagement is certainly relevant to Anne, since it has set Wentworth free and thus given her hope of happiness, yet, as she recognizes, its full details "could be properly interesting only to the principals" (230). "Anne," says the narrator, "felt that she did not belong to the conversation" (230). In one sense, of course, this is a simple statement of fact: Mrs.

Musgrove, despite her "powerful whisper," is involved in a moment of private chat with Mrs. Croft. But in a larger sense the comment is both significant and inapposite, since Anne's level of participation in the conversational activities that dominate the novel's narrative has already been transformed from a position of marginality and neglect to one of respected centrality. In fact this very conversation will soon move towards a subject—the desirability or otherwise of long engagements—in which Anne has a very lively interest. More importantly, as soon as Captain Harville *is* disposed to talk he and Anne will have the conversation about the relative constancy of women and men in which she takes control, not only of the conversation, but also of her own future.

Samuel Johnson, in his *Dictionary of the English Language* of 1755, defined conversation as "familiar discourse; chat; easy talk: opposed to a formal conference." One of the definitions of the current *Oxford English Dictionary* is very similar: "interchange of thoughts and words; familiar discourse or talk." Both emphasize the ease and informality inherent in conversation. The word "interchange"—with its implication of at least some degree of equality between participants—is important: conversation requires a reasonable balance between contributions and a relationship between participants that is both active and receptive. It is this aspect of conversation that is emphasized in one of the most recent accounts of conversational activity. In a rather more racy tone than either Samuel Johnson or *The Oxford English Dictionary* offers, Theodore Zeldin defines conversation as "an adventure in which we agree to cook the world together and make it taste less bitter" (3).

Implicit in all these definitions are some of the most striking features of conversation: its spontaneity and its fragmentariness—it is not rehearsed discourse, it has no defined beginning or end, it can occur naturally and accidentally, and it is always subject to change of tone, topic, or direction, to interruption or curtailment. *The Oxford English Dictionary*, however, makes explicit additional meanings that Johnson did not mention, but which were certainly current in his time: "The action of consorting or having dealings with others," even "Manner of conducting oneself in the world or in society; behaviour, mode or course of life." These definitions introduce quite other qualities of conversation. If conversation is central to the "action of consorting ... with others," if it genuinely represents "behaviour" and "mode or course of life," then it has a very important public and cultural role. This public role is one source of the conventions and formalities of conversational exchange that exist both alongside and in contradiction to the ease and informality already noted. After all, familiarity involves risk, particularly in societies depending on relatively rigid rules of conduct and behaviour for their smooth operation. In a society in which courtship was carried on largely through meetings at formal and public gatherings, a private conversation could carry heavy resonance. The eighteenth-century legal term for adultery was "criminal conversation," and any too private conversation could soon become prey to constructions or misconstructions of sexual transgression.[1] The same spectrum of meanings was attached to the word "intercourse," which nowadays refers more exclusively to sexual encounters.

Conversation is not without convention, even now. In Ian McEwan's recent novel *Enduring Love*, the protagonist is first alerted to suspicion of Jed Parry by Jed's rather bizarre failure to observe the proprieties of conversation: "I was old enough to dislike his presumption of first names, or, for that matter, of claiming to know Clarissa's state of mind. I didn't even know Parry's name at this point. Even with a dead man sitting between us, the rules of social engagement prevailed" (24). In less fraught circumstances than this, participants in a conversation expect to temper their discourse by considerations of each other's interests or attention span, the nature of their relationship to each other, and other factors.

But in Austen's time the rules and regulations involved in conversational activity were far more stringent and constricting than they are now, and maintaining a balance between observing niceties and achieving genuine interchange of ideas, opinions, and emotions was correspondingly more difficult. That Austen was acutely aware of the straitjacketing nature of formal conversation is clear in the way she satirizes it, particularly in the early novels, through Henry Tilney's mock-courtesy to Catherine Morland in *Northanger Abbey* ("I have hitherto been very remiss, madam, ... I have not yet asked you how long you have been in Bath; whether you were ever here before; whether you have been at the Upper Rooms, the theatre, and the concert; and how you like the place altogether" [25]) and Elizabeth Bennet's teasing of Darcy in the early chapters of *Pride and Prejudice*.

Austen's world turned on conversation. As Norman Page has pointed out in his useful book on Austen's language,

> Where the members of a society, and especially its female members, are virtually without prescribed duties, ... conversation takes on a significance that it can hardly afford to possess in a working community; and the ability to talk—to anyone, about anything, or nothing—becomes highly prized. (25)

The society described in Austen's novels is, as everybody knows, a leisured one. The only man with a significant speaking role in *Persuasion* to have what we would now call a proper job is Mr. Shepherd, the land-agent, since even the famous naval activities of Wentworth, Croft, Harville, and Benwick are all in the past by the time the action of *Persuasion* begins. All the women have servants to take care of the day-to-day domestic environment,[2] except for the poverty-stricken Mrs. Smith, who relies on the help of her landlady and Nurse Rooke.

These men and women spend their time not doing but talking: they attend dinners, balls, and concerts, and they make visits between households. At most of these events, the main activity, and the main medium of social interchange, is conversation. Austen's novels are full of conversations, and it is usually through them—the information they reveal, the ideas they raise, the tension they create or dissipate—that the action of the various narratives progresses. In this context my particular interest in the conversation in *Persuasion* is the way in which Austen explores the interplay between the proprieties of conversation and the attempts of honest and open people to achieve communication in a revealing, exciting, and intensely moving way.

All sorts of interchanges are described as conversation in *Persuasion,* from Mrs. Smith's long disquisition to Anne on the history of Mr. Elliot to Captain Wentworth's casual chat with one or other of the Miss Musgroves. However, since conversation depends on a readiness to exchange ideas and on some degree of ease and equality among the participants, it is hardly surprising that it does not exist in any recognizable form at Kellynch Hall. Here, as Laura Mooneyham has pointed out, "Sir Walter announces his prejudices ... and the two sycophants, Mr. Shepherd and Mrs. Clay, listen and approve"

(167). When Anne speaks she is either ignored or contradicted. Her earlier decision to remain silent, therefore, does not stem from excessive modesty (though there is a certain element of masochism involved: many of Anne's actions in the early part of the novel stem from her need to punish herself for her decision to give Wentworth up). Rather, Anne uses common sense, in the same way that Elinor Dashwood, in *Sense and Sensibility,* agrees to the preposterous opinions of Robert Ferrars on the grounds that "she did not think he deserved the compliment of rational opposition" (*SS* 252).

Things tend to the opposite extreme at Uppercross. The open communication between the Musgrove family at Uppercross Hall and their son and daughter-in-law at the Cottage is occasionally just *too* equal, *too* informal, omitting the proprieties that would serve to protect the privacy of individuals and households. However, there is never any doubt in Anne's mind or in the view of the narrator that, for all its drawbacks, the conversation at Uppercross is preferable to the non-conversation of Kellynch. In addition, the conversational style at Uppercross demonstrates, in its very difference from that at Kellynch, that the atrophied situation over which Sir Walter presides is willed rather than inevitable and that other, more desirable, forms of conversational communication may therefore still be possible.

And in fact such an option is offered by the naval characters and their families, all of whom live independent lives while enjoying easy, inclusive, and stimulating conversation whenever they meet. To take just one example, while at Uppercross there is a clear gender distinction between topics of conversation, topics that in any case are rarely very ambitious in scope (Charles with his guns and shooting, the girls with their music and dancing), the naval men and women share a much more equitable relationship in their conversation, as in their lives in general. Mrs. Croft is a full partner with her husband in the negotiations over the lease of Kellynch, and on the frequent occasions when "a little knot of the navy" forms in eager conversation in Bath, she is "as intelligent and keen as any of the officers around her" (168).

Significantly, there is considerable facility for overlap between the Uppercross and the naval groupings. The Crofts are welcome visitors to Uppercross, and so is Wentworth; Benwick (who will become part of the Musgrove family when he marries Louisa) and the Harvilles also enter easy conversational relationships with the Musgroves. By contrast, the Kellynch grouping cannot be assimilated. When Sir Walter and Elizabeth join the group at the White Hart, they cast a general chill: "The comfort, the freedom, the gaiety of the room was over, hushed into cold composure, determined silence, or insipid talk" (226). Fittingly, the Elliots have arrived to deposit their cards, the ultimate social substitute for verbal communication.

Not all conversation, of course, offers a free interchange of interesting views between intelligent people. Much of the talk in *Persuasion*, even between characters whom the reader is intended to respect, is reminiscent of what the narrator of *Emma*, in a jaundiced mood, called "the usual rate of conversation; a few clever things said, a few downright silly, but by much the larger proportion neither one nor the other—nothing worse than every day remarks, dull repetitions, old news, and heavy jokes" (*E* 219). However, as the authors of a recent linguistic study make clear, even this kind of exchange carries more significance than might appear:

> Despite its sometimes aimless appearance and apparently trivial content, casual conversation is, in fact, a highly structured, functionally motivated, semantic activity, ... [and] a critical linguistic site for the negotiation of such important dimensions of our social identity as gender, generational location, sexuality, social class membership, ethnicity, and subcultural and group affiliations. (*Eggins and Slade* 6)

This may seem a rather highfalutin way of describing the speech of Mary Musgrove or her mother-in-law (though Mary's attempts to maintain her position as her father's daughter through conversational attention would fall well into the definition), but in terms of the working-out of the central triangle of Anne, Wentworth, and Mr. Elliot—and more broadly in terms of establishing Anne's settled position in life—it is crucially relevant.

Anne's consciousness and her fate are at the heart of the novel. Many critics have noted the ways in which non-verbal matters—the lifting of little Charles from Anne's back at Uppercross Cottage, the admiring glances of Mr. Elliot at Lyme, the dropping of the pen from Wentworth's hands at the White Hart—determine the outcome of her narrative. Judy van Sickle Johnson has described the whole power of the novel residing in

"Austen's success in sustaining the credibility of a renewed emotional attachment through physical signs ... seductive half-glances, conscious gazes and slight bodily contact" (43). And yet, even while arguing strongly for the importance to the novel of "physical life" and "physical vulnerability" (164), John Wiltshire, in *Jane Austen and the Body*, acknowledges that ultimately "these bodily signs are not enough in themselves to achieve the final rapprochement" (190), that Anne's movement from nobody to somebody is crucially represented by her movement from silence to speech: "By having her speak, and speak eloquently and fully, if indirectly, of her own experience and love, the famous climactic scene at the White Hart grants Anne Elliot a central position for the first time in the novel" (191).

Significantly, Anne herself puts a high value on conversation. "My idea of good company," she tells Mr. Elliot, "is the company of clever, well-informed people, who have a great deal of conversation" (150). And this is one reason why Mr. Elliot is initially such an attractive and then such a disturbing figure for her. By all the rules of conversational propriety, especially in a society where what one says is one of the most important criteria by which individual worth is assessed, Mr. Elliot is a prize indeed: "His tone, his expressions, his choice of subject, his knowing where to stop,—it was all the operation of a sensible, discerning mind" (143). Moreover, while Anne is not "much attended to" by her own family (141), Mr. Elliot actually expresses an interest in what she has to say. On the first evening of his meeting with Anne in Bath, he converses eagerly with her, "wanting to compare opinions [about Lyme], ... to give his own route, understand something of hers, and regret that he should have lost such an opportunity of paying his respects to her" (143). It is not surprising that she needs help to make the discovery that this perfect conversationalist is, as Mrs. Smith declares, "a man without heart or conscience ... black at heart, hollow and black!" (199)—though it is interesting that his very perfection, his ability to control conversational formalities in order to promote a persona entirely at odds with his true character, first arouses her discomfort. Early in her relationship with Mr. Elliot, Anne recognizes the difference between his manners and those of Wentworth: "They were not the same, but they were, perhaps, equally good" (143). As time passes she comes to feel, with ever more conviction, that the openness and sincerity that mark Wentworth's speech, even when accompanied by signs of imperfect control of his emotions, offer a more reliable gauge of character than does a universally smooth conversational surface.

If Mr. Elliot represents the temptation to be taken in by facile words, and her own family represents the temptation to opt out of conversation altogether, Anne must also face a conversational impasse with Lady Russell, her second mother and mentor, the woman who persuaded her to give up Wentworth seven years before the story opens. Now, "they knew not each other's opinion, either its constancy or its change, on the one leading point of Anne's conduct, for the subject was never alluded to" (29). This admission is amazing for two women who purport to be so close; it makes Anne's claim to the "extraordinary blessing of having one such truly sympathising friend as Lady Russell" (42) seem a feat of self-delusion which might make the reader suspicious of some of her other assessments. So open with Lady Russell on other matters, Anne is awkward and inhibited when it comes to discussing her emotional life, and specifically her feelings about Wentworth. After her Lyme visit, Anne "could not speak [Wentworth's] name, and look straight forward to Lady Russell's eye" until she explains what she believes is his commitment to Louisa (124–25). Lady Russell listens composedly, while "internally her heart revelled in angry pleasure, in pleased contempt, that the man who at twenty-three had seemed to understand somewhat of the value of an Anne Elliot, should, eight years afterwards, be charmed by a Louisa Musgrove" (125). On both sides, therefore, the conversational surface is belied by a quite different, unspoken opinion. And nothing has changed by the time Anne watches Lady Russell scrutinizing Wentworth in Bath, only for the elder woman to declare that what has been fixing her eye was "some window-curtains, which Lady Alicia and Mrs. Frankland were telling me of last night" (179). No wonder Anne "sighed and blushed and smiled, in pity and disdain, either at her friend or herself" (179). In this ostensibly close and loving relationship the possibility for communication on the subject which is occupying Anne to the exclusion of almost everything else is apparently non-existent. One necessary outcome of the narrative, if Anne and Lady Russell are to heal the wounds of their relationship, is for Anne to tell Lady Russell the truth about her own feelings and, equally importantly, for Lady Russell "to admit she had been pretty completely wrong, and to take up a new set of opinions and of hopes" (249).[3]

But this is a Kellynch problem, and there is no real future for Anne at Kellynch. With her visit to Uppercross, her prospects, in a general sense, improve. "Anne had not wanted this visit to Uppercross, to learn that a removal from one set of people to another, though at a distance of only three miles, will often include a total change of conversation, opinion, and idea" (42), records the narrator in one of the most telling sentences in a novel that is so concerned with shifting and changing lives. At Uppercross Anne is literally a different person from who she is at Kellynch: regarded by Sir Walter as his youngest daughter (143), she is considered at Uppercross in Elizabeth's permanent absence as the eldest Miss Elliot (91, 92), and the difference is significant for the way in which she is regarded. Here she is no longer silent, and her views are respected; indeed she is appealed to on all sides for intervention in family rows and difficulties. But still she is not entirely at ease. Noticeably she hides behind conscious conversational strategies. She says "what was proper" (37); she exercises "patience, and forced cheerfulness" (39); she "could do little more than listen patiently, soften every grievance, and excuse each to the other" (46). When the Crofts visit, Anne's modest impact on the conversation is neatly encapsulated by Austen's narrative strategy of allowing Mrs. Croft direct speech, while describing Anne's responses in more general terms ("She could now answer as she ought" [49]).

Anne's conversational retreat during the Crofts' visit when Wentworth's name is mentioned is an ominous sign, and her concern is well founded, since his arrival results in the immediate displacement of her position in the company. Glamorous and successful, eager to talk of his adventures and his opinions, he dazzles the Musgrove family. He is immediately the centre of conversational attention, describing his career, giving his opinion of women on board ship, discussing midshipman Dick Musgrove with Dick's grieving mother. His central position in the Musgrove conversation forms an ironic contrast to Sir Walter's domination of the Kellynch grouping, but while the Musgrove sisters are quite as sycophantic as Mr. Shepherd and his daughter, Wentworth fortunately has a sister and a brother-in-law to puncture his wilder flights—"'Phoo! Phoo!' cried the admiral, 'what stuff these young fellows talk!'" (65)—and must take his place within the larger conversation in a way that Sir Walter, who cannot allow competing views in his presence, could not contemplate.

Wentworth's claiming of the limelight, however, relegates Anne to the outer periphery of the Uppercross conversational circle. He literally silences her: as he tells of his naval risks, "Anne's shudderings were to herself, alone: but the Miss Musgroves could be as open as they were sincere, in their exclamations of pity and horror" (66). She and Wentworth have "no conversation together, no intercourse but what the commonest civility required" (63). On the rare occasions when Wentworth does speak to her directly, the "studied politeness" with which he restricts his words to the most conventional and formal—"I beg your pardon, madam, this is your seat"— effectively stifles any possibility of active response (72). Anne's inner self is in constant and direct conflict with surface appearances, and she cannot stifle her deeper feelings in the cause of maintaining conversational smoothness. Unable to accommodate her past relationship to Wentworth or express her present feelings for him, she excludes herself, in deliberate abnegation, from the conversation. Indeed, she becomes almost a ghostly figure, present and yet absent, spoken of in her own hearing in the third person: "She has quite given up dancing," say the Miss Musgroves, "She had rather play. She is never tired of playing" (72).

The strain this imposes on both Anne and Wentworth is reflected by the way in which the most basic cultural and linguistic expectations break down when the two find themselves unexpectedly alone together, except for little Charles, at Uppercross Cottage. Convention dictates that two acquaintances in such circumstances converse with each other until other people arrive, but Wentworth, whose surprise has "deprived his manners of their usual composure," is awkward and flat-footed ("I thought the Miss Musgroves had been here—Mrs. Musgrove told me I should find them here"), while Anne's reply is hardly more composed (79). Yet this awkwardness, a sign of the disturbance caused by sincere feelings and so different from the conversational smoothness of Mr. Elliot, is the beginning of the thaw between them. Much later, in Bath, Anne, by now more confident in her feelings, correctly interprets "sentences begun which he could not finish" (185) as a sure sign of Wentworth's returning love for her.

But conversation between the two might never have developed beyond the "common civilities" stage if it had not been for the visit to Lyme, where genuine communication occurs unexpectedly in the high drama following Louisa's accident. The strong emotional bonds between the two reveal themselves in the heat of the moment, at a level of informality and trust in speech reminiscent of the fellow-feeling between Mr. Knightley and Emma Woodhouse in the novel Austen wrote before *Persuasion*:

> "I have been considering what we had best do. ... I have been thinking whether you had not better remain in the carriage with her, while I go in and break it to Mr. and Mrs. Musgrove. Do you think this a good plan?"
> She did: he was satisfied, and said no more. (*E* 117)

There is genuine intimacy in this little exchange, which is low-key in every sense, taking place during the late stages of a journey in a carriage, spoken in whispers to avoid waking Henrietta, embellished with very little in the way of formal niceties, concerned with an economically expressed agreement on a joint course of action between two people who need to say little to understand each other.

It has often been pointed out that the events at Lyme form the turning point in the renewal of the relationship between Anne and Wentworth and that from then onwards Anne begins to find her voice as Wentworth loses his. It is true that the relative situations of the two are reversed by the fall and its aftermath. The whole set of circumstances that established Wentworth as the complacent centre of conversational attention is swept away by Louisa's accident. In the new situation Wentworth can only maintain his dominance by becoming the declared lover of Louisa; since he is not prepared to do this, he can do nothing but remove himself completely from the action.

Meanwhile, Anne has room to consolidate the status of importance she assumed on the Cobb. She is so essential to the stricken Musgrove family that only she is in a position to "impart among them the general inclination to which she was privy, and persuade them all to go to Lyme at once" (122). The position of authority she assumes here has nothing directly to do with the renewal of her romantic relationship with Wentworth, though the two are indirectly related. She has begun at last to find a distinctive voice, one that offers her for the first time a settled place in her social environment as a mature and confident individual in her own right, as one who is highly regarded by those around her.

Of course it is from this basis that she summons the confidence to take the initiative in trying to reach an understanding with Wentworth—through a series of conversations in which the outer proprieties of what can be said exist in increasing, indeed sometimes unbearable, tension with the feelings and desires of the participants. After all, it is very unlikely there will be another crisis (such as Louisa's fall) during which the normal standards of politeness can be abrogated: Wentworth and Anne must now achieve communication within the normal parameters of conversation, and the question is how—and whether—they are able to do this.

In fact their reconciliation proceeds, as so much conversation does, in this novel and elsewhere, by obliquity and by fits and starts. The intensity of their efforts to reconcile propriety and sincerity, compounded with their fears of misinterpreting each other's responses, has rendered much "normal" conversation unintelligible to one or both of them from the beginning: when Anne first met Wentworth after their long estrangement, "the room seemed full—full of persons and voices" within which Anne could distinguish nothing specific (59). When they meet again after Wentworth has been released from his obligation to Louisa, "Mutual enquiries on common subjects passed; neither of them, probably, much the wiser for what they heard" (176). Their conversation concerns thoroughly predictable topics for British tourists: the health and well-being of their mutual acquaintance, how most conveniently to get home in the rain. Yet at the end of it Anne still doesn't know how long Wentworth intends to stay in Bath: "He had not mentioned it, or she could not recollect it" (178). Conversational niceties have been observed through a filter of "agitation, pain, pleasure, a something between delight and misery" (175).

When they meet again a few days later, at the concert, they seem locked in the same contradictory experience, to the extent that "after talking ... of the weather and Bath and the concert, their conversation began to flag" (181). By now, however, their increased ease with each other enables their conversation to become, albeit indirectly (he "looking not exactly forward," she "fixing her eyes on the ground" [182]), more personal, more concerned with topics that are absorbing them both. They talk of the accident, of the unexpected news of Louisa's engagement to Benwick, and—as a forerunner to the later conversation between Anne and Harville—of Wentworth's opinion of Benwick managing so speedily to alter the object of his affections.

Their conversations can now withstand the exhaustion of a topic, an event that could have easily signalled the end of the exchange. On one occasion Wentworth turns the subject "with renewed spirit" (181); on another, Anne, "feeling the necessity of speaking, and having not the smallest wish for a total change," draws the discussion back to Lyme (183).

And so the narrative advances to the two scenes at the White Hart Inn, which represent the conversational, as well as the emotional, climax of the narrative. Brilliantly representing the formal and yet fluid patterns of conversational exchanges among people who easily make and remake different conversational groupings, Austen presents these crucial scenes almost as a dance (one remembers that Anne was earlier said to have given up dancing), until, as John Wiltshire asserts, "the length and eloquence of Captain Harville's and Anne Elliot's speeches form a consummate duet, almost operatic in its final affirmative intensity, on the theme of constancy" (191). All kinds and levels of conversation are accommodated within these two scenes, beginning with the trivia of friendship and climaxing with Anne and Wentworth finally declaring their love. In stark contrast to the clumsy confrontation described in the cancelled chapters of the novel, Austen here pursues a pattern of obliquity: Anne speaks through the medium of a conversation with Captain Harville, ostensibly on the general subject of constancy, and Wentworth speaks by means of a letter written, he declares, because "I must speak to you by such means as are within my reach" (237).

Mrs. Musgrove and her daughter have welcomed Anne to the White Hart with "a heartiness, and a warmth, and a sincerity which Anne delighted in" (220): their high regard for Anne, completely on her own merits, is thus established. When plans for a visit to the theatre clash with an evening party at the Elliots, Mrs. Musgrove determines that the theatre tickets must be exchanged chiefly because of Anne: "I am sure neither Henrietta nor I should care at all for the play, if Miss Anne could not be with us" (224). Her importance to the naval group, represented at the White Hart by Captain Harville more than by the tormented Captain Wentworth, is equally emphasized: Harville's warm and homely description of Anne as "a good soul" and his extraordinarily intimate gesture of "putting his hand on her arm quite affectionately" (235) are clear magnifiers of her acceptance into the "little knot of the navy" (168) before there is any question of her joining it as Wentworth's wife.

As Anne is trying not to listen to Mrs. Musgrove's conversation with Mrs. Croft, Harville invites her to join him "with a smile, and a little motion of the head, which expressed, 'Come to me, I have something to say'" (231). Of all the conversations in this novel, the one that really matters is this one between Anne and Captain Harville. In his book on conversation, Theodore Zeldin asserts that

> real conversation ... is always an experiment, whose results are never guaranteed. It involves risk. ...
>
> What matters is whether you are willing to think for yourself, and to say what you think. Many people cannot, either because ... they assume they have nothing of importance to say, or because they have received too many knocks from life. (3, 15–16)

But, he adds, people can "suddenly come out with the most amazing statements when they find courage ... what matters most is courage" (16).

This seems a highly illuminating comment as far as Anne is concerned. She has indeed been silenced, and for a long time—a third of her life, as she herself notes (60)—by the emotional setbacks she has received. At the White Hart she is unexpectedly given the opportunity to articulate feelings she has never been able to share with anyone, and she takes courage, risks everything, and speaks. Her thoughts in determining to speak to Wentworth at the concert are expressed in terms very similar to those of Zeldin: "As to the power of addressing him she felt all over courage if the opportunity occurred" (180).

She is able to speak freely precisely because she is not speaking directly to Wentworth, but there is another reason why this conversation about the relative merits of the constancy of men and women is so powerful, and it is that the subject is one of great and personal relevance not only to Anne, but also to Captain Harville.[4] He, as he made clear in his earlier conversation with Anne at Lyme, has been finding it hard to come to terms with his sister's death; he must now adjust to the fact that his sister's lover, Benwick, has within a few months found happiness with another.

Both Anne and Harville are clearly deeply involved in their exchange with each other, as the intimate interplay between their speeches makes clear:

> "Songs and proverbs, all talk of woman's fickleness. But perhaps you will say, these were all written by men.'
>
> "Perhaps I shall.—Yes, yes, if you please, no reference to examples in books. ... I will not allow books to prove anything."
>
> "But how shall we prove any thing?"
>
> "We never shall." (234)

And yet their preoccupation with their personal experience also remains evident. Anne at one point forgets it is Benwick's conduct they are debating, arguing that men are more likely to forget women because of their professional exertions, a contention highly relevant to Wentworth, but quite inapplicable—as Harville points out—to Benwick.

At the end of this conversation, Anne makes her moving declaration of women's constancy—still addressing Harville certainly, but also putting into words for the first time things she has been brooding over for eight years, about which she could long have been "eloquent" (30)—and falls silent: "She could not immediately have uttered another sentence; her heart was too full, her breath too much oppressed" (235). Harville, listening intently to her views, equally feels the conversation has come to an end: "There is no quarrelling with you—And when I think of Benwick, my tongue is tied" (235–36).

But the conversation has fulfilled its secondary, and more important, function through the response of someone who both does and does not belong to it. Wentworth has heard and understood Anne's words, he responds with his own declaration, and the two finally reach an understanding—in a much more prosaic, but equally important, explanatory conversation in the gravel-walk, in which they renew their vows and explain their feelings and experiences over their years of estrangement. Unlike the high and rare drama of Anne's conversation with Harville (the conversational equivalent of Louisa's fall on the Cobb), this one is finally the paradigm for an easy exchange of views between equals: "They could indulge in those retrospections and acknowledgements, and especially in those explanations of what had directly preceded the present moment, which were so poignant and so ceaseless in interest" (241).

As this conversation elides into other, more fragmentary exchanges at the Elliots' party, Anne's personal confidence and sense of fulfilment is demonstrated through her conversation with her friends:

> With the Musgroves, there was the happy chat of perfect ease; with Captain Harville, the kind-hearted intercourse of brother and sister; with Lady Russell, attempts at conversation, which a delicious consciousness cut short; with Admiral and Mrs. Croft, every thing of peculiar cordiality and fervent interest, which the same consciousness sought to conceal;—and with Captain Wentworth, some moments of communication continually occurring, and always the hope of more, and always the knowledge of his being there! (246)

The sexuality inherent in the concept of conversation, and latent throughout the various conversations between Anne and Wentworth even at their least communicative, bubbles to the surface here, as the happy lovers achieve at last a state of unmediated communication and, in prospect, consummation—the ultimate belonging.

NOTES

1 The term is used, for example, in Sarah Fielding's *The Adventures of David Simple* when the evil Livia wishes to imply incest between the brother and sister Valentine and Camilla: "It is now some time since I found out there was a criminal Conversation between your Son and Daughter; to this was owing all that Love they talked of to each other," she tells her husband (148).

2   The tasks Anne describes as concerned with the Elliots' move to Bath, which left her
    "so busy, [with] so much to do"—duplicating her father's catalogue of books and
    pictures, instructing the gardener, packing and taking leave of the villagers (38–39)—
    are certainly matters of importance in the context of a move, but fall well short of
    full-time occupation.

3   On the more general point, it is true that Anne is still close to Lady Russell in many
    respects and that a life together—the most likely option for Anne in the event of her
    father remarrying, if she herself remained unmarried—would not be entirely unwel-
    come. It is simply that it would be a second-best, a limited alternative that would
    depend on Anne's continuing to bury her feelings not only about Wentworth, but
    also about Lady Russell's actions in putting an end to the engagement.

4   It was a subject that would have strong resonance for many readers of the novel, too,
    as, in addition to the normal high mortality rates of the time, England had begun to
    settle back into conditions of peace after more than twenty years of war, during
    which many men spent months and years away from their homeland fighting, while
    their women remained behind to watch and wait—or to find alternative sources of
    comfort and companionship.

11

"If I loved you less,
I might be able to talk
about it more"

~~~

Direct Dialogue and Education in the Proposal Scenes

AT THE EMOTIONAL CLIMAX of *Emma*, Mr. Knightley, the most eminently worthy of suitors, stands in front of Emma, who is in "the happiest dream" because he has just asked her, "Tell me, then, have I no chance of ever succeeding?" As Emma, for once, remains silent, Mr. Knightley continues:

> "I cannot make speeches, Emma:"—he soon resumed; and in a tone of such sincere, decided, intelligible tenderness as was tolerably convincing.—"If I loved you less, I might be able to talk about it more. But you know what I am.—You hear nothing but truth from me.—I have blamed you, and lectured you, and you have borne it as

no other woman in England would have borne it.—Bear with the truths I would tell you now, dearest Emma, as well as you have borne with them. The manner, perhaps, may have as little to recommend them. God knows, I have been a very indifferent lover.—But you understand me.—Yes, you see, you understand my feelings—and will return them if you can. At present, I ask only to hear, once to hear your voice." (*E* 430)

The emotional intensity of Mr. Knightley's impassioned words makes it difficult to believe Norman Page's claim that "Austen tends to renounce dialogue when events seem about to precipitate a scene with considerable emotional potential" (137). Mr. Knightley is not renouncing his considerable emotional potential—in fact, he seems to be revelling in it. However, with typical Austenian irony, Mr. Knightley's plea for Emma's voice provides the last words of direct dialogue in this chapter of reconciliation and exchange of love. Instead of a conversation between the lovers presented in direct dialogue, we read Emma's thoughts about Harriet's situation. As for Emma's response to Mr. Knightley's proposal, all we are told is: "What did she say?—Just what she ought, of course. A lady always does" (431). So although Austen represents Mr. Knightley's emotional declaration of love, she does not depict an exchange of vows between the hero and the heroine, thereby hinting that the reconciliation of the love story may not be the true purpose of this proposal scene.

In fact, in all of Austen's books, love is never directly exchanged between the hero and the heroine in full view of the reader. It is only exchanged during moments of quintessential Austenian irony, as in *Sense and Sensibility,* where "in what manner [Edward] expressed himself, and how he was received, need not be particularly told" (*ss* 361). Although the proposal scenes are superficially about love, through a close examination of Austen's manipulation of the narrative order of direct and indirect dialogue I argue that these scenes primarily provide the reader with a rare opportunity to experience the hero's understanding of his own moral education, unmediated by the narrator's words. Critics have focussed on the moral journey of Austen's heroines because access to their thoughts, and therefore to their education, is readily provided throughout the narrative. However, critics rarely examine the heroes' education that is equally necessary to the happy culmination of the novels, because Austen rarely reveals it directly. In fact, the proposal scenes are the only occasion Austen provides for the hero to tell both the reader and the heroine that he is worthy of the heroine's love because he is aware of and acting upon his capacity to change for the better.

I will first use *Pride and Prejudice* to prove my claim, not only because "it is a truth universally acknowledged" (*PP* 3) that Darcy experiences a moral transformation in order to overcome his pride, just as Elizabeth must learn to overcome her prejudice, but also because Austen's manipulation of direct and indirect dialogue in the two proposal scenes demonstrates what Darcy has learned. Darcy's disastrous first proposal begins with silence, indicating that these conversational sparring partners are not yet lovers, are not yet comfortable in each other's presence. However, the silence serves another function: after three paragraphs of descriptive prose, with no direct and little indirect dialogue, Darcy's bold statement of love emphasizes the paramount importance of every word that he says:

> After a silence of several minutes he came towards her in an agitated manner, and thus began,
> "In vain have I struggled. It will not do. My feelings will not be repressed. You must allow me to tell you how ardently I admire and love you" (189).

Darcy demonstrates his pride as soon as he opens his mouth. His struggles and his feelings are the first subjects of his words, not Elizabeth's worth as a lover and a wife. In fact, he goes so far as to order her to accept his declaration: "You must allow me to tell you ...". It can well be believed that

> Elizabeth's astonishment was beyond expression. She stared, coloured, doubted, and was silent. This he considered sufficient encouragement, and the avowal of all that he felt and had long felt for her, immediately followed. He spoke well, but there were feelings besides those of the heart to be detailed, and he was not more eloquent on the subject of tenderness than of pride. His sense of her inferiority—of its being a degradation—of the family obstacles which judgment had always

opposed to inclination, were dwelt on with a warmth which seemed
due to the consequence he was wounding, but was very unlikely to
recommend his suit. (189)

Blinded by his pride and certain of his suitability, Darcy misreads Elizabeth's
silence as encouragement, when it is actually the opposite. The remainder
of his proposal of marriage is presented by Austen with indirect dialogue
because, in his first direct words, he has managed to tell us all we need to
know—that he is proud and overbearing and that love has only made him
worse, not better.

The way in which Darcy's words are presented in the second proposal
scene indicates that he has learned all that he needs to know in order to
deserve and win his heroine, and that he is applying his knowledge:

> "If you *will* thank me," he replied, "let it be for yourself alone. That
> the wish of giving happiness to you, might add force to the other
> inducements which led me on, I shall not attempt to deny. But your
> *family* owe me nothing. Much as I respect them, I believe, I thought
> only of *you*."
>
> Elizabeth was too much embarrassed to say a word. After a short
> pause, her companion added, "You are too generous to trifle with me.
> If your feelings are still what they were last April, tell me so at once.
> *My* affections and wishes are unchanged, but one word from you will
> silence me on this subject for ever." (366)

Darcy prefaces his proposal with a direct expression of his new-found respect
for Elizabeth's family. After the manner in which he insulted them in his
first proposal, both Elizabeth and the reader need to be sure that his attitudes on this material point have changed. After a short pause, rather than
the long silence in the first scene, indicating their relative comfort with
each other but still emphasizing the importance of the ensuing words, Darcy
begins with a compliment to Elizabeth rather than to himself: "You are too
generous to trifle with me." And while he still orders her to tell him of her
feelings at once, he is ordering an action concerned with her comfort, rather
than his, as in the first scene. He finally alludes to the expression of love that

he made in the first proposal, but does not actually manage to commit the brave act of saying "I love you" as he did before. In fact, the expression of his love—"*My* affections and wishes are unchanged"—occupies the least space in the speech, demonstrating that he has learned and is expressing his knowledge that his feelings are of less importance than hers in this situation.

Elizabeth's acceptance of Darcy and their ensuing exchange of love is a masterpiece of Austenian irony and distance. Romantic convention dictates the characters' emotional expression in this type of scene, and Austen almost provides the expected, but Elizabeth's avowal of love and acceptance of Darcy's proposal are couched in distant terms, and Darcy's subsequent delight is ironically portrayed:

> Elizabeth feeling all the more than common awkwardness and anxiety of his situation, now forced herself to speak; and immediately, though not very fluently, gave him to understand, that her sentiments had undergone so material a change, since the period to which he alluded, as to make her receive with gratitude and pleasure, his present assurances. The happiness which this reply produced, was such as he had probably never felt before; and he expressed himself on the occasion as sensibly and as warmly as a man violently in love can be supposed to do. Had Elizabeth been able to encounter his eye, she might have seen how well the expression of heart-felt delight, diffused over his face, became him; but, though she could not look, she could listen, and he told her of feelings, which, in proving of what importance she was to him, made his affection every moment more valuable. (366)

In what is supposed to be the emotional culmination of the entire book, the characters' true feelings are uncertain: Darcy tells Elizabeth of "feelings," eliding the fact that they are *his* feelings; Darcy "probably" has never been this happy before, and Elizabeth might have seen his happiness if she had looked—but maybe not; Elizabeth's love for Darcy grows in proportion to his expression of her importance to him. Exquisitely biting as this paragraph is, it is not the typical novelistic exchange between lovers. Both the indirect dialogue and the narrator's irony distance the reader from the emotions that Elizabeth and Darcy might be feeling during this most important of scenes and therefore, by contrast, bring the reader closer to Darcy's subsequent direct and impassioned explanation of his moral progress, the true emotional culmination of this novel.

The first direct speech after this exchange of love is Darcy's discussion of his reaction to Lady Catherine's visit to Elizabeth: "'It taught me to hope,' said he, 'as I had scarcely ever allowed myself to hope before. I knew enough of your disposition to be certain, that, had you been absolutely, irrevocably decided against me, you would have acknowledged it to Lady Catherine, frankly and openly'" (367). His hope, implying a lack of hope before Lady Catherine's revelation, contrasts strongly with his certainty that Elizabeth would accept him during the first proposal, when she "could easily see that he had no doubt of a favourable answer. He *spoke* of apprehension and anxiety, but his countenance expressed real security" (189). Then, he felt himself to be irresistible; now, after he has admitted to himself the validity of her reproof, he cannot bring himself to think that he could ever find favour with her, precisely because of the nature of his first proposal. In this first paragraph of direct speech, we also hear that he knows and approves of her outspoken nature. In the first proposal scene, the first thing Darcy says after Elizabeth rejects him "frankly and openly" is to call her manner of rejection uncivil: "I might, perhaps, wish to be informed why, with so little *endeavour* at civility, I am thus rejected" (190). In the second scene, he now perceives her "little *endeavour* at civility" as frankness, outspokenness. Darcy has come to appreciate Lizzy's lively nature and cutting wit as much as the reader has, an appreciation that is a vital ingredient to their happy marriage.

Darcy's next words confirm that his representation of his education about his pride is the most important element of the scene. Having already experienced, through access to her thoughts, Elizabeth's painful process of realization that she was "prejudiced" against Darcy for incorrect reasons (208), the reader needs to hear from Darcy, in his own words, about his own process of realization of his "pride." Despite Elizabeth's attempts to turn away from the subject, Darcy returns again and again in his next speeches, not to love, but to the horror of his own earlier behaviour:

"What did you say of me, that I did not deserve? For, though your accusations were ill-founded, formed on mistaken premises, my behaviour to you at the time, had merited the severest reproof. It was unpardonable. I cannot think of it without abhorrence."

"We will not quarrel for the greater share of blame annexed to that evening," said Elizabeth. "The conduct of neither, if strictly examined, will be irreproachable; but since then, we have both, I hope, improved in civility."

"I cannot be so easily reconciled to myself. The recollection of what I then said, of my conduct, my manners, my expressions during the whole of it, is now, and has been many months, inexpressibly painful to me. Your reproof, so well applied, I shall never forget: 'had you behaved in a more gentleman-like manner.' Those were your words. You know not, you can scarcely conceive, how they have tortured me." (367)

Although Darcy talks of himself, he is describing the change that love has helped him undergo, rather than revealing, as he does in the first scene, what love has failed to achieve. Underlining how important direct speech is to revelation of education, Darcy's direct quotation of Elizabeth's words— "had you behaved in a more gentleman-like manner"—stresses his recognition of the validity of her reproach and reveals to the reader how important it was to his progress away from his pride.

My comparison of Austen's use of direct and indirect speech in the two proposal scenes of *Pride and Prejudice* reveals that the purpose of Darcy's speech in these scenes is to announce his moral education, not his love for Elizabeth. Before we return to the apparent anomaly of Mr. Knightley's impassioned declaration, however, I wish to turn to *Persuasion,* unique among Austen's novels because the manuscript of a previous version of the ending is still extant; this manuscript of the two cancelled chapters forming the original ending of *Persuasion* is the only portion of Austen's six completed novels to survive in manuscript. In comparing the ending Austen originally planned with the published version, we discover that Austen completely rewrote the reconciliation between Captain Wentworth and Anne Elliot, moving from one brought about by the contrivances of Admiral Croft to one controlled by both Anne and Wentworth. The result of the change that has received the most critical attention is Anne's direct expression of her opinions about love during her conversation with Captain Harville about the relative constancy of men and women. Anne's speech, overheard as it is by Wentworth, grants Anne a measure of control over her reconciliation with Wentworth. It also provides feminists with a powerful speech, written by a conservative, Tory, middle-aged woman, about the masculine ownership of history; Austen has Anne say, "Yes, yes, if you please, no reference to examples in books. Men have had every advantage of us in telling their own story. Education has been theirs in so much higher a degree; the pen has been in their hands. I will not allow books to prove anything" (*P* 234).

Less critically examined has been Wentworth's similarly increased control over their reconciliation through his hasty letter to Anne, allowing the reader to view an indirect, because written, but serious declaration of love from the hero to the heroine—a declaration noticeably lacking in irony. Wentworth's letter and Austen's further emendations to the subsequent dialogue between Anne and Wentworth, examined in the light of Wentworth's moral education, prove to be just as necessary to the novel's satisfactory resolution as Anne's powerful words to Harville. Reading Wentworth's letter to Anne again makes it difficult to believe that anyone could conceive of Austen as pulling her emotional punches:

> I can no longer listen in silence. I must speak to you by such means as are within my reach. You pierce my soul. I am half agony, half hope. Tell me not that I am too late, that such precious feelings are gone for ever. I offer myself to you again with a heart even more your own, than when you almost broke it eight years and a half ago. Dare not say that man forgets sooner than woman, that his love has an earlier death. I have loved none but you. Unjust I may have been, weak and resentful I have been, but never inconstant. You alone have brought me to Bath. For you alone I think and plan.—Have you not seen this? Can you fail to have understood my wishes?—I had not waited even these ten days, could I have read your feelings, as I think you must have penetrated mine. I can hardly write. I am every instant hearing something which overpowers me. You sink your voice, but I can distinguish the tones of that voice, when they would be lost on others.—Too good, too excellent creature! You do us justice indeed.

You do believe that there is true attachment and constancy among men. Believe it to be most fervent, most undeviating in

—F.W. (237)

Once again, however, this letter is still an indirect declaration of love—in one sense more emotionally stirring than the indirect, ironic representation of love exchanges in *Pride and Prejudice* and *Sense and Sensibility*, but in another sense even more indirect for the characters, because there is a necessary discontinuity between the times in which the hero and heroine feel their strongest emotions. And while their emotions emerge together during their stroll on "the comparatively quiet and retired gravel-walk," they are instead vastly impersonal for the reader:

> There they exchanged again those feelings and those promises which had once before seemed to secure everything, but which had been followed by so many, many years of division and estrangement. There they returned again into the past, more exquisitely happy, perhaps, in their re-union, than when it had been first projected; more tender, more tried, more fixed in a knowledge of each other's character, truth, and attachment; more equal to act, more justified in acting. (240–41)

At no time do the characters and the reader simultaneously share the emotional intensity of an exchange of love.

The double reconciliation in *Persuasion*—the letter and the ensuing conversation—is explained by the letter itself. When Wentworth declares at the climax of the letter, "I have loved none but you," he deftly deflects the major objection to his reconciliation with Anne—his relationship with Louisa Musgrove—onto the fault of resentment ("Unjust I may have been, weak and resentful I have been, but never inconstant"), indicating that there are actually two areas of education during the narrative, not just one as for his fellow heroes. Instead of learning either that his behaviour with Louisa was wrong or that his pride and resentment kept him apart from Anne longer than her persuadability, Wentworth must reveal to Anne and to the reader that he has learned both lessons equally well. In the letter he begins to communicate his reconsideration of his own behaviour by admitting to weakness and resentment, although not to his inconstancy to Louisa. Wentworth's admission of resentment is repeated at the end of the chapter, when he and Anne discuss whether Anne would have renewed their engagement if he had written to her after his posting to the Laconia:

> It is not that I did not think of it, or desire it, as what could alone crown all my other success. But I was proud, too proud to ask again. I did not understand you. I shut my eyes, and would not understand you, or do you justice. This is a recollection which ought to make me forgive everyone sooner than myself. Six years of separation and suffering might have been spared. (247)

The speech's position as the final one of this most important chapter grants his admission an additional narrative importance, confirming that Wentworth has truly learned his lesson about misplaced resentment.

However, in order to grant his admission of resentment the primacy that makes it believable, the lesson about his behaviour towards Louisa Musgrove must be revealed in a different manner—and one that is exposed by examining the differences between the representation of dialogue in the manuscript and in the published version of the reconciliation scene. In both versions, after the exchange of love, pages of descriptive prose relate the conversation in which Anne and Wentworth reveal to each other how they arrived at this moment. In the manuscript version, Wentworth's first direct words of the conversation discuss his jealousy of Mr. Elliot:

> "To see you," cried he, "in the midst of those who could not be *my* well-wishers, to see your Cousin close by you—conversing & smiling—& feel all the horrible Eligibilities & Proprieties of the Match!—to consider it as the certain wish of every being who could hope to influence you—even, if your own feelings were reluctant, or indifferent—to consider what powerful supports would be his! Was it not enough to make the fool of me, which my behaviour expressed? —How could I look on without agony?—Was not the very sight of the *Friend* who sat behind you?—was not the recollection of what had

could catch it" (61), without previous serious feelings as the cause of the attachment. Although Anne assures herself, and thereby the reader, that "it was the highest satisfaction to her, to believe Captain Wentworth not in the least aware of the pain he was occasioning" (82), Wentworth has ignored the fact that true love should be the only reason for marriage and is punished with uncertainty about his future. In fact, Austen changed more than the style of speech in Wentworth's explanation. In the published version of the speech, Austen has Wentworth utter four additional phrases that greatly increase its personal nature: "I was startled and shocked"; "I had been unguarded"; "I had no right"; "I had been grossly wrong, and must abide by the consequences." The manuscript version of this speech is more impersonal than the published one, not only because it is indirect speech, but also—and just as importantly—because it lacks these emotional declarations. The placement of Wentworth's direct speech as the first in the conversation and the addition of emotional statements that are the most personal and ardent of any of his speeches demonstrate that he understands why he suffered his punishment; by contrast, as we have seen, his first direct speech in the manuscript questions his education. In the published version, the reader and Anne can see that he is now an acceptable husband because he is finally truly moral: without resentment and forever constant.

This brings my discussion back to Mr. Knightley's impassioned outburst of love for Emma. Of all Austen's heroes, Mr. Knightley is the only one who is allowed to tell his heroine directly, in full view of the reader, that he loves her, making it seem that the book is much more about love than the rest of Austen's novels. Since Mr. Knightley apparently is the perfectly moral man, a man with almost nothing to learn about being good to others or about valuing his own worth, it is difficult to discover in what areas he needs improvement. "You might not see one in a hundred, with *gentleman* so plainly written as in Mr. Knightley" (*E* 33), Emma explains to Harriet, and she is right. Mr. Knightley is almost the embodiment of the perfect gentleman, as his name implies. He is a "knightly" character, even, it may be ventured, kingly or saintly; his first name is "George," after all. As Ronald Blythe elaborates: "Mr. Knightley is the timeless Englishman, the real thing, modest, unaffected, somewhat inadequate of speech (loquacity is not a masculine virtue in England), just, intelligent but not intellectual, loving rather than lover-like, and *landed*" (16). He is the best of hosts, thinking of everything for his guests' comfort, including, during the strawberry-picking picnic, having "done all in his power for Mr. Woodhouse's entertainment" in the form of "books of engravings, drawers of medals, cameos, corals, shells, and every other family collection within his cabinets" (361–62), and forestalling Mrs. Elton's idea about a meal out of doors, not only because his "idea of the simple and natural will be to have the table spread in the dining-room"(355), but also because he "wished to persuade Mr. Woodhouse, as well as Emma, to join the party; and he knew that to have any of them sitting down out of doors to eat would inevitably make him ill" (356). He is an active farmer and landlord, walks abroad in all weathers, is actually seen buttoning his gaiters, and greets his younger brother "in the true English style, burying under a calmness that seemed all but indifference, the real attachment which would have led either of them, if requisite, to do every thing for the good of the other" (99–100).

Part of Mr. Knightley's English perfection lies in his distinctly moral nature—after all, in Austen's novels a character's moral maturity is the primary basis for his or her suitability as a potential spouse. Darcy and Wentworth have too much pride. Both Edmund Bertram and Edward Ferrars love immoral women. Mr. Knightley, however, does not seem to need to learn any moral lessons. He already does what Emma terms "any thing really good-natured, useful, considerate, or benevolent. He is not a gallant man, but he is a very humane one" (223). He lends his carriage to Miss Bates and Jane Fairfax on the night of the Coles' party because he does not want Jane to catch a chill on a cold night, but in his "un-ostentatious kindness" (223), he refuses to tell Emma why his carriage was used. He sends gifts to and performs errands for the Bates, but not for the Coles, because they have servants to do their errands for them. He deplores all secrecy: "Mystery; Finesse—how they pervert the understanding!" (446). Most important of all, he saves Harriet from humiliation at the Crown Inn ball when she is slighted by the Eltons. Although he dislikes dancing, he recognizes his duty to help her and performs it without cavil. Anne Ruderman describes his morality in the simplest manner: "He is concerned with other people and is able to see what he might do for them" (26).

And if this were the full extent of Mr. Knightley's character, he would indeed have nothing to learn—his character would be stagnant. However, an examination of the novel reveals that while Mr. Knightley's moral *faux pas* are few and far between, they *do* exist, and all of them are related to his evolving love for Emma. He may tell Emma, "I ... have been in love with you ever since you were thirteen at least" (462), but Austen tells us, "He had been in love with Emma, and jealous of Frank Churchill, from about the same period, one sentiment having probably enlightened him as to the other" (432), giving us conflicting reports, since Frank has only been a part of their lives for one year, not eight. Although in existence, Mr. Knightley's love for Emma was unacknowledged by him until Frank Churchill became a threat to his "being *first*" with Emma, exactly as Emma did not recognize her love for him until Harriet threatened her "being *first* with Mr. Knightley, first in interest and affection" (415). Using the model I have established with *Pride and Prejudice* and *Persuasion,* it is possible to understand that the reason for Mr. Knightley's extraordinary and direct outpouring of love is that the very existence of his love for Emma is exactly the moral realization that Mr. Knightley has to make during the course of the novel in order for him to become the morally infallible character that his fellow characters and most critics think him.

Because of his unacknowledged love for Emma, Mr. Knightley creates in his mind a character for Frank that, although partly true, is not the fair representation that a completely moral character would build, but is instead the result of "ignorance, jealousy, ...' distrust" (432). Mr. Knightley's attempts at dissembling, both to himself and to Emma, are transparent. When he says "with a degree of vexation" that Frank "is a person I never think of from one month's end to another" (150), Emma's thoughts voice Austen's hint that Mr. Knightley is being unfair: she reflects, "To take a dislike to a young man, only because he appeared to be of a different disposition from himself, was unworthy the real liberality of mind which she was always used to acknowledge in him; for with all the high opinion of himself, which she had often laid to his charge, she had never before for a moment supposed it could make him unjust to the merit of another" (150–51). When an acquaintance between two men is "but trifling" (427), as Mr. Knightley admits his with Frank is, he should not describe Frank's handwriting as "like a woman's writing" (297) or call Frank himself a "trifling, silly fellow" (206). After Emma and Mr. Knightley are reconciled, Mr. Knightley admits, "I have never had a high opinion of Frank Churchill.—I can suppose, however, that I may have under-rated him" (427), and later says, "I was not quite impartial in my judgment" (445). Mr. Knightley's inconsistency in the important act of evaluating another person is not the sign of a character who has nothing to learn, who is never wrong. Rather, Mr. Knightley must acknowledge to himself his love for Emma and admit that his jealousy of Frank has made him almost as "clueless" as Emma in judging Frank's character.

To indicate that he does undergo the necessary education in morality by becoming aware of his love for Emma, Austen does not hide Mr. Knightley's words of love in a letter or behind ironic words, as she does with her other heroes. Mr. Knightley begins his declaration by revealing that he now understands his own mind and heart: "'My dearest Emma,' said he, 'for dearest you will always be, whatever the event of this hour's conversation, my dearest, most beloved Emma—tell me at once'"(430). Whether Emma accepts or rejects him, Mr. Knightley now knows that he will always love her. As we saw at the beginning of this essay, he continues, "I cannot make speeches, Emma," and then proceeds to make an eloquent one (430). This declaration acts in a similar manner to the silence before Darcy's proposals, making his avowal of love more powerful, more personal, more direct for the reader. And precisely because the consummation of Mr. Knightley's moral education is his realization that he loves Emma, Austen allows him to speak directly the words she denies her other heroes.

The final paragraph of the chapter presenting Mr. Knightley's proposal is Austen's quick summary of his regeneration to morality through an examination of his feelings for Frank Churchill in relation to his own position with Emma:

He had found her agitated and low.—Frank Churchill was a villain.—He heard her declare that she had never loved him. Frank Churchill's character was not desperate.—She was his own Emma, by hand and word, when they returned into the house; and if he could have thought of Frank Churchill then, he might have deemed him a very good sort of fellow. (433).

These few words serve to confirm what the reader already knows. Because he has come to terms with his love for Emma, as Darcy had to come to terms with his pride, as Wentworth had to come to terms with his impetuous actions, Mr. Knightley has learned his lesson, can return to full morality, and deserves his happy-ever-after.

NORA FOSTER STOVEL

12

Famous Last Words

Elizabeth Bennet Protests Too Much

"I BELIEVE, MA'AM, I may safely promise you *never* to dance with him" (*PP* 20). So Elizabeth Bennet declares to her mother in *Pride and Prejudice*. These are famous last words indeed. The astute Austen reader suspects the lady protests too much and anticipates witnessing her eat her words. The fact that she does protest too much, however, suggests that Elizabeth is impressed with Darcy from the outset, a theory that we will see borne out later in the book.[1] In fact, I suggest that we know all along that Darcy and Elizabeth are destined to be united at the end of the novel because the reader recognizes classic comic structure and Janeites recognize Austen's methods.[2] In order to make the plot intriguing, however, the author must place obstacles in the lovers' primrose path. So our pleasure lies in observing the skill with which the novelist overcomes these obstacles.

The occasion of this foolhardy promise is, of course, the famous, or infamous, snub that Darcy directs at Elizabeth on their first meeting at the

Meryton Assembly. Charles Bingley interrupts his dance with Jane Bennet to urge Darcy to dance with her sister Elizabeth, who is languishing for want of a partner. Looking around until he catches her eye, Darcy withdraws his own and replies coldly, "She is tolerable; but not handsome enough to tempt *me*; and I am in no humour at present to give consequence to young ladies who are slighted by other men" (12).

Admirers of Darcy have long been at pains to account for his rudeness: supposing that he must be aware that she *can* overhear him, since she *does* overhear him, his barb seems to be deliberately launched. Why is he so cruel? Shyness will not suffice to exonerate him. Nor will his dislike of dance or small talk. I suggest that he is offended: first, his friend has pre-empted him in monopolizing the most beautiful and eligible woman in the room, and, second, Elizabeth has had the effrontery to catch his eye, as if "to beg for a partner" (26). After all, "the single man in possession of a good fortune" (3) may not be Charles Bingley, but his friend, Fitzwilliam Darcy, his superior in birth, position, and fortune. We need only think of Miss Bingley's fawning flattery to see how Darcy must constantly repel advances from single women in want of a good fortune. I suggest that Darcy is attracted to Elizabeth and is resisting the attraction in the pattern of the eminently eligible single man of fortune—a theory borne out by subsequent developments. Colin Firth, who plays Darcy in the BBC/A&E TV adaptation of *Pride and Prejudice*, cites in an interview "a very helpful saying: 'A man who is eligible needs to entertain no one,'" and adds, "So out of both shyness and a lack of necessity [Darcy] remains aloof" (Birtwistle 102).

Whatever Darcy's reasons, Elizabeth imputes the worst possible interpretation to his words. But her "lively, playful disposition" (12) turns the slight into an amusing story. Mrs. Bennet, outraged by the snub, declares, "I quite detest the man" (13), and advises, "Another time, Lizzy, ... I would not dance with *him*, if I were you." Elizabeth goes one better by promising "*never* to dance with him" (20). Mrs. Bennet is scarcely the type for rational behaviour, and so, by allying herself with her mother, Elizabeth has put herself beyond the realm of reason. Just as Mrs. Bennet is said to be "beyond the reach of reason" (62) on the subject of the entail of the Longbourn estate, so Elizabeth has put herself beyond the reach of reason on the subject of Fitzwilliam Darcy.[3]

This phenomenon is, of course, the prejudice of Austen's title—a title one of my students referred to as *The Pride and the Prejudice*.[4] As Fanny Burney says in *Cecilia*, "The whole of this unfortunate business ... has been the result of PRIDE and PREJUDICE" (930). Modern psychology employs another term for this phenomenon: it is referred to as *mental schema*, whereby an individual forms a rigid mental framework that influences the interpretation of all data.[5] Elizabeth is a classic case of such schema: Darcy's snub, combined with her pride in her own perspicacity—what Walton Litz terms "Elizabeth's pride of her own quick perceptions" (102), a pride fostered by her doting father—results in an inflexible prejudice against Darcy that will require three volumes to dismantle.

Let us remember the original title of the novel—*First Impressions*.[6] What I might call "love at first impression" may inspire their prejudice. Darcy and Elizabeth, I argue, fall in hate, or, rather, fall into a love/hate relationship, as a result of offended pride. As Colin Firth explains, "[Darcy] hates [Elizabeth] because he fancies her" (100). Elizabeth acknowledges, "I could easily forgive *his* pride, if he had not mortified *mine*" (20). Mary, the pedantic Bennet sister, offers a useful definition: "Vanity and pride are different things. ... Pride relates more to our opinion of ourselves, vanity to what we would have others think of us" (20). This definition applies perfectly to Darcy and Elizabeth: he is proud while she is vain. Darcy refines this distinction further: "Yes, vanity is a weakness indeed. But pride—where there is a real superiority of mind, pride will be always under good regulation" (57). He acknowledges that his temper is unyielding, even resentful: Elizabeth concludes, "*Your* defect is a propensity to hate every body," to which he replies with ironic accuracy, "And yours ... is wilfully to misunderstand them" (58). Much of the reader's delight consists of witnessing Elizabeth being obliged to dismantle her prejudice and Darcy his pride—a process that provides the impetus for the novel.

Elizabeth proves as good as her word, and the fast-stepping that she is forced to execute to avoid dancing with Darcy, before he manages to outmanoeuvre her, affords the reader considerable entertainment—especially since the perverse author contrives to construct Volume I in terms of a series of dances. As Henry Tilney explains to Catherine Morland at the Bath Assembly in *Northanger Abbey*, in both matrimony and dancing "man has the advantage of choice, woman only the power of refusal" (77). As Elizabeth later notes to Colonel Fitzwilliam, who has been recounting Darcy's success in saving his friend Bingley from a most imprudent match, Darcy takes "great pleasure in the power of choice" (183). Whereas Darcy enjoys exercising his power of choice, Elizabeth can only exercise her right to refuse.

The second dance occurs at the gathering at Lucas Lodge, when Sir William flaunts his courtly manners by urging Darcy to dance with Elizabeth. Although Darcy has just expressed his disdain for the amusement, declaring, "Every savage can dance" (25), he is not unwilling to partner her.[7] But she remonstrates, "Indeed, Sir, I have not the least intention of dancing.—I entreat you not to suppose that I moved this way in order to beg for a partner" (26). Why, then, *has* she moved towards them, if not to seek a partner? Elizabeth is steadfast in refusing to accede either to Darcy's polite propriety or to Sir William's persistent persuasion, however. When the latter asks rhetorically, "Who would object to such a partner?" (26), Elizabeth "looked archly, and turned away" (26). Austen adds, "Her resistance had not injured her with the gentleman" (26–27). As Colin Firth notes, for once Darcy is "the pursuer rather than the pursued: it's irresistible" (Birtwistle 102).

Let us not fail to accord credit to Caroline Bingley for helping to dismantle Darcy's resistance to Elizabeth, for I suggest that he uses Elizabeth to protect himself from Miss Bingley's advances. He is hoist with his own petard, as the saying goes, however, for in attending to Elizabeth in order to offend Caroline, he falls under Elizabeth's spell. Upon Caroline's confronting him, he responds, "I have been meditating on the very great pleasure which a pair of fine eyes in the face of a pretty woman can bestow" (27). Darcy is learning the language of looks: the very glance that offended him at the Meryton Assembly now enchants. As Colin Firth says, "That's when he first notices her eyes. What starts off as intriguing becomes profoundly erotic for him" (Birtwistle 102). The glossary of glances is a vocabulary that Austen will pursue.

Darcy has further opportunity to admire Elizabeth at Netherfield when she goes to visit Jane, who, thanks to her mother's ingenuity, has fallen ill after getting soaked through while riding on horseback to Netherfield and must therefore remain there for a week to recover. Darcy persists in gazing intently at Elizabeth, who persists in misinterpreting his steadfast gaze:

> Mr. Darcy's eyes were fixed on her. She hardly knew how to suppose that she could be an object of admiration to so great a man; and yet that he should look at her because he disliked her, was still more strange. She could only imagine however at last, that she drew his notice because there was a something about her more wrong and reprehensible, according to his ideas of right, than in any other person present. The supposition did not pain her. She liked him too little to care for his approbation. (51)

The fact that men do not usually stare at women because they do *not* like the way they look serves to emphasize Elizabeth's rigid mind-set that will not admit any data that does not fit her schema.

When Elizabeth arrives with her petticoat inches deep in mud as a result of walking three miles to see her sister, Caroline Bingley attempts to denigrate her by observing, "She has nothing ... to recommend her, but being an excellent walker" (35). But being an excellent walker is a giant step towards being an exquisite dancer. When Miss Bingley attempts to call Darcy's attention to herself by playing "a lively Scotch air," he surprises Elizabeth by asking, "Do not you feel a great inclination, Miss Bennet, to seize such an opportunity of dancing a reel?" She is so surprised that she remains silent, provoking him to repeat his question, to which she replies, "I do not want to dance a reel at all—and now despise me if you dare." He replies, "Indeed I do not dare" (52). As Austen notes, "Darcy had never been so bewitched by any woman as he was by her. He really believed, that were it not for the inferiority of her connections, he should be in some danger" (52). Thus, Austen reinforces the idea that Darcy is resisting his attraction to Elizabeth because of his prejudice against her class. Her technique has the opposite effect from what is intended, however. Later Darcy acknowledges, "I believed you to be wishing, expecting my addresses" (369). Perhaps, at some level of which she is wilfully ignorant, she deliberately piques his admiration with her playful teasing. As she later declares, "Had I been in love, I could not have been more wretchedly blind" (208). Such passion may be at the root of her prejudice.

The grand finale of Volume I is, of course, the Netherfield ball on November 26. The Elizabeth–Darcy duo has by now become a trio and the antagonism rendered more complex by the arrival of George Wickham to join the ——shire Militia stationed near Meryton. In short, the plot thickens. Besides his handsome face, fine figure, easy manners, and *appearance* of virtue (Austen is always careful to include the word "appearance" to suggest that Elizabeth cannot see beyond surfaces), Wickham has the added advantage of being able to fuel Elizabeth's anger at Darcy. So blinded is she by her bias against Darcy that she cannot see the impropriety of Wickham's confidences to a virtual stranger nor the impudence of his vilifying his patron behind his back. Jane's tolerant nature provides the perfect foil for Elizabeth's intolerance: when she says, upon hearing Wickham's history of Darcy, "One does not know what to think," Elizabeth retorts, "I beg your pardon;—one knows exactly what to think" (86): "Attention, forbearance, patience with Darcy, was injury to Wickham" (89).

Anticipating "the conquest of all that remained unsubdued of [Wickham's] heart" (89) at the Netherfield ball—for "to be fond of dancing was a certain step towards falling in love" (9), as Austen reminds us at the outset— Elizabeth is crushed to discover that Wickham has avoided the ball by going to town, and her animosity towards Darcy is exacerbated accordingly. Consequently, she is so surprised by his voluntarily inviting her to dance that, "without knowing what she did, she accepted him" (90)—suggesting that her impulses are right, but her head in the form of her mental schema is at war with her heart. But when Charlotte Lucas remonstrates, "I dare say you will find him very agreeable," Elizabeth retorts, "Heaven forbid!—*That* would be the greatest misfortune of all!—To find a man agreeable whom one is determined to hate!—Do not wish me such an evil" (90). Austen suggests that Elizabeth is well aware of her prejudice: Darcy is the man she loves to hate.

Elizabeth, "amazed at the dignity to which she was arrived in being allowed to stand opposite to Mr. Darcy," employs first silence, then talk to torment him. Initially she maintains a steadfast silence, until, after they had "stood for some time without speaking a word," and "fancying that it would be the greater punishment to her partner to oblige him to talk" (for Darcy is taciturn, while Elizabeth is talkative), she speaks, adding, "It is *your* turn to say something now, Mr. Darcy.—*I* talked about the dance, and *you* ought to make some kind of remark on the size of the room, or the number of couples," provoking him to ask, "Do you talk by rule then, while you are dancing?" (90–91). She replies, "Sometimes. One must speak a little, you know. It would look odd to be entirely silent for half an hour together, and yet for the advantage of *some*, conversation ought to be so arranged as that they may have the trouble of saying as little as possible" (91). She adds, "We are each of an unsocial, taciturn disposition, unwilling to speak, unless we expect to say something that will amaze the whole room, and be handed down to posterity with all the eclat of a proverb" (91). Her catechism continues as she provokes Darcy by inquiring about his quarrel with Wickham, asking whether he never allows himself to be "blinded by prejudice": "It is particularly incumbent on those who never change their opinion, to be secure of judging properly at first" (93). Ultimately she succeeds in her design of offending him, and they separate in silence. What Reuben Brower terms "the poetry of wit" or "*jeux d'esprit*" (168, 171) Andrew Davies, screenwriter of the BBC/A&E adaptation, labels "a fencing match caught in dance" (Birtwistle 71). Indeed, Darcy and Elizabeth do resemble that reluctant couple, Beatrice and Benedick, from Shakespeare's comedy *Much Ado About Nothing*, who love to hate and hate to love, and who, in turn, inspired warring couples like Mirabel and Millamant in Congreve's *The Way of the World*.[8]

No sooner has she achieved her object, however, than circumstances conspire to challenge her complacency. Her admirer, Mr. Collins, on learning that he is in the presence of a relative of his patroness, Lady Catherine de Bourgh, announces to Elizabeth his intention of introducing himself to Darcy. Elizabeth is appalled at his effrontery in accosting a man so much his social superior and observes with embarrassment as Collins courts Darcy's contempt. A "most unlucky perverseness" (with the initials J.A.) seats Darcy where he can overhear Mrs. Bennet's insulting comments, just as Elizabeth overheard Darcy's insults at the Meryton Assembly: "What is Mr. Darcy to me, pray, that I should be afraid of him? I am sure we owe him no such particular civility as to be obliged to say nothing *he* may not like to hear" (99). After dinner, Mary regales the company with her songs. Finally, Collins displays his partiality for Elizabeth by monopolizing her in the dance, where he "gave her all the shame and misery which a disagreeable partner ... can give" (90). Austen concludes, "To Elizabeth it appeared, that had her family made an agreement to expose themselves as much as they could during the evening, it would have been impossible for them to play their parts with more spirit, or finer success" (101). It is Darcy's disapprobation that she fears the most, of course, for she does not wish to fuel his prejudice against her connections, indicating that his opinion is of the utmost importance to her. In short, she desires his approbation.

Collins's invitation to the dance proves to be a prelude to his proposal of marriage to Elizabeth. Recall Henry Tilney's comment to Catherine Morland at the cotillion ball in *Northanger Abbey*: "I consider a country-dance as an emblem of marriage" (76); so it proves in *Pride and Prejudice*. After cataloguing his reasons for marrying—not the least compelling being that it is the recommendation of his patroness, Lady Catherine de Bourgh—and assuring her "in the most animated language of the violence of [his] affection" (106), he is incapable of accepting her refusal, assuming that it is her natural delicacy that leads her to refuse, plus the coquetry of an elegant female who wishes him to repeat the offer. Finally, she is forced to insist: "I do assure you that I am not one of those young ladies (if such young ladies there are) who are so daring as to risk their happiness on the chance of being asked a second time" (107)—famous last words again. Remember them, for these are additional words that she will be obliged to eat. She then declares categorically, "Do not consider me now as an elegant female intending to plague you, but as a rational creature speaking the truth from her heart" (109)—a good example of self-deception, for Elizabeth is anything but rational at this point and has little interest in learning the truth, especially where Fitzwilliam Darcy is concerned.

Collins is, of course, a comic counterpart to Darcy, anticipating him first in dancing with, and then in proposing marriage to, Elizabeth. Even their proposals are parallel in some ways, as both detail their reasons for or against marrying. While Collins changes the object of his attentions and proposals with alacrity, however, Darcy stands firm in both his affections and his intentions.

Volume I ends with the overthrow of all Mrs. Bennet's dearest hopes of seeing her two eldest daughters well married—well, married. Elizabeth rejects the proposal of Mr. Collins, who redirects his attentions towards her friend, Charlotte Lucas, almost as readily as he redirected his intentions from Jane to Elizabeth. Jane's hopes are dashed by the news that the Bingley party is returning to London with no prospect of revisiting Netherfield. As a cheerless Christmas season approaches, Mrs. Bennet wallows in the winter of her discontent. Only the visit of the Gardiners consoles the Bennet women. When Aunt Gardiner hears of Elizabeth's preference for Wickham, she cautions her against encouraging such an imprudent attachment: "You have sense, and we all expect you to use it" (144). Elizabeth takes this appeal to her intelligence to heart, and, although she does allow herself one outburst—"Oh! *that* abominable Mr. Darcy!" (144)—she promises to "do [her] best" (145). When her aunt suggests a tour of the Lakes, she greets the prospect eagerly, exclaiming rhetorically, if disingenuously, "What are men to rocks and mountains?" (154).

Volume II does take the Bennet women far afield: Jane accompanies the Gardiners to London, where she is ignored by the Bingleys and left to languish alone; Elizabeth accepts Charlotte's urgent invitation to visit her new establishment at Hunsford Parsonage in Kent, where Elizabeth is able to admire Collins's conjugal felicity and the condescension of his patroness, Lady Catherine de Bourgh—all delights that she might have been able to call her own: "Words were insufficient for the elevation of his feelings; and he was obliged to walk about the room, while Elizabeth tried to unite civility and truth in a few short sentences" (216).

No sooner is Elizabeth established in Kent, however, than Darcy arrives at Rosings Park with his cousin, Colonel Fitzwilliam. The intercourse between the Park and the Parsonage provides many opportunities for Elizabeth to tease Darcy about his taciturn temperament: she even twits him about snubbing her at the Meryton Assembly. His excuse of shyness and dislike of small talk may impress the reader, who credits him with being "the strong silent type," but not the intolerant Elizabeth. As Darcy observes, "We neither of us perform to strangers" (176). Interestingly, this is the first time Darcy refers to himself and Elizabeth as *we*, suggesting a new level of intimacy.

The Rosings episode constitutes a turning point in Darcy's feelings for Elizabeth. I suggest that there are several reasons for this development. First, Darcy sees Elizabeth for the first time in isolation from her family. Secondly, he realizes that rank is no guarantee of good manners, for he is as embarrassed by the behaviour of his aunt, Lady Catherine de Bourgh, as Elizabeth could be by her own relations. Lastly, Colonel Fitzwilliam admires Elizabeth, and, although he makes it clear to her that he cannot afford to entertain any serious intentions towards her, his admiration must carry weight with his cousin, if only to arouse his jealousy.

Easter brings a renewal of Darcy's admiration of Elizabeth. Charlotte Lucas, unblinded by pride, prejudice, or passion, is able to interpret his "earnest, steadfast gaze" (181) and concludes, "My dear Eliza, he must be in love with you" (180). She is convinced that "all her friend's dislike would vanish, if she could suppose him to be in her power" (181). But Fitzwilliam's account of the decisive part played by Darcy in vanquishing all her sister Jane's hopes of happiness arouses Elizabeth's resentment: "If [Darcy's] own vanity ... did not mislead him, *he* was the cause, his pride and caprice were the cause of all that Jane had suffered" (186). Then, "as if intending to exasperate herself as much as possible against Mr. Darcy" (188), she rereads Jane's letters. It is in this mood of resentment that she greets Darcy's proposal of marriage.

"In vain have I struggled. It will not do. My feelings will not be repressed. You must allow me to tell you how ardently I admire and love you" (189). The reader, like the heroine herself, is in shock. The effect is as if a singer had changed register, moving from musical comedy to grand opera. The polite social mask is off. Darcy has long been the classic strong silent type, but still waters run deep indeed, and he is, unlike Collins, run away with by the violence of his affection. But where Austen allowed Collins to articulate his reasons for marrying in his own words, she wisely represses Darcy's reasons against marrying, summarizing them in the omniscient narrative. We can assume that his eloquence on the subject of his pride and her inferiority renders him just as rude, however, as did Bingley's initial invitation to partner Elizabeth in the dance, for he provokes her to incivility and accusations of his officious interference with regard to Bingley and Jane and his vicious behaviour to Wickham. Darcy cuts to the quick when he accuses:

"These offences might have been overlooked, had not your pride been hurt by my honest confession of the scruples that had long prevented my forming any serious design" (192). The gloves are off, and the wigs are on the green. She responds, "You could not have made me the offer of your hand in any possible way that would have tempted me to accept it" (192–93). These are famous last words, Volume II, and Elizabeth will devote all of Volume III to attempting to eat them. She expands her rejection eloquently:

> From the very beginning, from the first moment I may almost say, of my acquaintance with you, your manners impressing me with the fullest belief of your arrogance, your conceit, and your selfish disdain of the feelings of others, were such as to form that ground-work of disapprobation, on which succeeding events have built so immoveable a dislike; and I had not known you a month before I felt that you were the last man in the world whom I could ever be prevailed on to marry. (193)

The lady does indeed protest too much and in the process reveals, ironically, that she *has* considered marriage to Darcy. However, she does, as a result of this direct attack, achieve the last word. Darcy retires in defeat (or so it appears), leaving Elizabeth in a tumult of emotion, as she cries for half an hour—a torrent of tears that alerts the reader to the emotions Elizabeth refuses to acknowledge.

How curious it is, then, that, although she intends to avoid Darcy, her morning walk the next day takes her to the gates of Rosings Park, whence he emerges to give her a letter that the reader scans with almost as much impatience as the heroine herself. The missive provokes the process that his proposal failed to effect, namely the dismantling of her bias or schema. Darcy achieves this feat by appealing to her *reason* and her sense of *justice*, just as her Aunt Gardiner appealed to her *sense*. And a challenge to her reason and sense of justice must be answered:

> With a strong prejudice against every thing he might say, she began his account of what had happened at Netherfield. ... His belief of her sister's insensibility, she instantly resolved to be false, and his account

of the real, the worst objections to the match, made her too angry to have any wish of doing him justice. He expressed no regret for what he had done which satisfied her; his style was not penitent, but haughty. It was all pride and insolence. (204)

However, his desire to exonerate himself of blame and deserve her approbation by humbling his family pride to confess the scandal of his sister's intended elopement with Wickham ultimately has the desired effect. Like the figure of Justice herself, she "weighed every circumstance with what she meant to be impartiality" (205), in a manner that Reuben Brower calls her "judicial process" (176). Her eyes are opened, and she realizes that "she had been blind, partial, prejudiced, absurd":

> "How despicably have I acted!" she cried.—"I, who have prided myself on my discernment!—I, who have valued myself on my abilities! who have often disdained the generous candour of my sister, and gratified my vanity, in useless or blameable distrust.—How humiliating is this discovery!—Yet, how just a humiliation!—Had I been in love, I could not have been more wretchedly blind. But vanity, not love, has been my folly.—Pleased with the preference of one, and offended by the neglect of the other, on the very beginning of our acquaintance, I have courted prepossession and ignorance, and driven reason away, where either were concerned. Till this moment, I never knew myself." (208)

This epiphanic moment constitutes the turning point in Elizabeth's character development. Only when she achieves self-knowledge is she able to perceive Darcy's true character.

> Mr. Darcy's letter, she was in a fair way of soon knowing by heart. She studied every sentence: and her feelings towards its writer were at times widely different. When she remembered the style of his address, she was still full of indignation; but when she considered how unjustly she had condemned and upbraided him, her anger was turned against herself; and his disappointed feelings became the object of compas-

sion. His attachment excited gratitude, his general character respect; but she could not approve him; nor could she for a moment repent her refusal, or feel the slightest inclination ever to see him again. In her own past behaviour, there was a constant source of vexation and regret; and in the unhappy defects of her family a subject of yet heavier chagrin. (212)

Her reaction to his letter is a lesson in reading and interpretation.[9] It clarifies her continuum of reactions as she admits the justice of Darcy's prejudice against her relations' and her own defects.

Reunion with Jane tempts Elizabeth to "gratify whatever of her own vanity she had not yet been able to reason away" (218) by communicating Darcy's proposals to her sister. But, for once, she exercises restraint, until they are at leisure at Longbourn, where she reveals "Darcy's vindication" (225) in relation to Wickham. She concludes, "One has got all the goodness, and the other all the appearance of it" (225). She burlesques her bias in accounting for it to her more tolerant sister:

And yet I meant to be uncommonly clever in taking so decided a dislike to him, without any reason. It is such a spur to one's genius, such an opening for wit to have a dislike of that kind. One may be continually abusive without saying any thing just; but one cannot be always laughing at a man without now and then stumbling on something witty. (225–26)

Here she acknowledges her desire to employ her prejudice against Darcy as an opportunity to exercise her wit.

Volume II ends with the effective dismantling of both Darcy's pride and Elizabeth's prejudice. But it also ends with the renewed disappointment of both elder Bennet sisters' marital hopes, and only the prospect of the Gardiners' tour of the Lakes cheers Elizabeth until a change of schedule limits their tour to Derbyshire, the site of Darcy's country estate. "To Pemberley, therefore, they were to go" (241).

While Volume I staged the meeting of Elizabeth and Darcy in her home county of Hertfordshire, and Volume II reunited the pair on the relatively neutral ground of Kent, Volume III reunites them initially on Darcy's own turf of Derbyshire and finally in Hertfordshire once again, bringing their journeys full circle. Elizabeth is suitably impressed by Darcy's estate and thinks, "to be mistress of Pemberley might be something!" (245). The testimony to Darcy's good nature by his housekeeper, Mrs. Reynolds, makes an impression, and, upon viewing his portrait in the gallery, she "thought of his regard with a deeper sentiment of gratitude than it had ever raised before" (251). To her great surprise, no sooner does she view his portrait than she meets the man himself. Embarrassed by the perverseness of the meeting and amazed at the alteration in his manner, she is impressed by his civility to the Gardiners and his wish to introduce her to his sister. Elizabeth remains puzzled, but the Gardiners perceive his admiration for their niece and feel "the full conviction that one of them at least knew what it was to love. Of the lady's sensations they remained a little in doubt; but that the gentleman was overflowing with admiration was evident enough" (262). Even Elizabeth is impressed by the alteration in his behaviour and is obliged to adjust her attitude accordingly: "Such a change in a man of so much pride, excited not only astonishment but gratitude—for to love, ardent love, it must be attributed" (266). Her gratitude inspires her to review her feelings:

> She respected, she esteemed, she was grateful to him, she felt a real interest in his welfare; and she only wanted to know how far she wished that welfare to depend upon herself, and how far it would be for the happiness of both that she should employ the power, which her fancy told her she still possessed, of bringing on the renewal of his addresses. (266)

Collins is vindicated, for Elizabeth wishes for the very thing she assured Collins she would never desire—namely, to invite a man to repeat his proposals. Fate in the form of the novelist intervenes, however: no sooner is Elizabeth well on the way to a reconciliation with Darcy than her hopes are dashed in the cruellest manner by a letter from Jane informing her that her youngest sister, Lydia, has eloped with none other than George Wickham. A further perversity brings Darcy to wait on Elizabeth at the very moment when the shock of this catastrophe has thrown her into a tumult of emotions;

in the heat of the moment, she confesses her sister's shame to Darcy—a striking example of both her trust in his discretion and the level of intimacy that they have attained. His silence and hasty departure, the result of his apparent disapprobation, dash her nascent hopes of reconciliation:

> As he quitted the room, Elizabeth felt how improbable it was that they should ever see each other again on such terms of cordiality as had marked their several meetings in Derbyshire; and as she threw a retrospective glance over the whole of their acquaintance, so full of contradictions and varieties, sighed at the perverseness of those feelings which would now have promoted its continuance, and would formerly have rejoiced in its termination. (279)

Given the perversity of Elizabeth's nature, it is not surprising that the disgrace brought on the entire Bennet family by Lydia's shame ironically makes Elizabeth aware for the first time of her true feelings for Darcy, for it is human nature to value what we possess only when we have lost it. The achievement of Lydia's marriage to Wickham makes her regret that she ever informed Darcy of the affair (311). It also makes her realize that now "there seemed a gulf impassable between them" (311), for Darcy, even if he could overcome his repugnance at an alliance with the Bennet family, would never connect himself with a family that would make him brother-in-law of the man he so justly despised:

> What a triumph for him, as she often thought, could he know that the proposals which she had proudly spurned only four months ago, would now have been gladly and gratefully received! ...
> She began now to comprehend that he was exactly the man, who, in disposition and talents, would most suit her. His understanding and temper, though unlike her own, would have answered all her wishes. It was an union that must have been to the advantage of both; by her ease and liveliness, his mind might have been softened, his manners improved, and from his judgment, information, and knowledge of the world, she must have received benefit of greater importance.

But no such happy marriage could now teach the admiring multitude what connubial felicity really was. An union of a different tendency, and precluding the possibility of the other, was soon to be formed in their family. (312)

The reader, however, thanks to the author's narrative skill, is a better judge than Elizabeth of Darcy's character. Not until after Lydia's wedding does Elizabeth learn from her sister's foolish loquacity that Darcy was a witness to her marriage to Wickham. Petitioning Aunt Gardiner prompts a letter revealing all that Darcy has done to effect the marriage, from hunting down the couple to bribing Wickham to marry Lydia by offering to settle his debts and purchase his commission. The motive Darcy professes is regret that "his mistaken pride" led him to conceal Wickham's real viciousness (322). Elizabeth's vanity may be equally to blame, for publication of the truth would have rendered her previous preference for Wickham risible. But she begins to suspect his real motive: "Her heart did whisper, that he had done it for her" (326).

Finally Elizabeth listens to her heart. This Janus-faced heroine has often been led towards Darcy by her heart—at the Meryton Assembly, the Lucas Lodge ball, the Netherfield ball, and at Rosings Park—but has been driven away from him by her head, in the form of her mental schema. Elizabeth's own pride is finally humbled by Darcy's generosity; in a satisfying reversal, she is proud of *him*:

> They owed the restoration of Lydia, her character, every thing to him. Oh! how heartily did she grieve over every ungracious sensation she had ever encouraged, every saucy speech she had ever directed towards him. For herself she was humbled; but she was proud of him. Proud that in a cause of compassion and honour, he had been able to get the better of himself. (326–27)

The fact that Darcy proves himself to be not only generous, but also masterful in effecting this felicitous resolution of the situation may also, I suggest, influence Elizabeth's feelings.

September, surprisingly, brings the return of Bingley to Netherfield for the hunting season—to Mrs. Bennet's delight and Jane's distress. He comes to call, bringing that "tall, proud man" whom Mrs. Bennet so detests (334). Elizabeth is mortified by her mother's rudeness to their benefactor:

> To Jane, he could be only a man whose proposals she had refused, and whose merit she had undervalued; but to her own more extensive information, he was the person, to whom the whole family were indebted for the first of benefits, and whom she regarded herself with an interest, if not quite so tender, at least as reasonable and just, as what Jane felt for Bingley. (334)

The words "reasonable and just" counter "proud and prejudiced." Elizabeth's sense of shame as her mother boasts about Lydia's marriage is such that years of happiness could not compensate her, as she sees her own prejudice burlesqued in her mother's behaviour. Darcy's determined silence inspires her despair: "A man who has once been refused! How could I ever be foolish enough to expect a renewal of his love? Is there one among the sex, who would not protest against such a weakness as a second proposal to the same woman? There is no indignity so abhorrent to their feelings!" (341). Collins would be gratified at such a vision of hubris humbled.

Jane is more fortunate: with a little help from Mrs. Bennet, Mr. Bingley renews his addresses, and an understanding is reached between this well-suited, good-natured pair—but not until the influential Darcy has confessed to Bingley his subterfuge in concealing from him Jane's presence in London the previous winter and has communicated his approval of the match.

Elizabeth despairs of achieving equal felicity. But help comes from a most unexpected quarter. Lady Catherine de Bourgh proves to be an unlikely *dea ex machina* whose insolent interference backfires: descending on Longbourn in her chaise and four with the aim of exacting Elizabeth's promise to give up all pretensions to Darcy's hand in marriage in favour of her own daughter, her ladyship underestimates her antagonist's obstinacy, and her efforts achieve the opposite of their intended effect. "Are the shades of Pemberley to be thus polluted?" (357), Lady Catherine inquires rhetorically. The answer, apparently, is "Yes, they are," for Elizabeth resolutely refuses to refuse to marry Darcy. Ironically, her ladyship's complaints of Elizabeth's obstinacy lead Darcy to dare to hope (367). He returns to Longbourn to renew his addresses, but remains steadfastly silent.

Since, as Henry Tilney explained, woman does not have the advantage of choice but only the power of refusal, Elizabeth is driven to subterfuge to bring on the renewal of Darcy's addresses. She forms "a desperate resolution" to invite a proposal by thanking him for his kindness to Lydia: "Mr. Darcy, I am a very selfish creature; and, for the sake of giving relief to my own feelings, care not how much I may be wounding your's. I can no longer help thanking you for your unexampled kindness to my poor sister" (365). He responds, "If you *will* thank me, ... let it be for yourself alone. That the wish of giving happiness to you, might add force to the other inducements which led me on, I shall not attempt to deny. But your *family* owe me nothing. Much as I respect them, I believe, I thought only of *you*" (366). He accepts her invitation: "You are too generous to trifle with me. If your feelings are still what they were last April, tell me so at once. *My* affections and wishes are unchanged, but one word from you will silence me on this subject for ever." How different is this diffident address from his previous arrogant proposal! For once, Elizabeth is inarticulate, as she "immediately, though not very fluently, gave him to understand, that her sentiments had undergone so material a change, since the period to which he alluded, as to make her receive with gratitude and pleasure, his present assurances" (366). Austen writes, "The happiness which this reply produced, was such as he had probably never felt before; and he expressed himself on the occasion as sensibly and as warmly as a man violently in love can be supposed to do ... he told her of feelings, which, in proving of what importance she was to him, made his affection every moment more valuable" (366). Austen declines to repeat Darcy's words to the avid reader. Elizabeth learns that passion is more likely to render a man speechless than eloquent. Later, when she taxes Darcy with taciturnity, he has a ready reply: "You might have talked to me more when you came to dinner," she protests, and he responds, "A man who had felt less, might" (381).

Only when they have reached an understanding can they confess their previous prejudices; Elizabeth explains "how gradually all her former prejudices had been removed" by his letter (368). Colin Firth says, "He is so profoundly challenged by her that his old prejudices cannot be upheld" (Birtwistle 105). Their competition in conceit becomes a contest in contrition, a contest Darcy clearly wins. He then confesses, "What will you think of my vanity? I believed you to be wishing, expecting my addresses." Elizabeth replies, "My manners must have been in fault, but not intentionally I assure you. I never meant to deceive you, but my spirits might often lead me wrong." (369) This exchange suggests what the reader has suspected, namely that Elizabeth, unconsciously, was attempting to attract Darcy's addresses all along, but her prejudice or schema prevented her from interpreting his attentions and her own emotions correctly. She also offers a rational account of Darcy's falling in love with her that bears out our original theory:

> The fact is, that you were sick of civility, of deference, of officious attention. You were disgusted with the women who were always speaking and looking, and thinking for your approbation alone. I roused, and interested you, because I was so unlike them. Had you not been really amiable you would have hated me for it; but in spite of the pains you took to disguise yourself, your feelings were always noble and just; and in your heart, you thoroughly despised the persons who so assiduously courted you. (380)

In *Cecilia*, Fanny Burney writes: "Yet this, however, remember; if to PRIDE and PREJUDICE you owe your miseries, so wonderfully is good and evil balanced, that to PRIDE and PREJUDICE you will also owe their termination" (930). Tony Tanner observes, "During a decade in which Napoleon was effectively engaging, if not transforming, Europe, Jane Austen composed a novel in which the most important events are the fact that a man changes his manners and a young lady changes her mind" (103). But changing her mind has always been a lady's prerogative, and, in this case, the reader approves Elizabeth's change of heart. She is such an attractive heroine that the reader wishes to see her rewarded by marital happiness. As Austen writes to her sister Cassandra in 1813, "I must confess that *I* think her as delightful a creature as ever appeared in print" (*L* 201). Generations of readers have agreed.

Austen does not let Elizabeth off the hook so easily, however. She must run the gauntlet of family and friends, as each points to her well-known prejudice, and she is forced to eat her words repeatedly. First Jane remonstrates, "Oh, Lizzy! do any thing rather than marry without affection" (373). When her father protests, "Lizzy ... what are you doing? Are you out of your senses, to be accepting this man? Have not you always hated him?" (376), Austen comments, "How earnestly did she then wish that her former opinions had been more reasonable, her expressions more moderate!" (376). When he says, "We all know him to be a proud, unpleasant sort of man; but this would be nothing if you really liked him," she replies, with tears in her eyes, "I do, I do like him. ... I love him. Indeed he has no improper pride. He is perfectly amiable" (376). But the worst is to come: Mrs. Bennet's former fulminations against Darcy are nothing to her effusions once he has been accepted. Loquacity is a sure sign of foolishness in Austen's books. Mrs. Bennet's raptures, sprinkled with exclamation marks like a teenage girl's letter, are a comic inversion of her previous prejudices as she gushes:

> Good gracious! Lord bless me! only think! dear me! Mr. Darcy! Who would have thought it! And is it really true? Oh! my sweetest Lizzy! how rich and how great you will be! What pin-money, what jewels, what carriages you will have! Jane's is nothing to it—nothing at all. I am so pleased—so happy. Such a charming man!—so handsome! so tall!—Oh, my dear Lizzy! pray apologise for my having disliked him so much before. I hope he will overlook it. Dear, dear Lizzy. A house in town! Every thing that is charming! Three daughters married! Ten thousand a year! Oh, Lord! What will become of me. I shall go distracted. (378)

Just as Lady Catherine is a parody of Darcy, so Mrs. Bennet is a caricature of Elizabeth, and, just as Lady Catherine absorbs all Darcy's conceit, freeing him to be courteous, so Mrs. Bennet absorbs all Elizabeth's folly, freeing her to be rational, so that the couple can live happily ever after. As Elizabeth assures Jane, "It is settled between us already, that we are to be the happiest couple in the world" (373). One suspects that their union will be more interesting than Jane and Bingley's, however, for, although Darcy has no improper pride, he "had yet to learn to be laught at" (371). Elizabeth, however, *has* learned to avoid uttering famous last words.

Elizabeth Bennet is not the only Austen protagonist who protests too much, however. Emma Woodhouse insists to Harriet Smith, "I am not only, not going to be married, at present, but have very little intention of ever marrying at all" (*E* 84). Not until Harriet herself sets her cap at Mr. Knightley does Emma realize that "Mr. Knightley must marry no one but herself!" (408). But that is another story—and another essay.

NOTES

1 Farrer, for example, thinks that Elizabeth is "subconsciously ... in love with" Darcy from the outset (17).

2 Juliet McMaster, in "Talking about Talk in *Pride and Prejudice*," states that skill in language "marks Darcy out from the beginning as a man of intelligence, and a fit mate for Elizabeth" (82).

3 Reuben Brower foresees the conclusion in this beginning: "As all ambiguities are resolved and all irony is dropped, the reader feels the closing in of a structure by its necessary end, the end implied in the crude judgment of Darcy in the first ballroom scene" (179).

4 I wish to thank my students for many opportunities to discuss *Pride and Prejudice*. I also wish to thank my husband, Bruce Stovel, for discussing the novel with me over the years.

5 David Miall writes, "Within psychology, the analysis of narrative has been directed by an information processing approach, in particular by different versions of schema theory" (55).

6 See the Introductory Note in R.W. Chapman's edition of the novel (xi).

7 For a fuller discussion of this subject, see my essay, "'Every Savage Can Dance': Choreographing Courtship in the Novels of Jane Austen."

8 Interestingly, the anonymous reviewer of the novel in the *Critical Review* for March 1813 writes of Elizabeth, "She is in fact the *Beatrice* of the tale; and falls in love on much the same principles of contrariety" (Southam 13). For more on this, see Bruce Stovel, "'A Contrariety of Emotion': Jane Austen's Ambivalent Lovers in *Pride and Prejudice*."

9 This idea is developed in Gary Kelly's essay "The Art of Reading in *Pride and Prejudice*."

Speculations
and Possibilities

13

Words Not Spoken

Courtship and Seduction in Jane Austen's Novels

WHEN SHE WISHED, Jane Austen had few equals in the language of love. Listen to Mr. Darcy speak to Elizabeth: "In vain have I struggled. It will not do. My feelings will not be repressed. You must allow me to tell you how ardently I admire and love you" (*PP* 189). And when finally Elizabeth accepts him, he calls her "dearest, loveliest Elizabeth" (369). Here is Mr. Knightley addressing Emma in the language of love: "My dearest Emma, ... for dearest you will always be" (*E* 430).

It is interesting that Jane Austen so seldom exercised this particular gift. It is possible, I venture to suggest, that Mr. Darcy and Mr. Knightley are her favourite male protagonists (as they are for many of us) and that it gave her pleasure to put these words into their mouths. Perhaps they are words she herself would have liked to hear.

But as for the rest, Jane Austen is not always so explicit. In *Sense and Sensibility* Colonel Brandon "opened his whole heart," in the first place, to his Marianne's mama, but we don't hear him (336); Edward Ferrars is offstage, and so "in what manner he expressed himself [to Elinor], and how he was received, need not be particularly told" (*SS* 361), though we do have long speeches explaining Edward's entanglement with Lucy and his brother Robert's behaviour. We are not in the room when Bingley proposes to Jane. Edmund Bertram's proposal to Fanny Price is not laid out for us either. Henry Tilney spends his time with Catherine Morland relating the gross misconceptions of his greedy father, then they return home engaged (*NA* 243–48). Captain Wentworth writes his declaration (though here we do have appropriately fervent tones), and so does Robert Martin, first time around.

Two proposals she does give us in full are those of Mr. Collins to the fast-retreating Elizabeth Bennet and Mr. Elton to the outraged Emma. Both moments are comical, and both men are rejected. Mr. Elton is far away in Bristol when he proposes to Miss Hawkins only a few weeks later. Since most of the successful suitors' actual words are left to our imaginations, it is not surprising if we are tempted to supply them, and now, I must confess, I give way to that temptation. Here is the Reverend Philip Elton in his second attempt. He is to be imagined speaking with "a sort of sighing animation, which had a vast deal of the lover" (*E* 43):

> "Miss Hawkins—Madam—not that it can compare for a moment with Maple Grove—the Sucklings, the Braggs!—so liberal, so elegant—yet the home I offer has its advantages. Indeed, yes. I have renovated, Madam. I have improved. And I have an independent income. Indeed, you can be sure of everything in the greatest comfort. The neighborhood is one that—Our society is such that—
>
> [He seizes her hand.] "Madam, everything that I say and do—despite the shortness of our acquaintance—is with the sole view of marking my adoration of yourself. I am sure you have seen and understood my ardent attachment. I have not a doubt of your happiness if you would consider—only consider—pray do consider—the advantages of joining your life to mine. In short, granting me your hand in marriage? Let me entreat you, dear Miss Hawkins—It would be a delight—I should be the happiest of men. I hope—I fear—Miss Hawkins, be mine!

"Exactly so," said he happily, a moment later, with a tender sigh.

On most occasions Jane Austen sheers away from the actual declaration of love, and we are left to imagine, for example, what Edmund has to say to Fanny when he finally learns to prefer "soft light eyes to sparkling dark ones" (*MP* 470) and comes to wonder "whether it might not be a possible, an hopeful undertaking to persuade her that her warm and sisterly regard for him would be foundation enough for wedded love" (470). Once again we can invent our own version, and here is mine:

> Fanny, dear little Fanny, so long my friend and sweetest confidante, I have come to depend on your fondness for me—as a brother, a brother indeed. But we are older now, you and I, and sad experience has taught us much. This may be a shock to you, dear Fanny, but my heart has come to acknowledge it cannot do without your affection, your sweet company. That you are too good for me, I accept, yet I dare to hope I may with time deserve you. If ... oh my sweet Fanny ... *if* perhaps you can bring yourself to consider me in another light? No longer as a brother, but as a husband? Take time, if you choose, for consideration. I should not wish to disturb your delicate sensibilities for the world. But, if you can, give me just one word, Fanny, one word to encourage me, one word to ensure my happiness? Pray, do not faint!

I do not think she would keep him waiting long for that one word. But we do not hear it. And I will not supply her response. Jane Austen sets us straight: "Let no one presume to give the feelings of a young woman on receiving the assurance of that affection of which she has scarcely allowed herself to entertain a hope" (471).

If there is one thing evident, it is that Jane Austen's characters talk. Character and conversation intertwine in her novels. How could one describe Lady Catherine or Miss Bates as vividly as they describe themselves with every spoken word? Mr. Collins, Mrs. Bennet, Mr. Bennet, Mary Musgrove, Mrs. Elton, Mrs. Palmer (the list goes on): all come alive through their conversation. Whether a character is major or minor, the speech is fitted to the speaker. It is all the more surprising, therefore, that there are certain things we don't hear. There is in her novels little explicit courtship and still less explicit seduction.

Yet all the books deal with affairs of the heart. It is the main prop of the plot: who will marry whom? All end with weddings. And five of the books have a successful seducer: George Wickham in *Pride and Prejudice;* John Willoughby in *Sense and Sensibility;* Frank Churchill in *Emma* (his seduction is not physical, but he wins Jane Fairfax against the dictates of her conscience); William Walter Elliot in *Persuasion;* Henry Crawford in *Mansfield Park.* Even *Northanger Abbey* has a candidate for the seduction stakes, Captain Tilney, though perhaps it might be said of him, less severely, that he "toys with" a lady's affections. (I do not include Sir Edward Denham of *Sanditon,* that would-be seducer, in my survey. I cannot believe he would ever succeed in his "purpose all sublime.")

My point is that we seldom see, or hear, the seducers at their serious work. Why is this? Let us explore Jane Austen's omission. The underlying reason is, of course, that most of the actual incidents of seduction or attempted seduction take place offstage or in the past. They are background material, necessary to fill out characterizations and to provide motives for the happenings in the present, but they are not part of the main story-line.

They are an interesting and varied lot, these dubious gentlemen. Mr. Wickham is an excellent place to start. George Wickham is the son of the steward at Pemberley. His father was a diligent and well-respected man, held in high esteem by Mr. Darcy, Senior (81, 199). Although George is known by young Mr. Darcy as a dissolute, untrustworthy fellow, old Mr. Darcy, his godfather, retains an affection for him, hopes he will enter the Church, and leaves him a church living. George, it seems, has the ability to find favour with men as well as women—some men, at least. When we meet him in the company of Captain Denny, an officer of the ——shire Militia, he is introduced as someone the officers are anxious to have join them. They seem ready to find him a very fine fellow and, indeed, we are told that Wickham "wanted only regimentals to make him completely charming" (*PP* 72). He has "all the best part of beauty, a fine countenance, a good figure, and very pleasing address" (72). Elizabeth Bennet finds him someone "whose very countenance may vouch for [his] being amiable" (80–81).

If Elizabeth is well on the way to being caught in Wickham's web, how much more was Georgiana Darcy in danger? Georgiana was but fifteen, an orphan, not yet "out," quite unsophisticated. Moreover, we are told she is shy. To have a young man of George Wickham's poise and attractiveness— a young man she already knows, has been on casual childhood terms with— making his admiration obvious, seeking her out, turning on the charm, must have been intoxicating for the young, developing, lonely girl. We do not know that Georgiana has any friends of her own age at hand. She does not go to school; instead, she has a companion, Mrs. Younge, who is an admirer, if not an accomplice, of Wickham. Mrs. Younge can't have been bribed by him, since he has no money. Was he once her lover? Perhaps he offers her a share of the profits? Mrs. Younge encourages her charge in her interest in George. (To digress, I wonder how Mrs. Younge came to be employed. Did she have references?)

In any case, Mr. Wickham "so far recommended himself to Georgiana that," as her brother expresses it in his letter to Elizabeth, "she was persuaded to believe herself in love, and to consent to an elopement" (202). Wickham was aided in his efforts, of course, by the strong impression Georgiana retained of his kindness to her as a child. His sophistication, his appearance (even without regimentals), must certainly have influenced her at fifteen. But this is all we are told. There is no dialogue. What might have been said by Wickham to Georgiana? Perhaps ...

How delightful to find you alone, Miss Darcy. Dear Miss Darcy— Georgiana—Georgie—forgive my informality. I call you that in recognition of our childhood friendship, which lingers long in my memory, as I hope it does in yours. Ah, do you remember those days running free at Pemberley? The day you escaped your governess and fell in the lake—how glad I was that I was at hand to rescue you. Well, yes, your water spaniel did reach you first. But I do remember your petticoat was deeply splashed with water. It was trimmed with lace— Oh, do not draw back. Mrs. Younge is close at hand. You have no cause for alarm.

Oh, Georgiana, beautiful Georgiana, finding you here alone, temptation goes beyond my strength, my feelings are strong, and your blushes arouse me to hope that you regard me with something more than friendship?

Nay, my ardor makes me too impetuous. I ask too much of you. I move too fast. Pray, do not go. And do not speak. Let me gaze into your eyes and hope, for a moment longer! Dearest Georgiana! ...

Georgiana is, as I have said, but fifteen. Later Wickham makes strong inroads into the affections of the intelligent, amused Elizabeth Bennet, aged twenty. Address and appearance are used to good effect here. But the actual conversation between Wickham and Elizabeth that we are given, and at some length, deals mainly with the history of his complaints against Darcy (77–84). Surely Jane Austen has a double purpose here? Elizabeth is keenly interested in Wickham's discourse, and we can only wonder if she would be as interested if the villain of the piece were a stranger, or if she were not already aware of the very male Mr. Darcy's arrogant and intrusive personality. We hear Elizabeth declare to her aunt that she is *not* in love with Wickham and considering the possibility of what might happen if he became "really attached" to her (144), but we do not hear Mr. Wickham talking his way into her affections. Indeed, Wickham has no dialogue for several chapters.

Elizabeth Bennet, no fool and with a keen eye for the foibles of others, is almost completely taken in. Certainly Wickham openly admires her, and she enjoys that, just as she is provoked by Mr. Darcy's early dismissal of her attractions ("tolerable" [12], indeed). Mrs. Gardiner, visiting her favourite niece at Longbourn, is somewhat dismayed at Elizabeth's preference for Wickham, not because she sees through him (she does not), but because she knows him to have no resources. Mrs. Gardiner notes that "their preference of each other was plain enough to make her a little uneasy" (142). Indeed, Elizabeth admits to her aunt that Mr. Wickham "is, beyond all comparison, the most agreeable man I ever saw" (144).

But always, from the moment of his first introduction, Jane Austen has Wickham intertwined with Darcy. Here is the art of the novelist. Wickham does the speaking; he complains of Darcy's behaviour, he does his best to turn Elizabeth against Darcy, but in so doing he keeps Darcy before her eyes—"She could think of nothing but of Mr. Wickham, *and of what he had told her*, all the way home" (84; emphasis added).

In the end, of course, Wickham elopes with Lydia Bennet, whom he doubtless seduced by raising one eyebrow or lifting a finger (a wink and a nudge would probably have sufficed). Certainly, very few words would have been needed ("How about a bolt to the Village?"), or even a casual mention of the fact that he was taking off because of the pressure of his debts, followed by Lydia pouting and asking him not to go ("How can you leave me?") and Wickham replying, "Then come with me, baby doll. If you're good, I might even marry you. Gretna Green is charming in the spring. But don't nag."

I can hear Lydia giggle. But we do not hear *him*. The action takes place offstage, and these unheard words might be termed "noises off."

In *Sense and Sensibility,* we meet Willoughby when he rescues Marianne Dashwood from her damp hillside. Willoughby is the supposed heir of Mrs. Smith, an elderly lady living at Allenham Court. He has a small estate of his own but constantly outspends his income. He is described as "a young man of good abilities, quick imagination, lively spirits, and open, affectionate manners" (*ss* 48). Nothing there to alarm us; in fact, he seems quite admirable. But appearances are deceptive. Willoughby is a believer in instant gratification. He must have amusement, and what better amusement than an inexperienced and charming young lady? Again, here is a practised seducer. He had already persuaded Colonel Brandon's ward into an elopement and deserted her when she was pregnant. She, like Georgiana Darcy, is an orphan. She was fifteen when Willoughby met her (208) and a schoolgirl away from home. We don't meet her, but it is possible to imagine her a pretty, unformed girl, a little plump, perhaps, artless, eager for affection, carelessly chaperoned, without close relations, and with tenuous ties to home and guardian—and not, therefore, hard to flatter and coax. She easily succumbs. When Willoughby unburdens his soul to Elinor Dashwood, he does his best to share the blame for his affair with its object. He speaks of "the violence of her passions, the weakness of her understanding" (322). Yet obviously *he* approached *her*. He does not mention the child. When we compare the relative harm done—a girl of fifteen or sixteen left pregnant and alone, penniless, "ruined" forever, while Willoughby goes gaily on his way, romancing Marianne—it is hard indeed to forgive him.

Colonel Brandon, though conscientious and affectionate, is after all an army officer—even with the purchase of commissions, a man did not easily become a colonel—and must have been away from home a good part of his adult life and therefore not in touch with his ward. Indeed, we do hear that he was with his regiment in the East Indies when the cousin he loved was married to his brother (206). (We hear more from Jane Austen about sailors leaving for their ships than soldiers marching off to fight. But it was probably on the battlefield that Colonel Brandon developed rheumatism.) It is surprising that Marianne never considers him as a soldier, a man of action. And odd that in his duel with Willoughby, no one was hurt.

But back to seduction. With Marianne Dashwood, Willoughby has an instant effect since he rescues her after she sprains her ankle and carries her home. Prolonged physical contact with a handsome, stalwart young man in this way cannot but have a lasting effect on the well-brought-up, wholly untouched female of the times (and perhaps also on the less well-brought-up, not wholly untouched female of today). As well as an attractive person, Willoughby has social ease. He is already well known to Sir John Middleton, who says, "he is a pleasant, good humoured fellow, and has got the nicest little black bitch of a pointer I ever saw" (44). We know he is polite to Marianne's relatives, pays court to her, discusses favourite books and sings duets with her, shares her love of dancing into the small hours, takes her on carriage rides, devotes himself to her at parties. But what does he say to her that is personal? We hear very little (we are told he whispers [60]). Let us extrapolate a little. Willoughby might have said,

Marianne—my Juliet, my Isolde—what care we for convention? Let the faint of heart, the Colonel Brandons of this world, play by the rules. You and I shall brave disapprobation together. We are young, we believe in love. We need no formal ties, no binding vows. Trust is all. Give your heart into my keeping, my Marianne, as mine is yours. This will be our secret, our delicious secret. Take my hand...

Marianne makes a virtue of extreme emotion, of romantic imaginings, of recklessness. She is ready to "lose all for love" and count it a virtue. It is not hard to believe, despite her superiority of mind, that if their uncontrolled companionship had continued, Willoughby would have found her as easy a conquest, in the physical sense, as Colonel Brandon's ward.

In *Emma* we encounter Frank Churchill, by birth the son of Mr. Weston but the adopted son of the wealthy Churchills. He flirts with Emma, to her pleasure, seeks her out, dances with her, sings duets with her, is particular in his attention. It is no wonder she enjoys it. For all her local importance and decided *self*-importance, Emma does not have a very lively social life, and we know of no other young men whom she might consider her social equals who have been attentive in this way. It is all a matter of lighthearted jocularity, a meeting of eyes, an air of paying special attention. But all the time Frank is engaged to Jane Fairfax, whom he has seduced into an engagement through meetings, mainly in public, over a fairly short space of time: the duration of a seaside holiday. Presumably he behaved to Jane as he behaves to Emma, only more so.

We believe Frank Churchill handsome; he seems to have universal approbation (except from Mr. Knightley); he is used to the best and is decidedly self-assured. He must therefore have considerable address. But we do not hear him in loving conversation with Miss Fairfax. We hear him tease her by requesting her to play a waltz they both remember:

> "What felicity it is to hear a tune again which *has* made one happy! If I mistake not, that was danced at Weymouth."
>
> She looked up at him for a moment, coloured deeply, and played something else. (*E* 242)

This is not kind. And we hear him speak *of* her to Emma. He teasingly criticizes her complexion and her hair-style. But when we actually hear them exchange remarks, Jane is deeply hurt, dignified, and reproachful (372–73). He, on the other hand, though obviously keenly aware of everything she does and says, says little directly to her that is reported to us.

Towards the end of the book, in speaking to Emma, he does wax eloquent in regard to his admiration for Jane:

> She is a complete angel. Look at her. Is not she an angel in every gesture? Observe the turn of her throat. Observe her eyes, as she is looking up at my father.—You will be glad to hear ... that my uncle means to give her all my aunt's jewels. They are to be new set. I am

resolved to have some in an ornament for the head. Will not it be beautiful in her dark hair? (479)

But some time earlier, at Weymouth, he must have expressed his admiration for her beauty, her singing, her elegance of form. He captures her against the full force of her upbringing: a young lady should never consent to a secret alliance. And Jane has most upright principles. But seduced she is. These are his words to Jane, as I imagine them:

> Jane, if I may call you by that sweet name, believe me when I say you have my entire devotion. I give my heart into your keeping. Consent to marry me, and make me the happiest man of your acquaintance. Look at me, Jane. Believe in me.
>
> I must, I fear I must, ask you to wait. At the moment I am in no position to marry. My aunt, with her whims, her indisposition ... But if you will only consent to an engagement, secret but heartfelt, utterly binding! Jane, my beautiful Jane, be mine. Do not shake your head. Do you not love me a little? Your eyes persuade me that you do. Just trust me.
>
> Oh, Miss X approaches. Give me your hand, and let us escape into the dance once more. Jane, oh my dearest Jane ...

Etcetera, etcetera. It is interesting, in a time of formal manners, how potent the use of a lady's Christian name can become. We will return to this subject.

In *Persuasion* we meet the sophisticated William Walter Elliot. He is a widower and, one presumes, needed certain seductive powers to obtain his first, low-born but very wealthy, wife. She must have had protectors. Now, at one and the same time, he defers to Elizabeth Elliot, who takes it for granted that she holds his interest, and pays elegant court to Anne Elliot and, presumably, somewhat more earthy attention to Penelope Clay.

We do indeed hear him talking to Anne with suavity and charm (treating her as an attractive, intelligent woman of accomplishment, an approach pleasing in its originality and certainly a pleasant change for Anne) in a way that engages her attention and *might*, under different circumstances, have won her regard. He pays court to Anne by recognizing her intellect (when he talks to her of good company [*P* 150]), admiring her abilities (her knowledge of Italian, for instance [186]), and appealing to her fears for her father (151). He is a clever man.

But what does he say to Penelope? How did he begin? With arch looks and flirtatious remarks, at the same time he is telling Anne that Penelope is a danger to Sir Walter? It seems unlikely. Everyone is surprised when they elope together. Any exchanges in public must have *seemed,* at least, matter-of-fact. Perhaps he offered her admiration and appreciation when she is used to being taken for granted? In her position, she would be expected to *pay* compliments. To receive them would be a delightful change. For instance, "My dear Mrs. Clay, how infinitely patient you are. How tactful in your deference to my uncle and my cousin. They are fortunate indeed to have such a companion." And then, a few days later, with lowered voice, after perhaps some particularly tiresome exchange:

> I repeat, my uncle and cousin are fortunate to have your services. But I ask myself, how can you, with your lively mind and many social talents, confine yourself to the limited conversation of my demanding cousin (whose haughty looks, dare I say it, cannot compare with your own animated response) and my uncle? This should not be.

His manner would be such as not to arouse attention, but she must have been made aware. His eyes perhaps added footnotes to his speech. Later still, he might have ventured the personal:

> How your hair gleams in the candlelight. [Then, with planned impulsiveness:] You should live in London, the London of wit and cajolery, pleasure and pleasantry, in the company of those who can appreciate the full range of your abilities—your charms. I should enjoy undertaking to introduce you to the theatres, the salons, the ...

And when he began to despair of Anne, his importunities would increase. He meets her outside the house. The boredom he endured at the hands of Sir Walter and Miss Elliot must have threatened to overwhelm him with the removal of Anne. Penelope Clay must have been a relief after the self-importance and limited intelligence of Elizabeth Elliot. He does not have to watch his every word with her. He begins to long for a return to his London haunts and is not averse to taking an entertaining companion with him, especially when doing so would remove that companion from dangerously close contact with Sir Walter. Would he have bothered without this proviso? I believe not. William Elliot was not impulsive. He was a planner. But it does seem clear he enjoyed her company. And so he might have said:

> Mrs. Clay, a word with you. The time has come when I must think of my departure. I have affairs to attend to in London. Oh, do not sigh. It is not my wish to abandon you to the conceits and boredom of my uncle's house. ... [whispering:] Colonel Wallis draws near. Let us move to the window. [more loudly:] See, a remarkably handsome carriage is approaching. I wonder whose is the crest upon the door?
>
> [softly:] He has gone. [in normal tones:] Come, take a glass of Madeira with me before the others return and let me tell you again of my London house, oh, not to be compared with Kellynch (though that too, one day may be mine), but the neighborhood is good and the amenities of the best. Imagine yourself installed in such a house, mistress of such a house, dressed in the height of fashion, hostess to my friends? You will find them amusing, men and women of the world. Such relationships are understood. And I am rich. I can promise you a full life. ...
>
> [He looks deep into her eyes.] Over the past weeks we have been much thrown in each other's way. We deal well together, you and I. We understand each other.
>
> I speak with some detachment—dear Mrs. Clay—we have little time to ourselves, I must hurry over what I have to say—but can you not read what I leave unsaid? My appreciation? My admiration? You engage me, Penelope. Come with me to London. Trust me. Trust me. [His voice sinks.] Let me introduce you to the ... pleasures ... of city life. I promise you, you will not repine...

Mrs. Clay has hopes of becoming Sir Walter's wife; she has invested both time and trouble in him (one might term her a *female* would-be seducer).

Also, she has children to provide for. To take the huge step of leaving the Elliot household (it would be the end of her respectability; there would be no return), she must either have been very, very sure of what Mr. Elliot had to offer or persuaded into love—in other words, seduced. He must have been good at his job.

Lastly, we have Henry Crawford, and here is the exception that proves the rule, a vocal seducer—Henry is articulate in the extreme. We hear the reasons behind his attempted seduction, and we hear him in action. Crawford is a wealthy young man with his own estate who has been raised, with his sister, by a dissolute Admiral Crawford (does *he* ever go to sea? we don't know), who keeps a mistress and imports her into his home after his wife's death—not a good role model. Henry is clever, talented, conceited, and self-indulgent. Like Willoughby (and unlike the more complicated, calculating William Elliot), he likes to take his pleasure where he finds it and believes in instant gratification. But with Henry Crawford we have a very interesting twist. He sets out to seduce Fanny Price into loving him, out of vanity and idle amusement, and gets caught in his own trap. He falls in love with her, and he has the words to tell her how he feels.

Most of our seducers are surprisingly successful. Georgiana Darcy was quite willing to elope with George Wickham and was only stopped by her brother's sudden appearance. Later, Wickham has no trouble with Lydia Bennet. Willoughby seduces Colonel Brandon's ward, and would, I believe, have seduced Marianne if he had wished to continue—if, in fact, she had been rich. Frank Churchill has become engaged to Jane Fairfax after a short acquaintance, and, despite his reprehensible conduct, she is quickly reconciled with him after his aunt's death. William Elliot successfully removes Penelope Clay from Bath.

Henry Crawford, on the other hand, despite his undoubted abilities and the charm which works on others, is remarkably unsuccessful with Fanny Price. Like William Elliot, Henry Crawford undertakes three flirtations in quick succession: with Julia Bertram (mainly because she is considered his share of the ladies at Mansfield Park); with Maria Bertram, who is already engaged to Mr. Rushworth and is therefore a challenge (though in fact Maria is an eager participant); and lastly, in a total change of attack, with Fanny Price. He drops Julia when he has to choose whether she or her sister should play the part of Agatha opposite his Frederick in the Mansfield Park production of *Lovers' Vows*. And his courtship of Maria is, we understand, couched in the language of the play. It seems odd to modern eyes that they choose to act mother and son, but then there are, it seems, more opportunities for embraces that way.

After Sir Thomas's return from abroad and the *Lovers' Vows* debacle, followed by Maria's marriage to Mr. Rushworth and her removal, with Julia, to Brighton, Henry Crawford comes back to Mansfield and finds the only remaining young female is Fanny, now promoted to the role of companion for Mary Crawford. What is a man to do? Henry explains to his sister Mary his design on Fanny. He will exercise physically by walking and riding with Mary, but "*that* would be exercise only to my body, and I must take care of my mind" (*MP* 229). He says with a smile, "And how do you think I mean to amuse myself, Mary, on the days that I do not hunt? ... my plan is to make Fanny Price in love with me" (229).

No sooner said than done. But Fanny has double protection. She has long been in love with her cousin Edmund, and not only does she dislike Mr. Crawford from their previous acquaintance, but, as well, the moment she is back in his company she is confirmed in her aversion. Mr. Crawford talks with regret of the aborted playacting. "It is as a dream, a pleasant dream!", he exclaims. "I shall always look back on our theatricals with exquisite pleasure. ... I was never happier" (225).

> With silent indignation, Fanny repeated to herself, "Never happier!—never happier than when doing what you must know was not justifiable!—never happier than when behaving so dishonorably and unfeelingly!—Oh! what a corrupted mind!" (225)

And from that moment we, the readers, know what Henry Crawford is up against when he turns his attentions to Fanny. *He* has no idea. He is an accomplished flirt, and his recent triumph in making both Julia and Maria fall in love with him is fresh in his mind. He cannot believe that the quiet Miss Price, lacking social confidence and, for that matter, suitors, will be hard to conquer. He justifies his design to Mary by describing Fanny's charms:

You do not seem properly aware of her claims to notice. ... she is now absolutely pretty. I used to think she had neither complexion nor countenance; but in that soft skin of her's, so frequently tinged with a blush as it was yesterday, there is decided beauty; and from what I observed of her eyes and mouth, I do not despair of their being capable of expression enough when she has anything to express. (229–30)

Henry continues and tells us more of his motives:

I never was so long in company with a girl in my life—trying to entertain her—and succeed so ill! Never met with a girl who looked so grave on me! I must try to get the better of this. Her looks say, "I will not like you, I am determined not to like you," and I say, she shall. (230)

Mary objects, half-heartedly, to the idea of Henry making Fanny really unhappy, and he says:

It can be but for a fortnight, ... and if a fortnight can kill her, she must have a constitution which nothing could save. No, I will not do her any harm, dear little soul! I only want her to look kindly on me, to give me smiles as well as blushes, to keep a chair for me by herself wherever we are, and be all animation when I take it and talk to her; to think as I think, be interested in all my possessions and pleasures, try to keep me longer at Mansfield, and feel when I go away that she shall be never happy again. I want nothing more. (231)

How do these motives compare with those of our other seducers? Mr. Wickham determines to seduce Georgiana Darcy for money and for revenge; he takes Lydia Bennet with him as he might have taken a novel—for amusement on the journey. Willoughby seduces Colonel Brandon's ward for casual amusement and physical pleasure; Frank Churchill actually falls in love with Jane Fairfax—his problem is that he is not in a position to marry her (her seduction is against her conscience); William Walter Elliot removes

Penelope Clay from Sir Walter's vicinity "for his own interest and his own enjoyment" (*P* 250).

Henry Crawford is in it for the sport. He reminds me of Mr. Lovelace and other young men in Samuel Richardson's *Clarissa*, whose avowed aim, whose fashionable game, is seduction. But Henry is caught in his own trap. He sets out to ingratiate himself with Fanny, but she does not respond. And the less she responds, the more eager he becomes.

When Henry proposes to Fanny, the account is given us in the third person, and is interposed with Fanny's reactions—lack of understanding, disbelief, distress. We do, eventually, hear her actual words: "'No, no, no,'" she cried, hiding her face. 'This is all nonsense. Do not distress me. I can hear no more of this'" (300). Fanny feels sure Henry is behaving to her as he behaved to her cousins, and with as little sincerity. To quote from Shakespeare's *Henry V*, in the wonderful scene where that other, royal Henry avows his love for the French princess, Catherine, whom he has just met for the very first time:

> KING HARRY: An angel is like you, Kate, and you are like an angel. ...
> CATHERINE: *O bon Dieu! Les langues des hommes sont pleines de trumperies.*
> KING HARRY: What says she, fair one? That the tongues of men are full of deceits?
> ALICE: *Oui*, dat de tongues of de mans is be full of deceits. (V.ii.109–20)

Deceits, indeed. But, interestingly enough, we then hear Henry Crawford speak to Fanny with considerable charm:

> Yes, dearest, sweetest Fanny—Nay—(seeing her draw back displeased) forgive me. Perhaps I have as yet no right—but by what other name can I call you? Do you suppose you are ever present to my imagination under any other? No, it is "Fanny" that I think of all day, and dream of all night.—You have given the name such reality of sweetness, that nothing else can now be descriptive of you. (344)

Note the importance of the Christian name! These are not words of seduction—these are words of love! His speech is quite delightful. Why, I wonder, does Jane Austen pull out all the stops for Henry Crawford, when she knows he will not succeed? Why did she not bestow the speech on that eloquent speaker, Henry Tilney (but just how much does he love Catherine?)? Better still, why not Mr. Darcy, he of the fervent love, the correct manners, and the fatal honesty? Let's switch it over, just for the fun of it. Here's Mr. Darcy speaking to Elizabeth:

> Yes, dearest, loveliest Elizabeth—Nay—forgive me. Perhaps I have as yet no right—but by what other name can I call you? Do you suppose you are ever present to my imagination under any other? No, it is "Elizabeth" that I think of all day, and dream of all night.—You have given the name such reality of sweetness, that nothing else can now be descriptive of you.

Yes, indeed.

But to return to Mr. Crawford. The response to this winning speech is not what Henry would have hoped: "Fanny could hardly have kept her seat any longer, or have refrained from at least trying to get away ..." (344). Henry makes inroads when he is instrumental in effecting William Price's promotion; when he reads from Shakespeare with great dramatic ability; and when he meets Fanny in Portsmouth and deals with her distressing family with tact and good manners. She is ready to turn to him then. Jane Austen herself tells us that if Edmund had married Mary Crawford, Fanny would "within a reasonable period" have accepted Henry (467). But he is inveigled into eloping with Maria Rushworth, and all is at an end.

So, as I finish dealing with Fanny Price and Henry Crawford, I can only venture into fantasy. If—and it is a very big "if" indeed—if, even after the Maria Rushworth debacle, Mary had become engaged to Edmund, is there anything Henry could have said to Fanny that would have won her over? Imagine the conversation:

"Miss Price. I stand before you with such remorse in my heart, such sorrow for my behaviour. I can only bow my head and beg your forgiveness."

"Sir, I suggest you save your apologies for my cousin."

"Your cousin wants no more of me. My behaviour—and hers—has been the ruin of all my happiness with you. And without you my life can never be complete. Will nothing promote your forgiveness? Does not true repentance carry weight in your mind? Can I not, in time, given time, persuade you to accept me once more as your suitor? Oh, Fanny, sweet Fanny, send me away if you must. I will work on my estate. I will prove myself worthy. But give me some hope. Send me away—but allow me to return."

But no. It cannot be.

The language of Jane Austen is so delicious, so provocative, full as it is of constant surprises, variety, and wit, that it seems picky to base a paper on what she does *not* say. Why did I do it? Pure greed! I want more—the full courtship every time; all the language of love and seduction. We do not hear it. Shall we suppose it is not her favourite subject?

To conclude, we have, in *Mansfield Park*, one last seduction—and a successful one, though the female partner seems to have been the instigator and may have done all the talking. Julia Bertram is so dismayed at the thought of her father's reaction to Maria's behaviour that she elopes with Mr. Yates rather than return home. We hear nothing of the words that pass between them.

STEVEN D. SCOTT

14

Making Room
in the Middle

Mary in Pride and Prejudice

MARY IS A STRANGE, rather puzzling character. She is the middle sister
of five; one might think that in a novel by an author who is famous for her
preference for balance and moderation (even in her titles: *Sense and Sensibility,
Pride and Prejudice, Persuasion*), Mary would occupy a favoured middle ground.
She is a great reader in a family where reading was "always encouraged"
(165); she prefers books and study to almost anything else and has a father
who spends almost all of his time in a library. In addition, Mary is one of
only two of the sisters who can be considered "accomplished" in any way
(Elizabeth is the other, though we are told that she plays only "half so well"
[25] as Mary does). But while Mary might seem at first to be a prime place to
look for a heroine, Austen ignores her almost completely. The most striking
example of Mary's absence occurs during Charlotte's announcement of her
engagement to Mr. Collins. As you will recall, Charlotte makes her momen-

tous declaration to Elizabeth alone; then Sir William tells the rest of the Bennet family. We get a catalogue of the feelings of the members of the Bennet family, one after the other: Elizabeth immediately declares, "Engaged to Mr. Collins! my dear Charlotte,—impossible" (124); "Mrs. Bennet, with more perseverance than politeness, protested [Sir William] must be entirely mistaken" (126); Lydia exclaims, "Good Lord! Sir William, how can you tell such a story?" (126); "Mr. Bennet's emotions were much more tranquil on the occasion, and such as he did experience he pronounced to be of a most agreeable sort; for it gratified him, he said, to discover that Charlotte Lucas, whom he had been used to think tolerably sensible, was as foolish as his wife, and more foolish than his daughter!" (127); "Jane confessed herself a little surprised at the match" (127); "Kitty and Lydia were far from envying Miss Lucas, for Mr. Collins was only a clergyman; and it affected them in no other way than as a piece of news to spread at Meryton" (127). Notably absent from this catalogue of the reactions of the Bennet family is Mary's response, though a couple of pages earlier (124), there is some speculation that Mary herself might have been persuaded to accept a proposal of marriage from Mr. Collins.

One explanation for this treatment of Mary is that she is offered as a caricature rather than as a true character. Mary, in this view, is present in the novel merely for comic relief. But this is not a very satisfactory explanation. It would single her out as having a role that is very different from any of her sisters; in fact, it would single her out as having a role that is unique in the novel. Even Mr. Collins, who is there clearly to provide comic relief, also serves some very important purposes in plot development and illustration. Mary as a caricature is also too cruel a proposition. One does not usually get the emotional reactions of a caricature, and Mary is, the novel tells us near its end, "no longer mortified by comparisons between her sisters' beauty and her own" (386) once her sisters have all left home. Perhaps one of the reasons that I don't like the presentation of Mary in the film adaptations of the novel is that the films make a caricature out of her.

I argue that Mary does occupy a privileged space in the novel. Much of the time Mary speaks and acts like a writer, in fact. Mary is the closest we come in this novel to having a character who stands in for Austen herself.

She is a reader (of books and people), an observer, a surprisingly compassionate person who detects potential in the most unlikely places, refusing to condemn Mr. Collins outright, for instance, and staying at home with her mother at the novel's end. She is a young woman who is "plain" in a world that values only beauty; a young woman who pursues "accomplishments," not for the goal of catching a husband, as most of the young women in this novel do, from the opening sentence onward, but for the activity itself and for the personal satisfaction it offers. Mary pursues accomplishments apparently for the purpose of personal growth. Mary has educated herself despite her father's complete disregard for her; she has learned to play the piano despite having no governess to teach her. She is described as having "neither genius nor taste" (25), but she is reluctant to appear in the sort of company in which one acquires taste, because that sort of appearance also carries with it the inevitable comparisons of her with her more beautiful sisters. In her approaches and her attitudes, Mary reminds me more and more of Jane Austen herself, and, in fact, looks to be, in some ways, a model of what Gary Kelly elsewhere in this volume calls "a new or increased sense of identity that is inward and distinct from or even opposed to the social self" (Kelly 125–26).

As soon as Mary is mentioned, the reader of Austen's novels is likely to think along certain lines. Representations of Miss Mary Bennet have generally not been kind. Of the five Bennet sisters, she is, according to Austen, "the only plain one in the family" (25), but that "plainness" has often been exaggerated, sometimes into ridiculousness, in visual translations of the novel. The exaggerated tone was set in the 1940 film starring Laurence Olivier and Greer Garson, but Mary becomes progressively plainer and at the same time duller and less appealing as we move from the 1940 Hollywood adaptation to the 1979 BBC/A&E TV mini-series and the 1995 BBC/A&E mini-series. She is portrayed as not just the plain sister, but her plainness has been transformed in these adaptations until she is an object of ridicule. This kind of representation of her seems to me to be unkind and, more importantly, both inaccurate and overdone.

The first mention of Mary in the novel comes quite early on, in the form of a sarcastic gibe from Mr. Bennet:

"What say you, Mary? for you are a young lady of deep reflection I know, and read great books, and make extracts."

Mary wished to say something very sensible, but knew not how.

"While Mary is adjusting her ideas," he continued, "let us return to Mr. Bingley." (7)

Mr. Bennet has caught Mary by surprise and she is speechless, so he makes fun of her. He is engaged at the time in making fun of his wife in particular and of his family more generally. The incident occurs just after his surprising announcement that he has been to visit Bingley and anticipates being able to introduce Bingley to his family very soon.

Mr. Bennet, in fact, goes out of his way in the novel and in the film adaptations to single out Mary for ridicule. I would suggest that the best explanation for that singling out is that Mary is the first real disappointment of the Bennet family. The Bennets expected to have a son and break the entail on their estate. The first two daughters were treated as valued children, and Jane and Elizabeth act like cherished children; Mary, however, was clearly supposed to be a boy. The parents seem to have given up with the youngest two, who have no sense whatsoever and are essentially clones of their very foolish mother. Mary is the disappointment. This also explains why it is that Mary spends so much time reading. She would like to please a father who spends all of his time in the library. This explanation, of course, moves Mary from being silly and a comic character to being a sad, nearly tragic one.

Mary may be speechless at her father's unexpected thrust in the scene quoted above, but that is not always the case. She is capable of speaking at length; indeed, she does declaim from time to time in the novel, and those instances are part of what makes her sound ridiculous. But more of that later.

Mary is described as usually having more time for books than for social intercourse. She participates in few of the social activities that her sisters are constantly engaged in: walking, dancing, conversation, card-playing. When Miss Bingley says scornfully, "Miss Eliza Bennet ... is a great reader and has no pleasure in anything else" (37), she might have been speaking more accurately of Mary. Mary does take very little pleasure in anything but books, but why is that so self-evidently a bad thing in this novel? Why have readers and filmmakers alike consistently portrayed Mary in such an unflattering light? One explanation seems to be that she is an easy target. She certainly stands out: she is the only one of the Bennet sisters aside from Elizabeth who plays and sings, but when she does play and sing, that is, when she tries to be social, she tries too hard. At the very least she is consistently unsocial, and often very nearly antisocial, in a novel that is taken up entirely with social issues and situations.

When Elizabeth, confronted by Miss Bingley and accused of being unsociable because she takes no pleasure in anything but books, claims that she is "not a great reader" (37), one thinks immediately of Mary. Mary is a great reader. She is one of a very select group in this novel depicted actually reading, though many characters interact with books.

Elizabeth, of course, claims not to be a reader. In fact, in an evening episode at Netherfield, Elizabeth chooses to read while the other characters play cards; however, "Elizabeth was so much caught by what passed, as to leave her very little attention for her book; and soon laying it wholly aside, she drew near the card-table, and stationed herself between Mr. Bingley and his eldest sister, to observe the game" (38).

Mr. Bingley has this to say of books: "I wish my collection were larger for your benefit and my own credit; but I am an idle fellow, and though I have not many, I have more than I ever look into" (38). He is never shown actually engaged with a book; books are a kind of social enticement and badge of honour for him. Miss Bingley sees books only as an opportunity to impress Darcy:

> Darcy took up a book; Miss Bingley did the same; ...
>
> Miss Bingley's attention was quite as much engaged in watching Mr. Darcy's progress through his book, as in reading her own; and she was perpetually either making some inquiry, or looking at his page. ... At length, quite exhausted by the attempt to be amused with her own book, which she had only chosen because it was the second volume of his, she gave a great yawn. (54–55)

Mr. Collins, we are told, is "in fact much better fitted for a walker than a reader" (71). Mr. Bennet constantly seeks refuge in his library. He gets away from the world, from what he calls the "silliness" (7, 232) of his wife and his daughters, in his library, the place where he finds rationality and solace. But his escape from silliness is also a refusal of his own duties. His preference for books over the responsibilities of life is roundly critiqued. We are to like Mr. Bennet, in part because Elizabeth likes and admires him, but our liking of him must be tempered by the seriousness of his irresponsibility.

In these examples, books and reading in this novel are mocked, condemned, or at least seen as suspect because they are connected to individual, rather than social, activities. That condemnation, however, is not simple. Books and reading are also represented—more typically for Austen—as being very positive: Darcy is shown reading one evening in Netherfield, for instance, and his library at Pemberley is described as being very fine. Miss Bingley says to Darcy,

> "What a delightful library you have at Pemberley, Mr. Darcy!"
>
> "It ought to be good," he replied, "it has been the work of many generations."
>
> "And then you have added so much to it yourself, you are always buying books."
>
> "I cannot comprehend the neglect of a family library in such days as these." (38)

Darcy sees the culture represented by books as an important public and social responsibility.

For all the attention to reading that permeates this novel, the only book that is mentioned by name was written by James Fordyce. It is introduced in an amusing scene. Mr. Bennet invites Mr. Collins to read aloud: "Mr. Collins readily assented, and a book was produced; but on beholding it, (for everything announced it to be from a circulating library,) he started back, and begging pardon, protested that he never read novels. ... Other books were produced, and after some deliberation he chose Fordyce's Sermons" (68). The full title of this influential conduct-book is *Sermons to Young Women*; it was published in 1766 and frequently reprinted. The copy at the University of Alberta library is the "New Edition, 1787"; the inscription inside reads "Margaret Mary Chambers. Presented by my affectionate mother Sept 17, 1824."

Fordyce has this to say in his Sermon V, entitled "On Female Virtue, Friendship, and Conversation":

> That men are frighted at female pedantry, is very certain. A woman that affects to dispute, to dictate on every subject; that watches or makes the opportunity of throwing out scraps of literature, or shreds of philosophy, in every company; that engrosses the conversation as if she alone were qualified to entertain; that betrays, in short, a boundless intemperance of tongue, together with an inextinguishable passion for shining by the splendour of her supposed talents; such a woman is truly insufferable. (97)

Mary seems to be the incarnation of what Fordyce advises against. With her extensive reading and her "extracts," she is the embodiment of the "truly insufferable woman." That in itself should be enough to make her interesting.

I will now depart from *Pride and Prejudice* for a moment to cite a much-quoted passage about novels from *Northanger Abbey*. The narrator of that novel states,

> I will not adopt that ungenerous and impolitic custom so common with novel writers, of degrading by their contemptuous censure the very performances, to the number of which they are themselves adding—joining with their greatest enemies in bestowing the harshest epithets on such works, and scarcely ever permitting them to be read by their own heroine, who, if she accidentally take up a novel, is sure to turn over its insipid pages with disgust. Alas! if the heroine of one novel be not patronized by the heroine of another, from whom can she expect protection and regard? (37)

I think it is possible that one of the reasons that Mr. Bennet is inclined to include Mary in his blanket condemnation of his "silly" daughters is that she reads novels, along with other books; the condemnation of Mr. Collins by the novel and its narrator arises in part precisely because he does not read novels.

I have discussed books so much precisely because Mary is so infused with books. Mary's life is centred on books; it revolves around books. In what seems a typical instance, Lydia exclaims to Mary,

"Oh! Mary," said she, "I wish you had gone with us, for we had such fun!" ...

To this, Mary very gravely replied, "Far be it from me, my dear sister, to depreciate such pleasures. They would doubtless be congenial with the generality of female minds. But I confess they would have no charms for *me*. I should infinitely prefer a book." (222–23)

The influence of books is so strong and deep, in fact, that Mary speaks not as a speaker, but as a writer. Her speeches are lifted from books, both serious and sentimental: "Society has claims on us all; and I profess myself one of those who consider intervals of recreation and amusement as desirable for every body" (87). This is ponderous and moralizing, but it is not stupid; it is not, indeed, any worse than what can be found in any number of novels of the time. And it is not a speech from a caricature. Here is another example: "I admire the activity of your benevolence, ... but every impulse of feeling should be guided by reason; and, in my opinion, exertion should always be in proportion to what is required" (32). One thing that makes that speech amusing is the fact that it says so little—its own exertion is out of proportion to what is required. It is also enough to help condemn Mary as a caricature because it is unlike the more speech-like talk that is more typical of characters in this novel.

I usually teach this novel in my first-year classes as a representation of the movement of early nineteenth-century British culture from a world that is governed by neoclassical norms, ruled by writers like Swift, Pope, and Samuel Johnson, and summed up nicely in Johnson's maxim, "The business of a poet is to examine, not the individual, but the species" (*Rasselas* 352), to a Romantic world, one aware of feelings, one that celebrates emotion, and one that is much more concerned with the *individual* than with the species. *Pride and Prejudice* is, if you like, a novelistic example of what Thomas Kuhn in *The Structure of Scientific Revolutions* has called a paradigm shift.

This struggle between neoclassic norms and Romantic ideals comes out best in the scene near the end of the novel when Lady Catherine de Bourgh confronts Elizabeth, inquiring whether Elizabeth has any designs on Darcy. Lady Catherine's objections are entirely centred on Darcy's family and connections; her own hopes for the marriage of her daughter to Darcy are, in fact, neoclassical ones. They have nothing to do with Darcy or her daughter personally, but are based on the family and fortune that the two represent. Elizabeth, on the other hand, is steadfast in her refusal to acknowledge Lady Catherine's right to interfere in any way in her affairs:

> "I am only resolved to act in that manner, which will, in my own opinion, constitute my happiness, without reference to *you*, or to any person so wholly unconnected with me."
>
> "It is well. You refuse, then, to oblige me. You refuse to obey the claims of duty, honour, and gratitude. You are determined to ruin him in the opinion of all his friends, and make him the contempt of the world."
>
> "Neither duty, nor honour, nor gratitude ... have any possible claim on me, in the present instance." (358)

There are other places where these different worlds are particularly noticeable. Charlotte Lucas, for instance, proclaims that "happiness in marriage is entirely a matter of chance" (23) and later adds, "I am not romantic you know. I never was. I ask only a comfortable home; and considering Mr. Collins's character, connections, and situation in life, I am convinced that my chance of happiness with him is as fair, as most people can boast on entering the marriage state" (125). The rest of the female characters in the novel come out as variations on this theme. Charlotte would make a good neoclassical heroine. She is practical, social, straightforward. She understands the commercial nature of marriage. Elizabeth, on the other hand, is the epitome of the Romantic heroine. Between these extremes fall the rest of the women in the novel. Jane, in particular, is largely a Romantic heroine, although she has a number of old-fashioned characteristics. Her first thought, upon announcing her marriage plans, is taken up with how pleased she is that she can make her family so happy. Elizabeth repeatedly admires Jane's sweetness of temper; Mrs. Bennet exclaims, "I was sure you could not be so beautiful for nothing" (348).

Mary, however, does not fit very well into this scheme. She is "accomplished"; in fact, at the first dance in the novel, "Mary had heard herself mentioned to Miss Bingley as the most accomplished girl in the neighbourhood" (12). In a memorable exchange, Mr. Darcy and Miss Bingley compile the list of qualities of a truly accomplished woman:

> "Oh! certainly," cried [Miss Bingley], "no one can be really esteemed accomplished, who does not greatly surpass what is usually met with. A woman must have a thorough knowledge of music, singing, drawing, dancing, and the modern languages, to deserve the word; and besides all this, she must possess a certain something in her air and manner of walking, the tone of her voice, her address and expressions, or the word will be but half deserved."
>
> "All this she must possess," added Darcy, "and to all this she must yet add something more substantial, in the improvement of her mind by extensive reading." (39)

By this list, Mary is, of course, not "really" accomplished—as Elizabeth remarks, it would be remarkable if *any* woman could fit this definition (39). Mary is, however, making do with what she has, and working towards being as accomplished as her person and circumstances allow. She makes no attempt to lure men with her accomplishments; neither does she seem intent only on flaunting what she has achieved. Though we read that she "was always impatient for display" (25), she does not apparently "display" for purposes beyond the pleasures of the performance itself. She chooses a concerto before the "Scotch and Irish airs" that are preferred by her sisters (25). She plays and reads and pursues her accomplishments apparently to amuse and enrich herself, not as a way of laying a trap for a husband, and not even to show herself in public: she prefers books to balls, after all. In short, she has as her goals self-expression and self-improvement.

Her conversation is also distinctive. As we have seen, Mary, unlike the other characters, talks as though she were writing. Her speeches are not so much foolish as ponderously formal:

"Pride," observed Mary, who piqued herself upon the solidity of her reflections, "is a very common failing I believe. By all that I have ever read, I am convinced that it is very common indeed, that human nature is particularly prone to it, and that there are very few of us who do not cherish a feeling of self-complacency on the score of some quality or other, real or imaginary. Vanity and pride are different things, though the words are often used synonimously. A person may be proud without being vain. Pride relates more to our opinion of ourselves, vanity to what we would have others think of us." (20)

This is a speech that we would allow in narrative, but that we are quite ready to condemn when Mary says it.

Mary is the "plain" sister of five. She remains at home after her sisters have left, filling a domestic role as her mother's companion:

Mary was the only daughter who remained at home; and she was necessarily drawn from the pursuit of accomplishments by Mrs. Bennet's being quite unable to sit alone. Mary was obliged to mix more with the world, but she could still moralize over every morning visit; and as she was no longer mortified by comparisons between her sisters' beauty and her own, it was suspected by her father that she submitted to the change without much reluctance. (386)

Mary is not interested in marriage, apparently. Even in the case of Mr. Collins,

Mary might have been prevailed on to accept him. She rated his abilities much higher than any of the others; there was a solidity in his reflections which often struck her, and though by no means so clever as herself, she thought that if encouraged to read and improve himself by such an example as her's, he might become a very agreeable companion. (124)

Note that she thinks Collins has possibilities as a *companion*—not simply as a husband. Mary does not think in the ways that most of the women in the novel think. Mary is different; Mary is a problem. In a novel concerned with the construction of individual, authentic selves who still live in a world that considers marriage the only viable option for genteel young women, Mary stands out as an enigma. She is "accomplished" when, for everyone around her, being accomplished is really a way to catch a man, yet she shows no inclination to catch a man. She talks like a writer, rather than a character; her speeches sound written rather than spoken; she blurs the distinctions, smudges the lines, does not care for the matters that take up all of her sisters' time; she is very much like Austen herself, yet she is often silent when one would expect to hear Austen speak. She is inextricably a part of the double coding that goes on throughout this novel, and her problematic nature is precisely what makes her interesting.

The novel clearly condemns Mary as socially inept, someone who has spent too much time inside her own head and not nearly enough time in the company of good society. Accordingly, Mary's speech is of a curious kind. She does not speak easily or very well because speech is a social activity, along with walks, dancing, and cards, and she does not know how to play that game well; she really doesn't care to. She lives for herself and the part of the world that she touches. That seems to be enough for her. It seems to me that she displays the marks of a post-Romantic heroine and that, in her pursuits and interests and goals, Mary deserves not to be parodied, but admired as a precursor of a modern woman. In a sense, the novel has created a woman who is beyond itself. It condemns Mary for not following many of the social norms that it itself condemns at the same time. Mary seems, remarkably, capable of picking and choosing and making her own society. That individual capacity for self-determination is a fact of modern life that we now take for granted; I find it fascinating to discover it here, in this most unlikely of places.

JEFFREY HERRLE

15

The Idiolects of the Idiots

The Language and Conversation of Jane Austen's Less-Than-Savoury Suitors

AMONG THE MANY SUITORS that Austen presents in her six mature novels, John Thorpe and Mr. Collins are perhaps among the most memorable. Ironically, both characters are memorable not for their success as suitors, but rather for their utter failure to excite the interest of their would-be lovers. Though George Wickham, Mr. Elliot, and Henry Crawford also fail to win the hands of Austen's heroines, they nevertheless succeed in generating some romantic interest and arousing some curiosity. What, then, makes Thorpe and Collins so uninteresting as suitors? And what makes them so entertaining to us as readers?

Picking up on these issues in his book, *Mr. Collins Considered,* Ivor Morris remarks that Collins's name

> has become a byword for a silliness all of his own—a felicitous blend of complacent self-approval and ceremonious servility. Like Mr.

Bennet, we listen to him with the keenest enjoyment; ... we can never find the dose too much. If Mr. Darcy and Elizabeth Bennet are a pair of literature's classic lovers, Mr. Collins is surely one of its prize idiots. (1)

Whereas Wickham, Mr. Elliot, and Henry Crawford at varying points *seem* to possess, or to be capable of possessing, the cardinal virtues of the typical Austen hero—discernment, moderation, and sensibility—Collins and Thorpe never appear to be what they are not, both to the reader and to the heroines. Even before these laughable characters fully reveal the extent of their obscene self-centredness, Catherine Morland and Elizabeth Bennet have already rejected them as lovers because of their graceless social skills and their penchant for excessive language. Their talk initially confuses the people to whom it is directed, and then it is met with indifference, irritation, or giggles. It is unfailingly predictable, bizarrely excessive, and unabashedly self-centred. Indeed, their only attentive listeners, Lady Catherine de Bourgh and General Tilney, are individuals who have even more deluded notions of their own importance and talents.

In this essay, I argue that Austen renders these characters' moral, social, and romantic shortcomings and tawdriness in their relationships to language and talk. I approach these aspects of Thorpe's and Collins's talk by examining their conversational preoccupations and delusional attempts to render themselves as attractive, important, well-bred young gentlemen. Thorpe and Collins, I contend, are certainly capable of talk—or at least specific modes of talk—but they can never truly converse and have great difficulty listening.

Although Thorpe and Collins have been frequently identified by literary critics as "flat" or "two-dimensional" characters—characters that E.M. Forster identified as being built around a single idea or quality (103–04)—they play important roles in Austen's work. Henry James's notion, that fools are almost indispensable for any piece of fiction, is in my mind a valid one: these characters have enduringly consistent, familiar qualities that we witness in literature as well as in our own daily lives, and that in turn may partially explain our continuing fascination with them. We might easily imagine seeing John Thorpe on the street today, equipped with a cellular phone and a used sports car. Mr. Collins, on the other hand, we might imagine in a middle-management position of a multinational company, bedecked in a grey flannel suit, directing solemn compliments to his superiors. Though their clothes, accoutrements, accents, and verbal inflections might be different now, the substance of their talk would be much the same.

With this in mind, I begin by considering Thorpe's and Collins's voices— how Austen endows them with verbal mannerisms and patterns—and direct our attention to their intellectual hobby horses, which, in Thorpe's case, have much to do with horses. Indeed, when we first meet John Thorpe, in Chapter 7 of *Northanger Abbey*, he is driving his gig with "all the vehemence that could most fitly endanger the lives of himself, his companion, and his horse" (NA 44), not to mention the pedestrians on the street that include Catherine and Isabella. When he and James Morland finally dismount and engage in conversation, Thorpe sets the pattern for speeches to come, exaggerating the distance they have travelled and the speed with which his horses go; he then boasts the superiority of his carriage and emphasizes his magnanimity by telling Catherine that he was above haggling for it when he purchased it. Not surprisingly, when Catherine meets him again, Thorpe renews his conversation about his gig after a few minutes' silence, this time extolling its value and desirability (47); shortly after this, at the Upper Rooms, he enchants Catherine on the dance floor with the particulars "of the horses and dogs of the friend whom he had just left, and of a proposed exchange of terriers" (55). Although at this point Catherine is unable to read Thorpe for what he is, just as she is unable to discern the difference between gothic fiction and gothic reality, she already knows that she does not like him (50). In less than five pages a neutral opinion of Thorpe changes to one of increasing distaste.

There is, of course, more than talk of horses, gigs, and dogs in these five pages. After Isabella, James, Thorpe, and Catherine initially meet and agree to a drive in the country, Thorpe sidles up to Catherine. Having exhausted the topics of horses, travel, and gigs, he has less to say. His mind then fixes on his other masculine interest, the ladies. Notably, Austen's narrator conveys the rhythm and sound of Thorpe's manner of speaking here as well as what he says. His "discourse now sunk from its hitherto animated pitch, to nothing more than a short decisive sentence of praise or condemnation on the face of every woman they met" (48). We get a sense that Thorpe almost speaks like the animals with which he so enjoys spending time—he yelps, squeals, and whinnies wildly when he is excited, and barks and snorts at strangers. If he is like a horse, however, he is hardly one of Swift's Houyhnhnms in *Gulliver's Travels*. He seems much more like a Yahoo.

Not surprisingly, Catherine encounters similar discourse, both in substance and in delivery, again and again. If anything, Thorpe's speech degenerates upon further acquaintance. When they later discuss drinking at Oxford, another fine masculine pursuit in Thorpe's world, Catherine's assertion of her brother's sobriety provokes "a loud and overpowering reply, of which no part was very distinct, except the frequent exclamations, amounting almost to oaths, which adorned it" (64). When Catherine suggests that her brother does not have a horse and gig of his own because he cannot afford them, Thorpe "said something in the loud, incoherent way to which he had often recourse, about its being a d— thing to be miserly; ... which Catherine did not even endeavour to understand" (89).

Thorpe's departure from civilized discourse to a series of primordial grunts reaches its lowest point when he forces her, against her will, to go to Clifton. The credibility of his talk has by now been tarnished by his continual boasting and curt attacks on everyone else, as well as his lies about Blaize Castle and his lies to the Tilneys about Catherine's plans. Now, however, we finally see that behind the "rattle" there is something more ominous and brutal. This is, of course, already suggested with his lies and swearing— moral and social offences which clearly mark him as a menace in Austen's world. But what happens in the carriage on the way to Clifton is nothing short of a figurative rape:

> They passed briskly down Pulteney-street, and through Laura-place, without the exchange of many words. Thorpe talked to his horse, and she meditated, by turns, on broken promises and broken arches, phaetons and false hangings, Tilneys, and trap-doors. As they entered Argyle-buildings, however, she was roused by this address from her companion, "Who is that girl who looked at you so hard as she went by?"
>
> "Who?—where?"

"On the right-hand pavement—she must be almost out of sight now." Catherine looked round and saw Miss Tilney leaning on her brother's arm, walking slowly down the street. She saw them both looking back at her. "Stop, stop, Mr. Thorpe," she impatiently cried, … "Stop, stop, I will get out this moment and go to them." But to what purpose did she speak?—Thorpe only lashed his horse into a brisker trot; … Still, however, and during the length of another street, she intreated him to stop. "Pray, pray stop, Mr. Thorpe.—I cannot go on.—I will not go on.—I must go back to Miss Tilney." But Mr. Thorpe only laughed, smacked his whip, encouraged his horse, *made odd noises,* and drove on; (86–87; *emphasis added*)

I continue to find this scene the most disturbing in Austen's work. It does, however, forcefully emphasize how Thorpe's moral bankruptcy, lack of empathy, and sheer brutality manifests itself in his utterances and noises.

Interestingly, in the recent BBC/A&E version of *Pride and Prejudice,* Mr. Collins is characterized by non-verbal sounds; when Elizabeth Bennet stays at Hunsford, there is a memorable scene in which he grunts with pleasure as he devours his breakfast. The director's liberty is an interesting one, and I wonder if it was informed by a reading of *Northanger Abbey.* Regardless, while these "odd noises" are perhaps similar to Thorpe's insofar as they are effusions of self-contained pleasure, Collins's speech and rhetorical strategies, in both novel and film, are radically different. Whereas Thorpe commands and disparages others, Collins is almost always ready with an apology or a compliment; whereas Thorpe speaks in abrupt monosyllables and peppers his speech with profanity, Collins is floridly long-winded and solemnly formal. Finally, whereas Thorpe is recklessly unconscious of the manner in which he uses language and how people might respond to it, Collins seems acutely aware of his style and the social functions of rhetoric.

Of course, in *Northanger Abbey* and *Pride and Prejudice* we are also dealing with completely different heroines. While Catherine is initially confused by Thorpe's language and fails to recognize his Neanderthal methods of courtship, Elizabeth immediately sees from Collins's first letter that he must be utterly foolish and quickly comes to realize that he means to have her as his wife. Upon reading his letter, which introduces him in the text, she recognizes "something very pompous in his stile" and asks, "Can he be a sensible man?" To which Mr. Bennet gleefully replies, "No, my dear; I think not. I have great hopes of finding him quite the reverse. There is a mixture of servility and self-importance in his letter, which promises well. I am impatient to see him" (*PP* 64). Collins, as we all know, does not disappoint.

While horses, dogs, and carriages are Thorpe's enthusiasms, Collins revels in the grandeur of his patroness, his station in her household, and the art of compliment. And yet the two men are similar in that they fail to see beyond their own self-serving desires and sense of self-importance. Because they assume that the world naturally concurs with their lines of thinking, Thorpe and Collins also fail to discern the difference between desires and ambitions that can be appropriately spoken of and those that are better left concealed. Moreover, because these self-interested desires and ambitions are so unabashedly manifest in their talk—indeed they almost seem proud of them—they cannot even project the appearance of sympathy or compassion. This is what distinguishes them from the likes of Mr. Elliot, Wickham, and Henry Crawford.

Their inability to reflect on the difference between their own aspirations and those around them, and to tailor their speech accordingly, produces unusual results in talk. That Thorpe and Collins dislike novels is not so offensive as the *faux pas* of denouncing them in front of people who obviously enjoy them and of displaying their ignorance of the genre they decry. A striking instance of this type of obliviousness occurs in *Pride and Prejudice*: Mr. Bennet asks Collins about his verbal practices after Collins remarks,

> I am happy on every occasion to offer those little delicate compliments which are always acceptable to ladies. I have more than once observed to Lady Catherine, that her charming daughter seemed born to be a duchess, and that the most elevated rank, instead of giving her consequence, would be adorned by her.—These are the kind of little things which please her ladyship, and it is a sort of attention which I conceive myself peculiarly bound to pay. (67–68)

What is perverse here is not Mr. Collins's gallantry, nor his desire to ingratiate himself to a powerful patroness, but rather his implied pride in occupying the important role of chief sycophant at Rosings; he has enough pride in his role to speak of it as if it were a highly revered position of honour. Clearly incredulous, Mr. Bennet then decides to push the envelope, so to speak, to discover the limits of Collins's shamelessness. He does so with extreme care and, of course, great irony. With Collinsian solemnity and formal diction, he responds: "You judge very properly, ... and it is happy for you that you possess the talent of flattering with delicacy. May I ask whether these pleasing attentions proceed from the impulse of the moment, or are the result of previous study?" (68). To which Collins replies:

> They arise chiefly from what is passing at the time, and though I sometimes amuse myself with suggesting and arranging such little elegant compliments as may be adapted to ordinary occasions, I always wish to give them as unstudied an air as possible. (68)

The fact that there is no hint of apology in Collins's words here is significant, since, as Mr. Bennet has already observed, his language consistently balances servility and self-importance (64). Because compliments are his métier and praise his vocation, he need not apologize, I suppose.

Just as horses are the conversational hobby horse of Thorpe, we might see Lady Catherine de Bourgh as the deity whose gospel Mr. Collins preaches. Ivor Morris picks up on this when he suggests that "her opinions on small matters or great have for him the authority of Holy Writ, and are as religiously acquiesced in; and a person 'honoured with some portion of her notice' is but a step away from the vision beatific" (64–65). Mr. Collins is, indeed, her holy man, whose perpetual mission is to proselytize the unenlightened and to praise her ladyship. Collins repeatedly remarks on his veneration for his patroness (70). He cannot "think well of the man who should omit an occasion of testifying his respect towards any body connected with the family" (101). Naturally, Elizabeth is able to detect his religious zeal for Lady Catherine fairly quickly. She attempts to invoke Lady Catherine's omnipresent authority to dissuade Collins from attending

Bingley's ball; however, "she was rather surprised to find that he enter-tained no scruple whatever on that head, and was very far from dreading a rebuke either from the Archbishop, or Lady Catherine de Bourgh, by venturing to dance" (87). On the other end of things, Lady Catherine certainly lives up to her part. However, she is not the forgiving God of the New Testament, but instead the jealous God of the Old Testament who threatens to annihilate Israel for being led astray and who provides commandments for her people. When Elizabeth visits Rosings, she notes that she heard

> Lady Catherine talk, which she did without any intermission till coffee came in, delivering her opinion on every subject in so decisive a manner as proved, that she was not used to have her judgement controverted. She enquired into Charlotte's domestic concerns famil-iarly and minutely, and gave her a great deal of advice, as to the management of them all; told her how every thing ought to be regu-lated in so small a family as her's, and instructed her as to the care of her cows and her poultry. (163)

Here we might be reminded of God's specific commands regarding the daily living of the Israelites in Leviticus. But before Collins actually proposes to Elizabeth we find further resonances of the Old Testament. Invoking God's blessing, Isaac issues a command to his son Jacob: "Thou shalt not take a wife of the daughters of Canaan. Arise, go to Padan-aram, to the house of Bethuel thy mother's father; and take thee a wife from thence of the daughters of Laban thy mother's brother" (Genesis 28.1–2). Collins tells Elizabeth that Lady Catherine, in similar fashion, has given him a combined blessing and directive:

> Mr. Collins, you must marry. A clergyman like you must marry.—Chuse properly, chuse a gentlewoman for *my* sake; and for your *own*, let her be an active, useful sort of person, not brought up high but able to make a small income go a good way. This is my advice. Find such a woman as soon as you can, bring her to Hunsford, and I will visit her. (105–06)

Instead of his matrilinear cousins, though, Collins attempts to court his patrilinear cousins. Commanded by Lady Catherine, and perhaps encouraged by Elizabeth's "concern" prior to the ball at Netherfield, Collins loses little time in making his offer. Notably, it is in his proposal scene that the language of servility almost falls out of the picture completely and Collins's narcissism and self-centredness gain full ascendancy. In this scene, Collins does not attempt to supplicate, cajole, or persuade Elizabeth; he merely gives voice to his demands and his desires. In almost every sentence in his speech, he is the subject and the agent, and Elizabeth—when she is actually mentioned—is relegated to the status of an object. This is evident from the beginning of the proposal when he states,

> My reasons for marrying are, first, that I think it a right thing for every clergyman in easy circumstances (like *myself*) to set the example of matrimony in his parish. Secondly, that I am convinced it will add very greatly to my happiness; and thirdly—which perhaps I ought to have mentioned earlier, that it is the particular advice and recommendation of the very noble lady whom I have the honour of calling patroness." (105; *emphasis added*)

Where is Elizabeth in this passage? There are seven words that are variations of the first-person singular, but no references to the second-person singular. If this speech represents what Collins calls "the violence of my affection" (106), it is obviously violent self-love that he is talking about. After Elizabeth finally manages to get a word in, declining his offer, Collins's rhetorical strategy gradually changes. Not surprisingly, it takes her a while to begin to convince him that she is not following "the usual practice of elegant females" (108). Initially, he responds to this with the language of easy gallantry but then moves towards thinly veiled threats: he prognosticates for her a life of misery and poverty if she does not accept him, and then suggests that he will call on the force of parental authority to secure his claim to her.

Such well-articulated threats are a far cry from Thorpe's "odd noises" while driving Catherine away against her will, but the issues surrounding both scenes are the same: they both lay bare these characters' arrogance, their lack of empathy, and their inability to regard women as rational subjects. If Collins's proposal scene marks the point at which his language comes closest to the barefaced egocentrism of Thorpe's, we might argue that Thorpe's proposal scene marks the moment in which his speech most resembles Collins's. In Thorpe's proposal scene, his masculine bravado withers away as he attempts to speak in the genre of praise and concurrence. Anything beyond self-praise is foreign to Thorpe, so it is not surprising that he struggles. Only once does he tell Catherine that "there is no such confounded hurry" (NA 123), after she has responded literally to his song metaphor and wishes to go home. Instead, for the most part, he tries to put on his best talk and manners. He startles Catherine when he actually waits for an answer from her and atypically agrees with her about the pleasure of company. But what is most curious about his speech in this scene is his panegyric on Catherine's good nature. When she asks him why he is leaving Bath for so long, he responds,

> That is kind of you, however—kind and *good-natured.*—I shall not forget it in a hurry.—But you have more *good-nature* and all that, than any body living I believe. A monstrous deal of *good-nature*, and it is not only *good-nature*, but you have so much, so much of every thing; and then you have such—upon my soul I do not know any body like you. (123; *emphasis added*)

Just in case you did not get it: he really, really, really thinks she is good-natured. Thorpe clearly lacks Collins's wit and ability to compliment. His compliment follows the same pattern as his regular speech: it is disordered, repetitive, and ill-planned. Moreover, at this point in the novel it is obvious that the goodwill of his compliment is contingent on Catherine's receptivity to his suggestion.

That Collins and Thorpe are bold enough to propose to protagonists who are indifferent to them is in keeping with their arrogance and egotism. Nevertheless, one wonders what they think they have to offer as suitors. Collins's supposed strengths are made evident through his proposal: the paramount advantage is "the notice and kindness of Lady Catherine de Bourgh" (PP 106), and underlying this is his imminent inheritance of Longbourn. Conversely, in Thorpe's case it is unclear what advantage he offers. Though Mrs. Thorpe went to school with Mrs. Allen and Thorpe himself is at Oxford, his mother "was a widow, and not a very rich one" (NA 34), his family is from less-than-glamorous Putney, and in Bath they live in Edgar's Buildings, which in name sounds suspiciously like the Westgate Buildings where Mrs. Smith of *Persuasion* resides. Thorpe is, it seems, what would later be called shabby-genteel. In spite of Thorpe's lack of social advantages, I suggest that *both* characters seem to think that they can attract and impress the protagonists with their "class" and gentility. Through their talk they attempt to render themselves genteel, or at least what they construe to be genteel.

Naturally, what they construe as genteel or well-bred is something very different from what Jane Austen considers gentlemanly. This is immediately apparent with Thorpe's entrance in *Northanger Abbey*. Even before he attempts to impersonate a gentleman in his speech, he is targeted by the narrator, who describes him as

> a stout young man of middling height, who, with a plain face and ungraceful form, seemed fearful of being too handsome unless he wore the dress of a groom, and too much like a gentleman unless he were easy where he ought to be civil, and impudent where he might be allowed to be easy. (45)

Because Austen identifies "quality" and "good breeding" with proper moral and social conduct, as Juliet McMaster argues ("Class" 128–29), it is not surprising that she mentions talk in connection with class in this description of Thorpe. Fittingly, the two social positions that she identifies ("groom" and "gentleman"), like the polarities Mr. Bennet uses to describe Collins, speak to the ambivalences of Thorpe's self-fashioning in language. Try as he might to advertise himself as a well-bred young gentleman, Thorpe's stable-boy proclivities stubbornly reappear, and his supposedly squirely talk backfires. While Catherine may not recognize this, or for that matter recognize Thorpe's posturing, the narrator certainly does and emphatically points it out to the reader. In another instance, she exposes Thorpe in describing Catherine's bewilderment in the face of his blustery manner of speech. Thorpe's animated account of his carriage, his horse, and his driving skills is sharply deflated, as in the previous passage, by the narrator's deadpan summary:

> Catherine listened with astonishment; she knew not how to reconcile two such very different accounts of the same thing; for she had not been brought up to understand the propensities of a rattle, nor to know to how many idle assertions and impudent falsehoods the excess of vanity will lead. Her own family were plain matter-of-fact people, who seldom aimed at wit of any kind; ... they were not in the habit therefore of telling lies to increase their importance, or of asserting at one moment what they would contradict the next. She reflected on the affair for some time in much perplexity, and was more than once on the point of requesting from Mr. Thorpe a clearer insight into his real opinion on the subject; but she checked herself, because it appeared to her that he did not excel in giving those clearer insights, in making those things plain which he had before made ambiguous....
>
> Little as Catherine was in the habit of judging for her self, and unfixed as were her general notions of what men ought to be, she could not entirely repress a doubt, while she bore with the effusions of his endless conceit, of his being altogether completely agreeable. (65–66)

What Thorpe, like Collins, fails to recognize is that his boasting works as a double-edged sword. We, as readers, can clearly see that Thorpe's self-description as "the best coachman" in England (65) is a dubious honour, since it is a profession of the lower orders. Similarly, talking excessively about money, trading horses and dogs, and one's wealth—in this case imaginary—smacks of trade and the likes of Mrs. Elton. Thorpe's ostensibly gentlemanly interests in dogs, horses, and hunting are discussed by him with such zeal that he seems more like a gamekeeper than a country gentleman. Naturally, his incessant swearing and choppy speech do nothing to assist his attempts at projecting refinement and gentility. But Thorpe thinks differently; he models himself on the boorish Squire Western in *Tom Jones*, one of the few novels that he enjoys (48), failing to recognize that Fielding's character is a parody.

Mr. Collins's mode of projecting his gentlemanliness is almost antithetical to Thorpe's. It is important to recognize, however, that even though Collins is to inherit Longbourn, this was not always assured—and this lack of assurance, Austen suggests, contributes to the formation of his toadyism in speech. We discover early in our acquaintance with him that "the greatest part of his life [was] spent under the guidance of an illiterate and miserly father; ... The subjection in which his father had brought him up, had given him originally great humility of manner" (70). Indeed, Collins only learns "self-conceit" with "the consequential feelings of early and unexpected prosperity" that follow from his being appointed to the living of Hunsford by Lady Catherine de Bourgh (PP 70). But because of his humble beginnings and his reliance on Lady Catherine in the present of the novel, Collins retains his obsequiousness and can easily manipulate this posture.

One senses, from the exchange with Mr. Bennet that I discussed earlier, that Collins sees his modes of language as something that bespeaks his delicate refinement. Indeed, it would seem to me that his formality signifies not merely stiffness but a dogmatic attachment to the prescribed models of polite behaviour and talk of his day. In short, Collins speaks like a conduct book. While this is to some extent not surprising—he is, after all, a preacher— he seems to miss the point: good conduct is to regulate, and thus be a means towards, moral social intercourse; it is not an end in itself. But by making gallantry and zealous submission to his betters his chief study, Collins does achieve what he perceives to be a reward of upward mobility, the attention of Lady Catherine. He tells the Bennets, "She had always spoken to him as she would to any other *gentleman*; she made not the smallest objection to his joining in *the society* of the neighbourhood" (66; emphasis added).

Lady Catherine's attention is, at best, flighty; the paucity of invitations to Rosings after Darcy and Colonel Fitzwilliam arrive attests to this. But in Collins's mind her notice gives him a means of asserting his gentility by association and a licence to approach and converse familiarly with his social betters. Naturally, Collins invokes this reasoning when he informs

Elizabeth that he intends to approach Darcy at the Netherfield ball. But he takes a different line of argument when Elizabeth attempts "to dissuade him from such a scheme; assuring him that Mr. Darcy would consider his addressing him without introduction as an impertinent freedom, rather than a compliment to his aunt" and that if any introduction should take place "it must belong to Mr. Darcy, the superior in consequence, to begin the acquaintance" (97). In response to this, he remarks that

> there must be a wide difference between the established forms of ceremony amongst the laity, and those which regulate the clergy; for give me leave to observe that I consider the clerical office as equal in point of dignity with the highest rank in the kingdom—provided that a proper humility of behaviour is at the same time maintained. (97)

Collins's conviction that the famously hierarchical Anglican Church is a great leveller and that he shares the dignity of the King is just as preposterous as his imagined intimacy with Lady Catherine. But in his typically ambivalent, self-important, and servile way Collins undermines this claim by asserting it to be his own humble opinion and by referring to the "humility" that the clergyman must inevitably convey. Yet there is a grain of *realpolitik* truth in Collins's disclaimers, and his "early and unexpected prosperity" (70) attests to it. Herein lies the difference between John Thorpe and Mr. Collins as pompous, chattering fools: Collins clearly recognizes that to rise up the ranks, he must take advantage of human vanity by cajoling and caressing. And in a world inhabited by Sir Walter Elliots, Augusta Eltons, and Mrs. John Dashwoods, he has every chance of success. Taking this a step further by considering Austen's readers, Ivor Morris poignantly remarks,

> What is insidious in Mr. Collins is that, vain himself, he is responsive to the vanity of all around him, making it the medium and means of his socialising and advancement. He operates at the level which we pride ourselves on having left behind, but where we are in fact just as vulnerable to his blandishments. In reality, we draw upon our self-

contempt in deriding him, sensing, with an instinctive recognition, that our own shame is written into his progress. (67)

While it is Mr. Collins's vanity and his cultivation of other people's vanity that equips him for worldly success, it also prevents him from ever having a real conversation. Samuel Johnson, Jane Austen's favourite moralist, once remarked that ideal conversations are ones in which "there is no competition, no vanity, but a calm quiet interchange of sentiments" (Boswell 623). There is, of course, much evidence to suggest that Jane Austen inherited this ideal of conversation. We get an inkling of this when Austen's narrator in *Northanger Abbey* remarks that Mrs. Allen spent most of the day "by the side of Mrs. Thorpe, in what they called conversation, but in which there was scarcely ever any exchange of opinion, and not often any resemblance of subject" (NA 36). We also see this ideal of conversation in the discursive movement of Austen's heroes and heroines; their social interaction frequently culminates in scenes prior to a proposal, scenes in which they mutually disclose to each other their takes on the turn of events, finally being able to speak to each other with candour. This being the case, it becomes readily apparent why Austen's heroines find Thorpe and Collins so unsavoury. Too self-serving and egotistical to listen sympathetically to others and to exchange ideas, Thorpe and Collins exhort, denounce, and proclaim their own personal enthusiasms and desires, but never converse. Austen herself makes the distinction between talk and conversation with Thorpe, remarking that "all the rest of his conversation, or rather talk, began and ended with himself and his own concerns" (NA 66). And the same distinction is of course implied by the narrator of *Pride and Prejudice* when she refers to Collins's talk as "pompous nothings" (PP 72) or as "his speech" (101).

While Thorpe and Collins prove to be ineffectual in their attempts to master Catherine and Elizabeth with their selfish rhetoric, through them Austen is able to allude to different endings for her heroines, endings in which marriage does not involve the equality and companionship implied in "the calm quiet interchange of sentiments." Fools' talk, then, is more than simply rattle and something to laugh at. It speaks to a range of social and moral concerns that were important to Jane Austen and that continue to have relevance today.

Works Cited

Abrams, M.H. *A Glossary of Literary Terms*. 7th ed. Fort Worth, TX: Harcourt Brace, 1999.

Anderson, Benedict. *Imagined Communities: Reflections on the Origin and Spread of Nationalism*. 2nd ed. London and New York: Verso, 1991.

Aristotle. *Politics*. Ed. Steven Everson. Cambridge and New York: Cambridge University Press, 1987.

Astell, Mary. *Some Reflections upon Marriage Occasion'd by the Duke and Duchess of Mazarin's Case; which is also considered*. London, 1700.

Austen-Leigh, James Edward. *A Memoir of Jane Austen*. 1870. Ed. R.W. Chapman. Oxford: Clarendon, 1926.

Babb, Howard S. *Jane Austen's Novels: The Fabric of Dialogue*. Columbus, OH: Ohio State University Press, 1962.

Bakhtin, Mikhail. *The Dialogic Imagination: Four Essays*. Ed. Michael Holquist. Trans. Caryl Emerson and Michael Holquist. Austin: University of Texas Press, 1981.

—————. *Speech Genres and Other Late Essays*. Ed. Caryl Emerson and Michael
  Holquist. Trans. Vern W. McGee. Austin: University of Texas Press, 1985.

Bateson, Gregory. *Steps to an Ecology of Mind: Collected Essays in Anthropology,
  Psychology, Evolution, and Epistemology*. New York: Ballantine, 1972.

Benger, Elizabeth. *The Heart and the Fancy, or Valsimore, a Tale*. London, 1813.

Birchall, Diana. *In Defense of Mrs. Elton*. Santa Monica, CA: JASNA, 1999.

Birtwistle, Sue, and Susie Conklin. *The Making of* Pride and Prejudice.
  London and New York: Penguin, 1995.

Blythe, Ronald. Introduction. *Emma*. By Jane Austen. Harmondsworth,
  England: Penguin, 1985. 7–32.

Boswell, James. *The Life of Samuel Johnson, LL.D.* 1791. Ed. R.W. Chapman.
  London and New York: Oxford University Press, 1980

Brink, André. *The Novel: Language and Narrative from Cervantes to Calvino*. New
  York: New York University Press, 1998.

Brower, Reuben A. "Light and Bright and Sparkling: Irony and Fiction in
  Pride and Prejudice." *The Fields of Light: An Experiment in Critical Reading*. New
  York: Oxford University Press, 1951. 164–81.

Brunton, Mary. *Self-Control: A Novel*. Edinburgh, 1811.

Burney, Frances. *Cecilia, or Memoirs of an Heiress*. 1782. Ed. Margaret Anne
  Doody and Peter Sabor. Oxford and New York: Oxford University Press,
  1988.

—————. *The Wanderer; or, Female Difficulties*. 1814. Ed. Margaret Anne Doody,
  Robert L. Mack, and Peter Sabor. Oxford and New York: Oxford
  University Press, 1991.

Butler, Judith. *Bodies That Matter: On the Discursive Limits of "Sex."* New York:
  Routledge, 1993.

Butler, Marilyn. *Jane Austen and the War of Ideas*. Oxford: Clarendon, 1975.

"Conversation." *The Concise Oxford Dictionary of Current English*. 9th ed. Oxford:
  Clarendon, 1995.

"Conversation." *The Oxford English Dictionary*. 2nd ed. 20 vols. Oxford:
  Clarendon, 1989.

"Conversation." *The Oxford English Dictionary*. 2nd ed. CD-ROM. Oxford:
  Oxford University Press, 1992.

Dickens, Charles. *The Life and Adventures of Martin Chuzzlewit*. 1843–44. Ed. Margaret Cardwell. London and New York: Oxford University Press, 1998.

Duckworth, Alistair M. *The Improvement of the Estate: A Study of Jane Austen's Novels*. Baltimore, MD: Johns Hopkins University Press, 1971.

DuPlessis, Rachel Blau. *Writing Beyond the Ending: Narrative Strategies of Twentieth-Century Women Writers*. Bloomington, IN: Indiana University Press, 1985.

Edgeworth, Maria. "The Absentee." *Tales of Fashionable Life*. London, 1812.

Eggins, Suzanne, and Diana Slade. *Analysing Casual Conversation*. London: Cassell, 1997.

Farrer, Reginald. "Jane Austen." *Quarterly Review* 228 (1917): 1–30.

Fergus, Jan. *Jane Austen and the Didactic Novel:* Northanger Abbey, Sense and Sensibility, *and* Pride and Prejudice. London: Macmillan, 1983.

Fielding, Sarah. *The Adventures of David Simple*. 1744. Ed. Linda Bree. Harmondsworth, England: Penguin, 2002.

Finch, Anne. "The Apology" and "The Introduction." *Poems by Anne, Countess of Winchilsea, 1661–1720*. Selected and introduced by John Middleton Murry. New York and London: Jonathan Cape, 1928.

Fludernik, Monika. *The Fictions of Language and the Languages of Fiction: The Linguistic Representation of Speech and Consciousness*. London and New York: Routledge, 1993.

Flynn, Carol Houlihan. "The Letters." *The Cambridge Companion to Jane Austen*. Ed. Edward Copeland and Juliet McMaster. Cambridge: Cambridge University Press, 1997. 100–14.

Fordyce, James. *Sermons to Young Women*. 1766. Philadelphia, 1787.

Forster, E.M. *Aspects of the Novel*. 1927. New York: Harcourt Brace, 1954.

Foucault, Michel. *Power/Knowledge: Selected Interviews and Other Writings, 1972–1977*. Ed. and trans. Colin Gordon. New York: Pantheon, 1977.

———. "The Political Technology of Individuals." *Technologies of the Self: A Seminar with Michel Foucault*. Amherst, MA: University of Massachusetts Press, 1988. 145–62.

Freud, Sigmund. "From *Jokes and Their Relation to the Unconscious* (1905)." *Theories of Comedy*. Ed. Paul Lauter. Garden City, NY: Anchor, 1964.

Furet, Francois, and Jacques Ozouf. *Reading and Writing: Literacy in France from Calvin to Jules Ferry*. Cambridge and New York: Cambridge University Press, 1982.

Harris, Jocelyn. *Jane Austen's Art of Memory*. Cambridge and New York: Cambridge University Press, 1989.

———. "Sappho, Souls, and the Salic Law of Wit." *Anticipations of the Enlightenment in England, France, and Germany*. Ed. Alan Charles Kors and Paul J. Korshin. Philadelphia: University of Pennsylvania Press, 1987. 232–58.

Harvey, Jane. *Memoirs of an Author*. Gainsborough, England, 1812.

Hayley, William. *A Philosophical, Historical, and Moral Essay on Old Maids. By a Friend of the Sisterhood*. London, 1875.

The Holy Bible. King James Version. 1611. London and New York: Collins, 1953.

Johnson, Claudia. *Equivocal Beings: Politics, Gender, and Sentimentality in the 1790s, Wollstonecraft, Radcliffe, Burney, Austen*. Chicago and London: University of Chicago Press, 1995.

Johnson, Judy van Sickle. "The Bodily Frame: Learning Romance in *Persuasion*." *Nineteenth-Century Fiction* 38 (1983): 43–61.

Johnson, Samuel. *A Dictionary of the English Language*. London, 1755.

———. *Rasselas*. 1759. In *Samuel Johnson*. Ed. Donald Greene. Oxford: Oxford University Press, 1992.

Kelly, Gary. "The Art of Reading in *Pride and Prejudice*." *English Studies in Canada* 10 (1984): 156–71.

———. *English Fiction of the Romantic Period 1789–1830*. London and New York: Longman, 1989.

———. "Jane Austen's Real Business: The Novel, Literature, and Cultural Capital." *Jane Austen's Business: Her World and Her Profession*. Ed. Juliet McMaster and Bruce Stovel. London: Macmillan and New York: St. Martin's, 1996. 154–67.

Kuhn, Thomas. *The Structure of Scientific Revolutions*. Chicago: University of Chicago Press, 1962.

Langer, Suzanne K. "'The Great Dramatic Forms: The Comic Rhythm,' from *Feeling and Form* (1953)." *Theories of Comedy*. Ed. Paul Lauter. Garden City, NY: Anchor, 1964.

Lascelles, Mary. *Jane Austen and Her Art*. 1939. London: Oxford University Press, 1965.

Le Faye, Deirdre. *Jane Austen: A Family Record, by William Austen-Leigh and Richard Arthur Austen-Leigh,* revised and enlarged by Deirdre Le Faye. London: The British Library, 1989.

Leapor, Mary. "Man the Monarch." *Eighteenth-Century Women Poets.* Ed. Roger Lonsdale. Oxford and New York: Oxford University Press, 1989.

Litz, A. Walton. *Jane Austen: A Study of Her Artistic Development.* New York: Oxford University Press, 1965.

Locke, John. *An Essay Concerning Human Understanding.* 1690. Ed. Peter H. Nidditch. Oxford: Clarendon, 1975.

————. *Two Treatises of Government.* 1690. Ed. Peter Laslett. 2nd ed. Cambridge and New York: Cambridge University Press, 1967.

McEwan, Ian. *Enduring Love.* London: Vintage, 1998.

McMaster, Juliet. "Class." *The Cambridge Companion to Jane Austen.* Ed. Edward Copeland and Juliet McMaster. Cambridge: Cambridge University Press, 1997. 115–30.

————. "Clothing the Thought in the Word: The Speakers of *Northanger Abbey.*" *Persuasions: The Jane Austen Journal* 20 (1998): 207–21.

————. *Jane Austen the Novelist: Essays Past and Present.* London: Macmillan and New York: St. Martin's, 1996.

————. "The Secret Languages of *Emma.*" *Persuasions: The Journal of the Jane Austen Society of North America* 13 (1991): 119–31.

————. "The Talkers and Listeners of *Mansfield Park.*" *Persuasions: The Journal of the Jane Austen Society of North America* 17 (1995): 77–89.

————. "Talking about Talk in *Pride and Prejudice.*" *Jane Austen's Business: Her World and Her Profession.* Ed. Juliet McMaster and Bruce Stovel. London: Macmillan and New York: St. Martin's, 1996. 81–94.

Miall, David. "Beyond the Schema Given: Affective Comprehension of Literary Narratives." *Cognition and Emotion* 3.1 (1989): 55–78.

Milroy, James. *Linguistic Variation and Change: On the Historical Sociolinguistics of English.* Oxford and Cambridge, MA: Blackwell, 1992.

Milton, John. *Paradise Lost.* 1673. In *John Milton: A Critical Edition of the Major Works.* Ed. Stephen Orgel and Jonathan Goldberg. Oxford: Oxford University Press, 1991.

Moler, Kenneth L. *Jane Austen's Art of Allusion.* Lincoln, NE: University of Nebraska Press, 1968.

Mooneyham, Laura G. "Loss and Language of Restitution in *Persuasion*." *New Casebooks: Mansfield Park and Persuasion*. Ed. Judy Simons. Basingstoke: Macmillan, 1997. Rpt. from Mooneyham. *Romance, Language, and Education in Jane Austen's Novels*. New York: St. Martin's, 1988.

Morris, Ivor. *Mr. Collins Considered: Approaches to Jane Austen*. New York: Routledge and Kegan Paul, 1987.

Ong, Walter J. *Orality and Literacy: The Technologizing of the Word*. London and New York: Methuen, 1982.

Page, Norman. *The Language of Jane Austen*. Oxford: Basil Blackwell, 1972.

Philips, Katherine. *The Collected Works*. Ed. Patrick Thomas. Vol. 2: *The Letters*. Stump Cross, Essex: Stump Cross Press, 1998. 3 vols.

Phillips, K.C. *Jane Austen's English*. London: André Deutsch, 1970.

Pride and Prejudice. Dir. Robert Z. Leonard. Wr. Aldous Huxley and Jane Murfin. With Laurence Olivier and Greer Garson. MGM feature film, 1940.

Pride and Prejudice. Dir. Cyril Coke. Wr. Fay Weldon. With David Rintoul and Elizabeth Garvie. BBC/A&E mini-series, 1979.

Pride and Prejudice. Dir. Simon Langton. Wr. Andrew Davies. With Colin Firth and Jennifer Ehle. BBC/A&E mini-series, 1995.

Richardson, Samuel. *Clarissa, Or The History of a Young Lady*. 1747–48. Ed. Angus Ross. Harmondsworth, England: Penguin, 1985.

———. *The History of Sir Charles Grandison*. 1753–54. Ed. Jocelyn Harris. Oxford and New York: Oxford University Press, 1986.

Ruderman, Anne Crippen. *The Pleasures of Virtue: Political Thought in the Novels of Jane Austen*. Lanham, MD: Rowman and Littlefield, 1995.

Shakespeare, William. *The Complete Works*. Ed. Stanley Wells and Gary Taylor. Oxford: Oxford University Press, 1986.

Smith, Sidonie. *A Poetics of Women's Autobiography: Marginality and the Fictions of Self-Representation*. Bloomington, IN: Indiana University Press, 1987.

Society Small Talk: Or What To Say and When to Say It. 8th ed. London, n.d.

Stovel, Bruce. "'A Contrariety of Emotion': Jane Austen's Ambivalent Lovers in *Pride and Prejudice*." *International Fiction Review* 14 (1987): 27–33.

Stovel, Nora Foster. "'Every Savage Can Dance': Choreographing Courtship in the Novels of Jane Austen." *Persuasions: The Jane Austen Journal* 23 (2001): 29–49.

Southam, B.C., ed. *Jane Austen: The Critical Heritage*. London: Routledge and
Kegan Paul and New York: Barnes and Noble, 1968.

Tanner, Tony. *Jane Austen*. Cambridge, MA: Harvard University Press, 1986.

Tave, Stuart. *Some Words of Jane Austen*. Chicago: University of Chicago Press,
1973.

Walpole, Horace. *The Castle of Otranto*. 1765. Ed. W.S. Lewis. World's Classics
Edition. Oxford and New York: Oxford University Press, 1996.

Wiltshire, John. *Jane Austen and the Body: 'The Picture of Health.'* Cambridge:
Cambridge University Press, 1992.

Wimsatt, William K., ed. *The Idea of Comedy: Essays in Prose and Verse. Ben Jonson
to George Meredith*. Englewood Cliffs, NJ: Prentice-Hall, 1969.

Wittgenstein, Ludwig. *Philosophical Investigations*. 2nd ed. Trans. G.E.M.
Anscombe. Oxford: Basil Blackwell, 1963.

Young, Kay. *Ordinary Pleasures: Couples, Conversation, and Comedy*. Columbus,
OH: Ohio State University Press, 2001.

Zeldin, Theodore. *Conversation: How Talk Can Change Your Life*. London: Harvill,
1998.

Index

first-person narration, 128–29

flattery, 84, 93, 98, 115, 243, 251

Fludernik, Monika, 138

Flynn, Carol Houlihan, 56

fools, 238, 241–42, 250, 251

Fordyce, James, *Sermons to Young Ladies*, 230–31

formality in speech, xxii, 234–35, 236

Forster, E.M., 238

Foucault, Michel, 104, 107, 126

Frantz, Sarah S.G., xi

free indirect discourse, xx, 17–18, 124–25, 129, 131, 133, 135, 136, 137, 138, 142, 147, 171

French Revolution, 88, 128, 130, 201; British responses to, 128–29, 130, 138

Freud, Sigmund, 121

Furet, Francois, and Jacques Ozouf, 138

Gardiner, Mrs. (*PP*), 195–96, 197, 212

Garson, Greer, 227

gender stereotypes, 16–17, 118–20, 121

generalizations, 105–06, 107, 118–19

gentleman, 118–19, 120, 178, 247–49

Genesis (in Bible), 4, 244

gestures and body-English, 69–70, 154–55

Godwin, William, 129

Goldsmith, Oliver, *She Stoops To Conquer*, 42

"good" prose style, 132, 136

gossip, 50

Grundy, Isobel, xix–xx, 87

Hall, Ronald, xxi

Hamilton, Elizabeth, 55

happiness, 55–56

Hardy, Thomas, xvii

Harvey, Jane, *Memoirs of an Author*, 55

Harris, Jocelyn, xix, 11, 16, 22, 138

Harville, Captain (*P*), 162–63

Hayley, William, *Essay on Old Maids*, 48

Hays, Mary, 129

Herrle, Jeffrey, xxii

hierarchy, 87–88

Hobbes, Thomas, *Leviathan*, 104, 121

hobby horses, 239, 242, 243

Holcroft, Thomas, 129

idiolects, xxii, 130, 131, 237–51

indirect dialogue, 168, 171, 176, 177–78, 208, 222

Ingram, Patricia, 120

Irigaray, Luce, 106

irony, xxi, 106–09, 115, 119, 120, 133, 135, 137, 143, 147–48, 168, 171, 174, 183–203

James, Henry, 125, 238

Jane Austen Society of North America (JASNA), xviii–xix, 22, 56

Jasper, Alberta, conference, xviii, xix, 22, 56

Jennings, Mrs. (*SS*), 29

Johnson, Claudia L., 118, 120

Johnson, Judy van Sickle, 154–55